University of WARRINGTON CAMPUS
Chester LIBRARY
01925 534284

This book is to be returned on or before the last date stamped below. Overdue charges will be incurred by the late return of books.

Research Highlights in Social Work series

This topical series examines areas of particular interest to those in social and community work and related fields. Each book draws together different aspects of the subject, highlighting relevant research and drawing out implications for policy and practice. The project is under the general direction of Professor Joyce Lishman, Head of the School of Applied Social Studies at the Robert Gordon University.

Social Work and Evidence-Based Practice
Edited by David Smith
ISBN 1 84310 156 4
Research Highlights in Social Work 45

The Changing Role of Social Care
Edited by Bob Hudson
ISBN 1 85302 752 9
Research Highlights in Social Work 37

Managing Frontline Practice in Social Work
Edited by Daphne Statham
ISBN 1 85302 886 X
Research Highlights in Social Work 40

Reconceptualising Work with 'Carers'
New Directions for Policy and Practice
Edited by Kirsten Stalker
ISBN 1 84310 118 1
Research Highlights in Social Work 43

Risk Assessment in Social Care and Social Work
Edited by Pyhllida Parsloe
ISBN 1 85302 689 1
Research Highlights in Social Work 36

of related interest

Social Perspectives in Mental Health
Developing Social Models to Understand and Work
with Mental Distress
Edited by Jerry Tew
Foreword by Judy Foster
ISBN 1 84310 220 X

Good Practice in Adult Mental Health
Edited by Tony Ryan and Jacki Pritchard
ISBN 1 84310 217 X

Mental Health Services for Minority Ethnic Children and Adolescents
Edited by Mhemooda Malek and Carol Joughin
ISBN 1 84310 236 6
Part of the Child and Adolescent Mental Health Series

RESEARCH HIGHLIGHTS IN SOCIAL WORK 28

Mental Health and Social Work

Edited by Marion Ulas and Anne Connor

Jessica Kingsley Publishers
London and Philadelphia

Research Highlights in Social Work 28
Editors: Marion Ulas and Anne Connor
Secretary: Anne Forbes
Editorial Advisory Committee:

Professor Joyce Lishman	Robert Gordon University, Aberdeen
Ms M. Buist	Independent researcher, Edinburgh
Mr P. Cassidy	Social Work Department, Aberdeen City Council, representing the Association of Directors of Social Work
Ms A. Connor	Independent researcher, Edinburgh
Mr D. Cox	Robert Gordon University, Aberdeen
Mr M. King	Northern College, Aberdeen
Dr F. Paterson	Social Work Services Group, Scottish Office
Dr A. Robertson	University of Edinburgh
Ms C. Smith	Scottish Council for Voluntary Organisations, Edinburgh

Robert Gordon University
School of Applied Social Studies
Kepplestone Annexe, Queen's Road
Aberdeen AB15 4PH

First published in the United Kingdom in 1999 by
Jessica Kingsley Publishers
116 Pentonville Road
London N1 9JB, UK
and
400 Market Street, Suite 400
Philadelphia, PA 19106, U S A
Copyright © Robert Gordon University, Research Highlights Advisory Group,
School of Applied Social Studies 1999

Printed digitally since 2005

Library of Congress Cataloging in Publication Data
A CIP catalog record for this book is available from the Library of Congress

British Library Cataloguing in Publication Data
A CIP catalogue record for this book is available from the British Library

ISBN-13: 978 1 85302 302 6
ISBN-10: 1 85302 302 7

Contents

List of figures

List of boxes

List of tables

CHAPTER 1

Introduction and Overview

Anne Connor and Marion Ulas

Background and context of this book

In 1985 the Research Highlights series published a volume on mental illness (Horobin 1985). This new book builds on many of the ideas described in that volume. It also marks both the similarities and the changes in the social work responses to people with mental health problems that have occurred over the intervening years.

The first change worth noting is reflected in the title: 'mental health' rather than 'mental illness'. The last few years have seen a shift in thinking about mental health among many social workers and others planning and providing services (examples include Department of Health 1992, 1994; Scottish Office 1997). There is now wider recognition of a broader range of circumstances and needs, encompassing people who have spent substantial periods in hospital and who have severe and/or long-term needs and those whose mental health problems are less marked but still disabling (Tilbury 1993). Many writers have presented these two situations as opposite ends of a continuum, but feedback from users and those who care for them highlights the ways in which an individual will move between periods of severe and of less acute phases of some illnesses, with changing levels and types of need. There is increasing emphasis on the factors that contribute to a mental health problem being more or less disabling, with a consequent increased focus on prevention and health promotion. Underpinning many of these issues is the way in which the people who are experiencing mental health problems perceive themselves and their own well-being.

The second change is reflected in the scope of this volume. Over the past decade there has also been a change in the way the needs of older people with dementia are perceived. Social work support for this group and their carers was the subject of a single chapter in the previous mental illness volume, which noted the difficulties in offering a response when services were underdeveloped (Gilleard 1985). Now there is a well-established network of targeted services for people with dementia, although support for younger adults with dementia is more patchy. Indeed, the social work response for people with dementia is now the subject of a separate book in the Research Highlights series (Hunter 1997).

A third development is the increasing extent to which the assumptions and actions of the medical professions are being questioned. For many years mental health user groups and some voluntary organisations have challenged and/or rejected the medical model as the cornerstone of mental health services, and these views were reflected in the earlier volume. The debate which has emerged more recently centres on the values and attitudes of psychiatrists and those planning and providing health care services, and the impact these values and attitudes have – intentionally or not – on the way individual people with mental health problems are treated, or receive or are denied services. Several specific examples – racism, sexism and ageism – are outlined in chapters in this volume. Related concerns are also being raised about other groups of people who do not fit easily into the parameters of traditional psychiatric services – for example, people who are home-less, and people who have mental health problems and substance misuse problems. The other important shift is that those endorsing and stimulating these debates now include national and local policy makers and leading members of the medical professions.

The fourth change is the increasing impact of the user movement. This has been a significant feature of services for people with mental health problems for some time, and the campaigning and related activities of this group of service users are more widespread than is the case so far for most other groups of users of health and social work services. One important element is the place of self-help groups and a range of user-led services. There is a growing body of research evidence to under-line the effectiveness of these approaches, but they have tended to stay separate from the statutory services (Chamberlain 1988). Recent developments have seen more user involvement in the statutory services. This applies both to people with mental health problems in respect of the services they use and to carers in respect of both the main mental health services provided to the people they care about and for the way services support them in their caring role. Recent statements of national policy and good practice have emphasised the central importance of service users and their carers, and this development will have a long-term influence on the type of services offered by other providers and the way those services are delivered.

The fifth change is the impact on mental health services of policies with a wider focus. Arguably, the most notable policy and resource change in the last decade has been community care. Other policies which are having a far-reaching, if less visible, impact include:

- the way social work services are organised
- the separation of, and relationship between, those deciding which services will be delivered with local authority or NHS funds and those providing the services
- the increasing role of the voluntary and private sectors in social care.

At the same time there are many – some argue too many – similarities in the issues addressed in the two Research Highlights volumes on mental health, despite the intervening decade. Readers will be able to form their own views on whether the ways of tackling those issues have changed to reflect the changed context. The main similarities are:

- the realities of living with chronic and severe mental illness for those affected and for their families
- the importance of external and independent checks on the provision of services to people who, by the nature of their circumstances, may not be able to challenge on their own account
- the role of social workers in providing specialist input, especially on compulsory admissions to hospital care
- access to resources within social work and social services departments for mental health services, and especially for qualified social workers' time, when pressure from other demands continues unabated
- the emphasis placed by policy statements and by social workers and others on the need for inter-disciplinary collaboration and good communication, and the struggle to make this a reality in day-to-day practice and in strategic planning.

Structure and content of the book

The chapters in this book reflect the current state with regard to policy and practice in social work services for people with mental health problems. Many have a Scottish context which is applicable to the broader UK-wide picture, but it is refreshing also to have the opportunity to consider a collection of work in mental health which offers contrasting perspectives in policy and practice to other parts of the UK.

The chapters chart the move away from separate, specialist services, with the associated problems of more people potentially seeking access to social work support which can address the consequences of mental health problems; concerns about a dilution of expertise; and the organisational and other factors which can improve or diminish the quality of the response.

Some themes run through many of the chapters:

- the ways in which mental health problems, and the people affected, are perceived by social work professionals and by their organisations

- the different ways in which social work services to people with mental health problems are organised, including the impact of community care arrangements

- the circumstances of groups of people with mental health problems who are, or could be, in contact with social work services but who are often 'hidden' or perceived in another way

- evidence of a mismatch between the needs of people with mental health problems and the provision offered, which may be caught up with the issues of empowerment and assessment of risk as well as with resources and confidence in models of care

- the place and extent of interaction between different agencies and professional groups in responding to the needs of people with mental health problems

- the ways in which research has addressed the policy and professional aspects of social work and mental health. Aspects include the sources and levels of available funding, which is mostly from central government and associated with particular policy agendas; the differing cultures of social science research on the one hand and the medical research tradition with its emphasis on large-scale clinical trials on the other; and the difficulties for research funders and practitioners in keeping pace with the rate and scale of change in mental health needs and services, and in the requirements of service users and those providing and planning services.

In the following chapter on the policy context of social work services, in order to explore the tensions involved in translating policy into practice, Allyson McCollam describes the evolution of mental health services in Scotland over the past ten years and considers the joint working of the statutory agencies with responsibility for community care, health, social work and housing. The second part of this chapter describes the complexity of existing models which provide a balance in service provision between the majority of those mental health service users who are living in the community and those receiving institutional care.

Following on from this overview, Anne Connor's chapter addresses current research findings on the community-based services which social workers use to provide support to those living in the community. The chapter provides useful information on a range of service models and ways in which to apply the research findings for practitioners and managers.

In the light of increased recognition of the need to review services, Christine McGregor's chapter describes the inspection role of the Mental Welfare Commission for Scotland and the functions and remit of the Commission at the interface of social work services. Case examples are used well to illustrate how the Commission liaises with individual workers within social work departments across a range of issues to protect people suffering from a mental disorder.

The chapter by Marion Ulas gives an account of the research on the role of the Mental Health Officer, the social worker who assesses the need for compulsory detention, and summarises other related research studies in mental health social work. The chapter demonstrates the value of research to inform managers, policy makers and practitioners about the organisational limits to a consistent role in statutory mental health social work.

The chapter by Fiona Myers describes the implications for practitioners of trying both to function in a social work role and operate as a Mental Health Officer. The hidden tensions that surface for social workers who take part in the compulsory detention process are illustrated using data from the interviews with the Mental Health Officers themselves.

Suman Fernando's chapter addresses how the complex issues of ethnicity and race are related in mental health practice, how these issues can be tackled in social work practice, in the organisation of training and in service provision, and how to take them into account in research. The first part of the chapter clarifies the meaning of the concepts of race, culture, ethnicity and the manifestation of racism. The second part of the chapter addresses how minority ethnic communities experience racism in services. This is followed by an overview of current research with suggestions for social work practice to address in future.

On a similar theme, Maureen O'Neill's chapter highlights the discrimination experienced by older people suffering from depression, in that it is seen as an inevitable part of ageing by professionals, carers and the older people themselves. The extent of depression in old age, the contributory factors, and the main social work and multidisciplinary practice issues requiring implementation are also discussed.

Michael Sheppard has described in detail the extent of the research that demonstrated links between maternal depression and problems in caring for children. Following a description of the theoretical and conceptual aspects, his chapter describes the design and use of a case review questionnaire and the rationale for it to be used by social workers to identify the key issues in planning work supporting mothers who are suffering from depression.

In their chapter on the evaluation and outcomes of social work services for people with mental health problems, Allyson McCollam and Julia White describe the process of evaluation and those issues that arise out of the process which are particularly relevant to a mental health setting. Aimed at service users and social workers, the chapter gives examples of considerations to take into account when carrying out evaluations in practice across different settings, and findings from a project evaluation where service user satisfaction was measured.

The last two chapters focus directly on the service user perspective. In their chapter, Julia White and Allyson McCollam summarise a history of the mental health service user movement, which is perceived as being at the forefront of users' organisations. The chapter identifies how changes within services can be achieved by involving service users at the levels of planning, assessment of services, and service provision and evaluation. Examples of user participation in practice are demonstrated, together with indicators for social workers to note to enable participation.

Jim Kiddie was asked to comment on chapters to give a critique from the perspective of someone who has used mental health services. His comments on, for example, researchers' views of issues such as user participation grounds the discussion in another level of experience. Drawing on his own experiences, he supplies a test of relevance of the material, offering different conclusions from the professional view – for example, on the social work role and aftercare.

Other current and emerging mental health issues

Other aspects of the mental health needs of social work clients are not included in this volume. The main reason is that little research into these particular topics, and especially into the social work aspects, had been published at the time the book was being put together. In part, this reflects the rapidly changing policy and practice agenda highlighted by the chapters in this book. One of the challenges here is to those funding and carrying out research to keep pace with emerging needs and practice in the field. It is hoped that by the time the next volume of Research Highlights is prepared there will be a sound body of research to support and inform social work practice.

One area which is of growing importance is support to children and young people with mental health problems (Health Advisory Service 1995).

The scale of the need is gaining increasing recognition:

- about 40 per cent of children and young people experience periods of mental distress
- ten per cent of children and young people have marked behavioural difficulties or severe worries which they need help to overcome
- two per cent of children and young people have problems or disturbed behaviour that would benefit from input from child and adolescent mental health services
- within this last group, a small number have a psychiatric illness: this is very low among children and increases with adolescence
- a disproportionate number of children and young people in contact with the social work services will have a mental health problem or behavioural difficulties.

As among adults, mental health problems are more common where children:

- live in urban and/or deprived areas
- are experiencing homelessness
- have family pressures such as unemployment
- have an ill or disabled parent
- are experiencing a period of stress.

The majority of children and young people who have less severe mental health problems are best served by support from services with which they and their families are already in touch. This means that social work services are likely to be an important source of potential support to the young people and their families.

This has been identified as an area where the interaction of planning for mental health and community care on the one hand, and for children's services on the other, can either support or act as a barrier to the development of appropriate supports for young people, particularly those who are likely to have longer-term needs.

Similar issues arise in relation to people in touch with the court or criminal justice services who have mental health problems. The term 'mentally disordered offender' is generally used as shorthand for a large group of people with various and usually complex needs:

- a small proportion of people with severe and enduring mental health problems who have committed offences, where the offending behaviour is linked to their mental illness
- other people who are detained in a special hospital or other secure setting, where there is a 'personality disorder' rather than a mental illness
- people with mental health problems who have committed less serious offences or where their behaviour has brought them into contact with the police, and where the aim is to divert away from prosecution or penalty and to address their mental health needs
- people who are in prison or in touch with probation services, who have a mental health problem that is not associated with their offending behaviour, but who will need access to appropriate health care and may benefit from access to social work services which address their mental health needs.

For those with very high needs, social work services will be part of a network of services aimed at meeting the needs of the individual and protecting other people from potential harm. It is this group, and their needs, which has tended to receive the greatest attention. Practice and planning issues for both those with the highest needs and others with both offending and mental health needs, are:

- the interaction of planning and service delivery for the two client groups which, as with children's services, can ease or complicate effective delivery of social work services
- the circumstances of people who are caught up in the criminal justice system, including the impact for people from black and minority ethnic communities (highlighted by Fernando in Chapter 7 and in his recent research on forensic psychiatry)
- the extent to which local mental health services interact with diversion schemes, and the link with the role of Mental Health Officers and Approved Social Workers
- the potential impact of mainstream community mental health services such as housing and support schemes and day services, when part of a joint care plan
- the extent to which social work and social care services have explained and demonstrated their actual and potential role in respect of this group of clients.

Many of the chapters in this book refer to users of mental health services, but there are fewer references to the family and friends who identify themselves as carers. To some extent this reflects the debate in mental health services about the role of family members in contributing to some individuals' mental health problems, however unintentionally. It also reflects the wishes of some people with mental health problems not to involve family or friends in the management of their illness or care arrangements, to which those providing services have responded. A separate factor is the nature of the 'carers' movement': although the distinct needs of carers have had growing recognition over recent years at both policy and practice levels, this has to some extent been at the expense of attention to the distinct and additional needs of people caring in particular situations. Recent policy statements and work nationally and locally have sought to gain greater recognition of the needs and contribution of carers of people with mental health problems, and are addressing both these root issues.

Other specific points to note concerning carers of people with mental health problems are:

- aspects of serious mental health problems which place additional difficulties are the stigma associated with mental health, which means they are less likely to get emotional and practical support from other people in their community; the less predictable course of the illness, with a crisis potentially happening at any time; the feeling of being always 'on call', even when the person with the mental health problem does not live with their carer

- the contact between people with mental health problems and one or more significant carers may be underestimated in assessments of need which are influenced by either the expectation that carers live with service users, or that people with mental health problems will avoid contact with family members

- the carer may not be living in the area where their relative or friend is, and this can present further barriers in getting access to information and support

- the ways in which services respond to a crisis is one of the areas on which carers place high priority. The well-being of the person with the mental health problem in these situations is one of carers' greatest concerns. Also, even when the carer and the person with the mental health problem do not live together, the service user may still contact or return to familiar people and places at times of crisis

- carers are themselves more likely to experience mental health problems such as depression and stress

- children of parents with mental health problems often find it difficult to get meaningful information about mental illness and what is happening to their parent

- the priorities identified by carers and service users for mental health services, and suggested ways of tackling issues, are very similar.

Conclusion

Mental health services form an area where both the policy and practice context is changing rapidly. Ten years from now another volume of Research Highlights will be needed to review the impacts of those changes.

Acknowledgements

We wish to thank Joyce Lishman for her support and advice, and Anne Forbes at the Research Highlight project. Our thanks also go to the contributors.

References

Chamberlain, J. (1988) *On Our Own: Patient-Controlled Alternatives to the Mental Health System.* London: MIND.

Department of Health (1992) *Health of the Nation.* London: HMSO.

Department of Health (1994) *Health of the Nation: Second Key Area Handbook.* London: HMSO.

Gilleard, C. (1985) The psychogeriatric patient and the family. In G. Horobin (ed.) *Responding to Mental Illness. Research Highlights in Social Work 11.* London: Jessica Kingsley Publishers.

Health Advisory Service (1995) *Child and Adolescent Mental Health Services – Together We Stand.* London: HMSO.

Horobin, G. (ed.) (1985) *Responding to Mental Illness. Research Highlights in Social Work 11.* London: Jessica Kingsley Publishers.

Hunter, S. (1997) *Dementia: Challenges and New Directions. Research Highlights in Social Work 31.* London: Jessica Kingsley Publishers.

Scottish Office (1997) *A Framework for Mental Health Services in Scotland.* Edinburgh: The Stationery Office.

Tilbury, D. (1993) *Working with Mental Illness.* Basingstoke: BASW/Macmillan.

CHAPTER 2

Policy into Practice:
Creative Tension or Deadlock?

The Policy Context of Social Work Services
for People with Mental Health Problems

Allyson McCollam

Introduction

For most social work practitioners and managers, services for people with mental
health problems are planned and delivered within the wider framework of general
community care policies and services. However, these services are also affected by
a range of other policy developments and need therefore to be set in context. This
chapter will focus on the evolution of mental health policy in Scotland over the last
ten years, as a case study to examine and consider some of the major issues involved
in translating policy into practice.

 The discussion will reflect in particular on joint working among the statutory
agencies with responsibilities for community care – health, social work and housing – and with the independent sector. It will be argued that many of the difficulties experienced 'on the ground' in providing the mythical seamless service to
those whose needs straddle several agencies originate at policy level or are at least
exacerbated by the tensions between policies. One of the underlying themes of the
chapter is that, for a variety of reasons, social work activity in the field of mental
health – from service planning and purchasing to individual assessment and service delivery – is heavily influenced by policies and practices within the health service. What is more, particular structural and organisational features of local

government in Scotland impact on the implementation of community care policies in mental health.

Part one: mental health policy in Scotland

Local context

Care in the community has been an objective of Scottish mental health policy for several decades, as in the rest of the UK. However, Scotland differs in a number of important ways from other parts of the UK. At a general level it has its own system of governance. The Scottish Office has responsibility for community care policy through its health, social work and housing departments. Until May 1997 these departments were separate – social work came under the Home Department, housing was part of the Development Department and health was a department in its own right. Since May this has altered, with a closer alignment of health and social work, which now report to the same minister, although housing remains part of the Development Department under a different minister. In other areas, such as taxation and social security, however, policy is determined at UK level.

The system of local government in Scotland has recently undergone reorganisation to create 32 unitary authorities, whose structure, funding mechanisms and responsibilities differ from counterparts elsewhere in the UK. There are also various differences in the legislative framework, for example the Social Work (Scotland) Act 1968 and the Mental Health (Scotland) Act 1984.

More specifically, there are discernible differences in practices between Scotland and other parts of the UK. Scotland spends a proportionately higher amount per capita on health services and its local authorities receive a higher per capita grant from central government than England and Wales. This partly reflects differences in responsibilities and the inflated costs associated with serving a population dispersed across a wide geographical area, and is partly the result of historical factors (Midwinter 1997). The total figures for councils' allocations for all social work services–including community care–in 1996–97 were £950 million for Scotland and £7446.5 million for England (Scottish Office, Social Work Services Group 1997).

The Scottish allocation is over 20 per cent higher per capita. However, direct comparisons are somewhat misleading as expenditure for English and Scottish councils is calculated using different methods.

Historical perspective

There has been a tendency in Scotland to rely heavily on institutional models of care for a range of vulnerable groups (Checkland 1980). In relation to mental health, Scotland has adopted a distinctive approach to both policy development and to the provision of services. One of the tenets of the philosophy of community care is a shift in the axis of care away from hospitals to ensure the availability of a range of community-based services, in accordance with the particular needs of the local population and with local circumstances (e.g. geography). Scottish mental health policy has tended to reflect an ambivalence towards hospital provision, and has never actively pursued a closure programme of the scale and pace adopted from the 1980s in England. Hospital-based services still continue to play a predominant part in mental health provision, as we shall see below.

The SHAPE Report, which reviewed health priorities for the 1980s, made recommendations on changes required to make the most effective use of resources (Scottish Home and Health Department 1980). The conclusions of the working group prioritised health service programmes and patient groups into three categories. Community care groups were among the top priorities (Category A), and the expectation was that expenditure on these groups would show the greatest increase over the coming decade.

In 1985, the Scottish Office published its first review of adult mental health services (Scottish Home and Health Department 1985), which stated that psychiatric hospitals would continue to play a major role in the future but failed to elucidate how that imperative was to be reconciled with the pursuit of community care objectives (Drucker 1986).

The SHARPEN Report assessed progress towards the achievement of SHAPE objectives with a view to revising guidelines for the period up to 1992 (Scottish Home and Health Department 1988). This review found that Category A programmes had increased their share of overall expenditure, but within Category A, there had actually been a decline in the share of expenditure allocated to services for people with mental illness.

A number of reasons can be adduced to explain Scotland's hesitancy to develop and implement a more robust policy on community mental health service development:

- the predominant role played by the medical profession in policy formulation (Drucker 1986; Hunter and Wistow 1987)

- an absence of legitimate challenges to the status quo and, until recently, little public debate on mental health. Whereas a succession of scandals in long-stay hospitals in England and Wales precipitated an examination of existing arrangements, this was not mirrored in Scotland (Martin 1984)

- the separation between health and social work at policy and service delivery levels and, perhaps more importantly, the continuing imbalances (in terms of resources and power) between the two sectors. This means that the development of community-based services is predicated on health relinquishing some resources and control to local authority social work departments

- the political culture in Scotland which has tended to favour an approach which devolves responsibility to local agencies, rather than the centre (i.e. the Scottish Office) taking a more proactive, directive role in propelling forward policy objectives

- a genuine concern to ensure that the development of community mental health care should proceed at a measured pace and not jeopardise the well-being of people with mental health problems. Experiences elsewhere in the UK and further afield are alleged to provide useful lessons in the benefits of pursuing closure with 'cautious optimism' (speech by the Minister for Health to Annual Conference of the Scottish Health Advisory Service, 1995).

Set against this ambivalent attitude towards community care, there are a number of compelling arguments for reviewing the role of hospitals (Turner-Crowson 1993):

- evidence of negative impact of institutionalisation on patients

- preference of service users and carers for more individualised, less stigmatising approaches, if adequately funded and coordinated

- people have often been admitted to, and have remained in, hospital because that is the only source of treatment and support available

- many long-stay hospitals are in remote and inaccessible locations

- many old hospitals are in poor physical condition and refurbishment would be a very expensive option

- evidence of the effectiveness of community-based treatment and support

- closure can release funding to develop new alternative services in the community

- growing recognition by professionals and policy makers of the importance of consumer choice. (adapted from Turner-Crowson (1993))

Current trends in policy

Until recently, the Scottish Office had produced a series of circulars and guidance to reinforce the implementation of the 1990 community care legislation, but had issued no overarching policy statement to parallel the publication of the *Health of the Nation* in England in 1992. (The nearest equivalent, *Scotland's Health, A Challenge to Us All,* features dental rather than mental health!)

However, since the early 1990s there has been a discernible sharpening of focus in mental health policy in Scotland. This has had a number of precipitants. To some extent, it has been a reaction to policies in England; in the wake of the Bottomley ten-point plan, for example, Scottish policy makers and advisers set out to devise responses which fitted with the particular needs of the Scottish situation and were in line with existing Scottish mental health legislation and how it is applied. Thus community care orders came into being, under the Mental Health (Patients in the Community) Act 1995, but at the same time further measures, such as supervision registers, were rejected for Scotland.

The need to ensure that the most vulnerable people received coordinated care and treatment, with agencies working cohesively together, was recognised as the linchpin of an effective mental health care system and translated into a systematic process in the care programme approach. Again, this has been operationalised differently in England and Scotland, with the latter taking a narrower and more focused approach on those deemed to be most at risk.

There has also been a recognition that mental health services account for a substantial proportion of overall expenditure on health and social services. In 1990 in Scotland, patients with mental illnesses (excluding learning disabilities and dementia) accounted for 18 per cent of NHS inpatient days (Kendrick 1993). The annual expenditure on adult mental illness inpatient beds alone amounted to £187.4 million in 1995/96 (Scottish Health Service Costs 1996).

In addition, recent epidemiological evidence on mental health problems among the population at large indicates the enormous costs involved, both in terms of the distress caused to individuals and families, and in terms of the financial implications (Office for Population and Census Studies 1995; Scottish Needs Assessment Programme 1994). In the light of such considerations, the Scottish Health Service has made mental health a priority, along with cardiovascular disease and cancer, since 1995.

Interestingly, and this will be discussed in more detail later, this priority status is not mirrored directly in the social work or housing sectors. Within community care, mental health must therefore compete with other client groups; in the wider context, services for people with mental health problems must contend with other, statutory responsibilities of social work and housing. Consequently, there is little impetus to indicate how the historical pattern of the predominant role of the health sector in mental health might be challenged.

A number of financial mechanisms have been introduced to further policy objectives, and these have added to the momentum of community mental health services development. The operation of bridging finance and resource transfer mechanisms has provided incentives and opportunities for local health, social work and housing agencies to plan and deliver community-based mental health services in conjunction with the voluntary sector. Some areas of Scotland, such as Glasgow, were in the vanguard of this process and have been able to reconfigure their local mental health service. However, this has led to widening differences between areas in the patterns and levels of service provision, concern about the equity of the financial mechanisms and the variable prioritisation of mental health service development by local agencies (see below).

The introduction of the Mental Illness Specific Grant (MISG) under the NHS and Community Care Act in 1990 and the initial year-on-year increase in the sums available, reaching £18 million in 1995/96, were highly significant for the development of a diversity of community-based services. Not only did MISG provide the means to fund such services, it also indicated clearly that the Scottish Office was prepared to back up its avowed commitment to mental health with resources – albeit ring-fenced and top-sliced. The development of services through MISG has helped to shift the axis of provision from hospital to community; it has also encouraged innovation and generated expertise and experience in such activities, especially among voluntary organisations. However, the overall sum available has remained static for three years and uncertainty about the longer-term prospects of MISG-funded services has only been exacerbated by the funding difficulties facing the newly created local authorities. Equally, the intention that MISG-funded projects would be absorbed into mainstream local authority budgets has not been realised (Nuffield Centre for Community Care Studies 1995).

Until recently, the infrastructure was lacking to ensure research and expertise in clinical and social care aspects of mental health provision informed service development in Scotland. The work of bodies such as the Sainsbury Centre for Mental Health and the Centre for Mental Health Services Development, King's College in England, have no direct equivalent in Scotland, except in the field of dementia with the Dementia Services Development Centre, University of Stirling.

However, good practice initiatives have recently begun to emerge in Scotland. These include:

- a series of reports produced by the Clinical Resources and Audit Group working group on mental illness (CRAG final report 1996)

- other UK-wide initiatives, such as the Clinical Standards Advisory Group, which have a Scottish dimension (CSAG 1995)

- the establishment in Scotland of a good practice database for community care – Community Care Works – at the Nuffield Centre for Community Care Studies, University of Glasgow, which includes examples of a wide spectrum of services and approaches across community care groupings

- a review by the Accounts Commission of adult mental health services, modelled on similar work by the Audit Commission in England (Audit Commission 1994). This is a unique development for Scotland.

Against this background, the user movement in Scotland has become more firmly established, both locally and nationally, and increasingly commands the attention of practitioners, researchers and policy makers. Experience is gradually accumulating across Scotland of user and carer participation in planning, providing and monitoring services (Scottish Needs Assessment Programme, 1998). The number of advocacy projects and posts has grown, providing opportunities for service users to make their views known, individually and collectively.

There has also been an increase in lobbying by voluntary sector campaigning organisations – including user groups – for greater clarity on mental health policy and firmer direction from the centre on its implementation (Scottish Association for Mental Health (SAMH) 1994–97). Such demands were furthered by an inquiry in 1994 by the Scottish Affairs Committee into the future of Scotland's psychiatric hospitals (House of Commons Scottish Affairs Committee 1995). In its report, the Committee called on the Scottish Office to produce a fully costed strategy for the closure of long-stay beds and the development of community-based alternatives. The Scottish Office responded by declaring its intention to produce a statement of the aims and key points which should be addressed in local mental health strategies.

The publication of the *Framework for Mental Health Services* affirmed the commitment of the Scottish Office to mental health as a key component of its community care policies (Scottish Office 1997). The *Framework* affords an opportunity to set the scene for the coming six years, and to generate consensus about the key principles and elements in a comprehensive local mental health service. The clear expectation is that in drawing up and implementing local mental health strategies, health and local authority partners must give priority to the needs of those with severe and/or enduring mental health problems.

Issued jointly by health, social work and housing departments within the Scottish Office, the document acknowledges the need for mental health policy to be implemented on a solid interagency basis. Expectations of local agencies are premised on the need for joint planning and joint working among health, housing and social work, and a recognition that, while good practice exists, this has not been universal.

As a means of supporting the implementation of the *Framework* and of assisting the continuing development of mental health services in Scotland, the Scottish Office has recently established a Mental Health Development Fund and a Scottish Development Centre for Mental Health Services.

All these initiatives are promising indications that mental health is being accorded higher priority by policy makers. The next section goes on to consider some of the current issues and likely future challenges in translating policy into practice in Scotland.

Part two: policy into practice
Striking a balance

As the previous section illustrated, there is evidence to support the view that Scotland is in the throes of developing a more coherent mental health policy. However, the import of policy must be gauged ultimately by considering the extent to which it has an impact – on service development and on the quality of life and well-being of people with mental health problems.

Community care is not just about closing hospitals or paring them down. It is a philosophy which entails a radical shift away from reliance on large psychiatric institutions to establish a spectrum of services in the community to respond to the particular needs of local people. There are many tensions inherent in the philosophy of community care; balance has to be struck, for instance, between the provision of health and social care, since often needs will span both, and between short-term interventions and long-term support. The complexity of closing a large and out-moded institution and resettling individuals into alternative settings can dominate the agenda to the extent that a mental health strategy becomes a hospital closure strategy, and the needs of the majority of people with mental health problems who are already in the community are overlooked.

In addition, experience from the United States illustrates that it is imperative to ensure that mental health services accord explicit priority to the needs of those with severe and/or enduring mental health problems (Turner-Crowson 1993). This group constitutes only a small proportion of the overall total population who experience some kind of mental health problem in their lifetime, but tends to make the greatest demand of services. Where adequate care is not provided on a coordinated basis for individuals with severe and enduring problems, the results can be devastating and potentially tragic (Blom Cooper, Hally and Murphy 1995; Ritchie, Dick and Lingham 1994). This group requires access to a network of treatment, care and support services to avoid individuals becoming entrapped as inpatients because no alternatives exist. Their support needs may be long term.

By contrast, the vast majority of those who experience mental health problems at some time in their lives may not require input from specialist mental health services. Their support needs may be short term or intermittent. As we shall see, social work authorities in Scotland have not played a major role in relation to the delivery of mental health services for the group with severe and enduring mental health problems. However, much social work activity has an implicit mental health component, in the context of interventions with other client groups – for example, family work – or in more general preventive work with individuals and communities (Sheppard 1994; Watkins *et al.* 1996).

Finally, there is a balance to be achieved between the different components of local mental health services. Research has shown that reductions in the number of long-stay beds increase demand for acute beds (Leff 1993). Similarly, in both Scotland and England it has been found that a shortage of suitable support services in the community can lead to inordinate pressure on acute psychiatric beds and result in over-occupancy.

Mental health services in Scotland

In reviewing the development of mental health services, it is important to note the dearth of comprehensive information which makes it difficult to make any authoritative statement about the adequacy of current provision.

INPATIENT SERVICES

The level of inpatient provision for people with mental health problems has decreased dramatically over the last decade and continues to fall:

Adult mental illness beds

	1985	1990	1995
Available staffed beds	12,551	8351	4906

Source: Scottish Health Service, 1996.

Part of this reduction can be attributed to a reclassification of some adult beds as psychogeriatric beds. Undoubtedly there has also been a real decrease in adult bed numbers, although the figures available make it difficult to estimate the true scale of the change. Nor is it possible to distinguish different categories of bed in the national statistics, for example to identify the number of acute beds.

As bed numbers have been declining, there have been parallel changes in patterns of usage, with increases in admission and discharge rates, and a rise in out-patient attendances (Scottish Health Service 1996).

HOUSING

The number of residential places for people with mental health problems has risen over the last decade, as shown below:

Residential places for people with mental health problems

1985	1991	1993	1995
238	446	692	1105

These figures include places in homes run by local authorities (5%) and in registered homes run by the private (7%) and voluntary (88%) sectors.

Accommodation with support can also be provided in unregistered settings. A database of supported accommodation provision in Scotland compiled by Scottish Homes indicates a total of 1014 places for people with mental health problems in 1995. The same source estimates a shortfall of almost 12,000 places for this client group and questions the extent to which current patterns and models of housing with support reflect the needs of the individuals concerned (Scottish Homes 1996).

DAY ACTIVITIES

Day activity services perform a number of different but vital functions for people with mental health problems (McCollam 1994; Pozner *et al.* 1996). There are, however, very few day centres either run by local authorities or registered with them:

Day centres for people with mental health problems

	1985	1990	1995
Centres	1	4	16
Places	35	225	469

Source: Scottish Office Statistical Bulletin, Social Work Series, 1996

By 1995, the voluntary sector provided 48 per cent of these places. These figures appear to reflect considerable variations in the recording of information as much as variations in levels of provision. Of the 16 centres operating in 1995, 12 were in the former region of Tayside, one was in Highland and two were in Strathclyde.

Most mental health day services are not formally registered with the local authority and therefore do not show up in these figures. In the report of an inspection of day services, the Scottish Office estimated that in 1995 there were some 2000 day service places across Scotland, used by around 4000 people (Social Work Services Inspectorate 1996). This inspection highlighted significant gaps in the range of day services available – including information and advice, home support, education, training and work. It also identified the importance of developing services capable of responding more satisfactorily to the needs of specific groups such as women and ethnic minorities (see Chapter 7).

The information systems currently in place and the data generated are not adequate to build up an accurate picture of mental health provision across Scotland, either in terms of what exists or of how the different service elements interlink. Comprehensive community-based mental health care requires the provision of an array of services to fulfil certain core functions (as described in the Scottish Office *Framework*). At present there are considerable variations in the pattern and level of provision across the country, and it cannot be assumed that such variations are a rational response to the particularities of local circumstances. Interestingly, the Audit Commission found in England that areas which had previously been serviced by a large mental hospital had higher than average expenditure on mental health services, even after that institution was closed. Areas which had no local hospital did not have access to the same volume of resources to develop alternative services in the community.

Resources

The Scottish Office has acknowledged that there is currently no accurate information on overall expenditure on mental health services across all sectors (Consultation Seminar on Draft *Framework,* Dundee 1996).

In 1992–93 the Mental Health Foundation estimated that UK expenditure on mental health by the health service amounted to £2887 million, compared with £273 million from social services. Available figures indicate that the health sector in Scotland spends in the region of £220 million annually on adult mental health services (Scottish Health Service, 1995/96), with social work expenditure on people with mental health problems amounting to almost £25 million (Scottish Office Statistical Bulletin 1996).

Local authority per capita expenditure on people with mental health problems has risen substantially from a low baseline, with the introduction of the MISG, from £0.52 in 1985 to £7.54 in 1995. However, this includes only those costs which are directly attributable to mental health cases and masks the hidden mental health element in social work mentioned above. Nevertheless, mental health fares badly when compared with learning disability, where the equivalent per capita expenditure in 1995 was £27.30. There are also striking differences across authorities in per capita expenditure on mental health.

In addition to this 'visible' expenditure, services funded through various European and national government programmes, such as urban aid and employment training programmes, include projects targeted at people with mental health problems. Spending in these areas is not easily disaggregated, although such projects are known to provide support to a substantial number of individuals with mental health problems (SAMH 1996a).

The development of comprehensive local mental health services hinges to a large extent on the ability and willingness of health authorities to release resources locked up in expensive institutions and channel these into more appropriate forms of provision. Where responsibility shifts from health to a local authority to provide care, there should be an accompanying shift in resources. In 1995/96, £52 million was transferred across from health to social work for a range of priority groups including people with mental health problems, rising to £80 million for 1996/97. However, there is no openly available information on what proportion of the overall sum was in mental health, what percentage of the savings has been reinvested in health care or how the money transferred is being spent by the local authority. In addition, there are indications that some social work departments have been put at a financial disadvantage by the workings of resource transfer (House of Commons 1977, Vol. I). The Association of Directors of Social Work has expressed concern at the apparent disparities in levels of resource transfer between health boards and about the difficulties local authorities have experienced in reaching agreement with their local health partners about numbers of beds closed and the level of resource transfer involved (House of Commons, Vol. II).

The impetus at policy level to develop comprehensive mental health service has, ironically, coincided with local government reorganisation in Scotland and with severe budgetary constraints on the spending of the new councils. Many have been obliged to introduce a package of measures, such as more stringent criteria for service eligibility, reducing grants to voluntary organisations and revising charging policies for services such as domiciliary care.

Joint working

Joint working among the various agencies involved directly and indirectly in community care has long been recognised as a prerequisite for the delivery of high quality services to individuals (Department of Health 1989; Scottish Home and Health Department 1988). Yet the gap between rhetoric and practice persists in Scotland, ostensibly because of inherent differences between health and local authority services (both social work and housing) in:

- the ways in which policy is formulated and implemented in general
- the extent to which mental health in particular is accorded priority status
- accountability and performance management processes
- financial rules and the overall resource base.

The barriers to solid interagency collaboration are considerable and are largely (but not entirely) structural in nature. Prompted by similar concerns about mental health provision in England and Wales, the Department of Health produced a Green Paper in 1997, outlining four options to rectify the situation entailing varying degrees of structural alignment between health and local authorities. The paper identified key features of successful partnerships as follows:

- clear vision of service development
- effective leadership
- commitment at all levels within the partner organisations
- coterminous boundaries

- formal mechanisms for bringing people together and sharing information
- understanding of each organisation's culture, roles, values and constraints. (Department of Health 1997)

The debate generated by the Green Paper has not been pursued with any great vigour in Scotland. Recent experiences of local government reorganisation and health board restructuring (Shields Report 1996) have undoubtedly made the prospect of further structural change unwelcome. The fact remains that the community care legislation assigns social work departments a lead role in assessing the needs of their local population and devising appropriate care plans in conjunction with other agencies as appropriate. This has the appearance of creating an anomalous situation in mental health where health agencies have traditionally had the main input either by default or as a result of needs being interpreted in predominately clinical terms, and where they continue to command greater resources.

Sterile debates about who should lead contribute little to the quality of the service to users. There are welcome signs of a greater maturity emerging, with more of a willingness among statutory authorities to operate in concert, with agreement on the roles and responsibilities of the agencies and practitioners involved. This approach has been encouraged in Scottish Office guidance – for example, in relation to the care programme approach, the guidance is not prescriptive on the issue of lead responsibility, but stresses the overriding importance of local agreement being achieved. Similarly, the *Framework for Mental Health Services* proposes the establishment of a local joint commissioning body to coordinate service development.

Collaboration between agencies takes place at different levels – ranging from joint planning and commissioning, to joint management and to joint service delivery; it also relies on the combined effectiveness of formalised arrangements for joint working and more informal approaches, evolving out of the experience of working together (Hill and Shepherd 1997). Higgins (1994) observe that progress is mixed, with the most encouraging signs of a more joint approach at strategic level. Although joint commissioning tends to be regarded as a panacea, it appears to remain an aspiration rather than a common practice (Towards 2001 Conference, Edinburgh, 1997). Effective joint working at the level of service delivery is still relatively rare. Despite the fact that the care programme approach was first introduced in Scotland in 1992, many authorities are still in the throes of setting up a joint system. A recent survey of community mental health teams across Scotland found that only 36 per cent of teams were participating in the approach (Health Services Research Unit 1996).

However, examples are now emerging of a range of successful interagency initiatives, which have consciously addressed the barriers between agencies by developing structures and practices which actively promote and sustain joint working (National Association of Health Authorities and Trusts 1997).

The creation of 32 local authority areas in Scotland adds to the complexities of joint working. The disaggregation of the large regional authorities has resulted in health boards having to collaborate with up to five local authority partners and some of the new authorities fall into two health board areas.

The local authority area may not always be the most appropriate for the planning and delivery of all services for people with mental health problems, particularly more specialist services. There is therefore likely to be a need for collaboration and coordination between local authorities. As yet the new authorities are primarily concerned with planning and provision within their area. However, the interface between authorities is likely to emerge as an important dimension, not least because of the financial pressures councils face in meeting community care needs. The proliferation of local authorities has imposed a heavy burden on voluntary organisations, particularly those whose operations span a number of different authorities or extend across Scotland. This has reduced their capacity to engage fully in joint planning activities and their opportunities to contribute the experience they have amassed in service development and delivery.

Commissioning

The implementation of the community care legislation has been accompanied by policies which promote the model of a market economy in health and social welfare, premised on a clear distinction between the functions of service commissioning/purchasing and service delivery. This has called into question the desirability of local authorities' traditional multiple roles as purchaser, provider and regulator of services (Social Work Services Inspectorate 1996).

However, in view of the relatively low profile local authorities have tended to play in Scotland as providers of mental health services, a more pertinent concern is their relative lack of experience in commissioning mental health services (Scottish Human Services 1996) and the increasing importance of that function as resource transfer monies become available. The shift from institutional services to community-based patterns poses significant challenges for commissioners of services in terms of identifying desirable and effective models which will be feasible and affordable in their local context.

The availability of resources released through the closure or 'downsizing' of large psychiatric hospitals provides a unique opportunity for those commissioning health and social care services for people with mental health problems. The Accounts Commission has drawn attention to the tension between value for money considerations and the need to ensure that the services purchased do not lock resources into models of provision which will become less appropriate over time (Accounts Commission 1994).

There is also a tension between the perceived needs of service users and professional views of what is required, feasible and affordable; this is perhaps most marked in relation to the debate about crisis responses (Consultation and Advocacy Promotion Service 1995). User groups are increasingly vocal about the range of services to which they wish to have access and the features of service provision which they value (Eastwood Mental Health Forum 1996).

Increasingly, mental health services commissioners are under pressure to ensure that the services developed can respond to the specific needs of particular sectors of the population, such as:

- black and ethnic minority communities (Glasgow Association for Mental Health 1996)

- older people (Age Concern Scotland/Edinburgh Assocation for Mental Health 1996)

- children and adolescents (House of Commons Health Committee 1997)

- rural and remote communities (White 1995)

- groups with more complex problems, especially mentally disordered offenders (Chiswick, in SAMH 1996b).

In responding to these various demands, social work departments have to seek to 'manage the market' and encourage both voluntary and private sector providers to develop the range and quality of services required. The private sector accounts for only a very small part of adult mental health provision, apart from dementia services. On the other hand, the voluntary sector is a major provider of community-based mental health services in Scotland – over two-thirds of MISG-funded projects are managed by voluntary organisations. The operation of the contract culture and latterly the impact of resource constraints have severely curtailed the capacity of the voluntary sector to be innovative and visionary. Voluntary organisations report mixed success in securing access to local community care planning structures and opportunities to feed their experience as both providers and advocates for service users into the commissioning process (House of Commons Scottish Affairs Committee 1997, Vol. II).

Provider organisations find themselves increasingly beset by the insecurities of short-term multiple funding. Funding is becoming contingent on the attainment of quality standards and outcomes, but these are defined and assessed in different ways by different funders. The costs to the provider of negotiating and preparing contracts are high, and are not necessarily covered in the formal contract (Scottish Council for Voluntary Organisations 1997).

Primary care

It is encouraging to note that in some areas, specific initiatives have been undertaken to ensure that primary care is integrally involved in community care planning. This is important for several reasons. First, the vast majority of those with a mental health problem are seen by a GP, not by secondary mental health services (Goldberg and Huxley 1992). GPs are therefore at the heart of any local mental health service. Second, GPs act as gatekeepers to specialist services and are therefore at the hub of local mental health provision.

In addition, the development of GP fundholding (GPFH) has introduced an additional group of players with the capacity to commission services for people with mental health problems. This reflects a wider policy emphasis on a primary care-led NHS and an extension of the market economy model of health care. Since the inception of fundholding, concerns have been expressed about the potential for GPFH purchasing decisions to cut across the strategic intentions of health boards and their community care planning partners. The Scottish Office has recently sought to address this by setting out a clear accountability framework within which fundholders and health boards would be expected to ensure the consistency of their respective purchasing intentions (Shields Report 1996).

Housing

The importance of the housing input to community care planning has not always been sufficiently recognised. It was not until 1994 that the Scottish Office issued a circular emphasising the equal status of housing as a planning partner in community care. Experience of reprovisioning in areas such as Glasgow, where several long-stay hospitals have closed, has illustrated very forcibly the importance of involving housing from the earliest possible stage in view of the long lead-in times required to identify and develop suitable sites (Scottish Association of Health Councils Annual Conference 1996). Currently efforts are being made by the Scottish Office to bring housing planning cycles into step with community care planning cycles.

One of the positive effects already emerging from local government reorganisation is the potential for closer working relationships between housing and social work. However, ironically, the availability of decent, affordable housing with access to appropriate support for people with mental health problems (among other community care service users) has become increasingly difficult: the consequences of wider housing policies which have reduced both the stock of local authority housing for rent and the resources available to maintain and upgrade remaining stock. Even where there may be capital available for housing developments, authorities are not always able to guarantee the availability of revenue to sustain the longer-term costs of providing support, particularly in the light of the possible outcomes of the current review of housing benefit (House of Commons Scottish Affairs Committee 1977, Vol II.).

Professional training and development

The changing models of care for people with mental health problems have practice implications for each of the professions involved, as roles and responsibilities evolve. Within social work, core functions, such as assessment and care management, have been developed in various ways (Scottish Office 1996). At the same time, boundaries between professions are becoming more fluid (Poole and Broderick 1995). More and more mental health care is being coordinated and delivered via a multidisciplinary team or network. This raises issues about support, supervision and management for social workers, along with other professional groups such as nurses (Health Services Research Unit 1996).

Staff from various disciplines stress the value of joint training – pre- and post-qualification – to draw out the commonalities among professions and to encourage mutual understanding of roles and skills (McCollam *et al.* 1997; Sheppard 1991). The implementation of the care programme approach in Scotland has provided an impetus and a focus for such joint training initiatives at local level.

There is also a need to ensure that expertise and skills are not diluted and lost. There is a need, for example, to ensure that Mental Health Officers not only fulfil their statutory responsibilities, but also carry out wider specialist tasks and act as a resource within the local mental health service (see Chapter 5).

In social care, the training agenda is running to keep up with the pace of change and with the development of a widening range of services for people with mental health problems. There are indications that staff do not always possess the competencies and skills to work effectively in such settings and that vocational training qualifications do not relate directly to the practicalities of mental health work (JICC 1996).

Increasingly, mental health service users are seeking to be involved in developing training curricula and in delivering training. However, such involvement still remains the exception rather than the rule (see Chapter 11).

Conclusion

The implementation of community care policies for people with mental health problems is inevitably complex and invariably contentious. This chapter has sought to highlight some of the recent trends in policy and practice in Scotland to reflect on their inter-relationship and to set social work activities in context. This final section will consider briefly challenges and opportunities which must be confronted to ensure the continuing development of community-based mental health services. The points raised are of relevance in Scotland but also beyond.

Information, research and evaluation

Community care implementation requires effective information systems to perform the core tasks of needs assessment, planning, resource allocation and so on (Bovell 1997). As we have seen, attempts to build up an accurate picture of current mental health services founder because of the lack of information and inconsistencies in the way in which information is recorded. There is an urgent need for local data sets which are compatible with national requirements (Accounts Commission 1994) and which are developed and utilised on an interagency basis.

To ensure that scarce resources are used optimally requires sound evidence of the effectiveness of different models and approaches. A solid body of research evidence has been accumulated (e.g. Leff *et al.* 1997). However, such research and evaluation needs to be harnessed more closely to service development, both to promote good practice and strengthen accountability to those who use services (see Chapter 10). In addition, it is important that mechanisms are in place to link practice to policy, to ensure that the lessons emerging from policy implementation are fed back into the policy-making machinery.

Policy coordination

Probably the greatest challenge for mental health agencies is to achieve a coordinated approach to service planning and delivery, avoiding fragmentation. The policy lead from the Scottish Office as laid out in the *Framework* reiterates the imperative of joint working. This in turn places an onus on the Scottish Office to ensure that appropriate arrangements are in place to monitor the implementation of policy on a joint interdepartmental basis, rather than in a fragmentary and partialised manner, as has tended to be the case hitherto.

The effective provision of mental health services is influenced by many factors beyond the realms of mental health policy. In the first place, wider government policies – such as housing and social security – can impede the effectiveness of services. Coordination is as vital at national policy level as at local service delivery level. There is a paradox in the effort central government has invested in exhorting and encouraging local agencies to work together, when the same 'seamlessness' is far from apparent within and between the Scottish Office and Whitehall.

Equally, it is striking that government policy on mental health is concerned with services to provide care and treatment for individuals, principally the small minority who have severe and enduring mental health problems. This largely ignores the impact of wider social and economic factors on the mental health of individuals and communities. It also overlooks valuable work undertaken in mental health promotion to broaden people's understanding of mental health problems as experienced by themselves and others (Tudor 1996).

There is a major issue around the public's perceptions of mental health and support for community care initiatives. Service developers continue to face hostile reactions from local communities, leading on occasions to the revision of plans to move people out of hospital. To carry through a major piece of social change such as the closure of the old-style psychiatric hospitals requires a strategy to inform and educate the public and to gain their support. This has particular significance at local authority level, where elected members, who play a key role in deciding how resources should be allocated, are influenced by public attitudes. Nationally defined policy priorities may therefore be at odds with local intentions.

Last, and perhaps most important, the policy of creating and maintaining comprehensive community-based mental health services is a long-term undertaking. Its implementation is beset by the difficulties of funding arrangements which are short term and insecure. Local agencies are expected to produce strategies for service development against a background of budgetary uncertainty and pressure. In addition, the environment of constant change in organisations and structures is not conducive to the establishment of robust working relationships between agencies, itself the prerequisite of effective community care for people with mental health problems.

References

Accounts Commission (1994) *Squaring the Circle. Managing Community Care Resources.* Edinburgh: Accounts Commission.

Age Concern Scotland/Edinburgh Association for Mental Health (1996) *Older People with Mental Health Difficulties. User Preferences and Housing Options.* Edinburgh: Age Concern Scotland.

Audit Commission (1994) *Finding a Place: A Review of Mental Health Services for Adults.* London: HMSO.

Blom Cooper, L., Hally, H. and Murphy, E. (1995) *The Falling Shadow: One Patient's Mental Health Care 1978–1993.* London: Duckworth.

Bovell, V. (1997) The implications for social services departments of the information task in the social care market. *Health and Social Care in the Community 5,* 94–105.

Checkland, O. (1980) *Philanthropy in Victorian Scotland.* Edinburgh: John Donald.

Clinical Audit and Resource Group (CRAG) (1996) *Final Report. Working Group on Mental Illness.* Edinburgh: The Scottish Office.

Clinical Standards Advisory Group (1995) *Schizophrenia.* London: HMSO.

Consultation and Advocacy Promotion Service (1995) *Research into Mental Health Crisis Services for Lothian.* Edinburgh: CAPS.

Department of Health (1989) *Caring for People. Community Care in the Next Decade and Beyond.* London: HMSO.

Department of Health (1997) *Developing Partnerships in Mental Health.* London: HMSO.

Drucker, N. (1986) Lost in the Haar. A critique of mental health in focus. In D. McCrone (ed) *Scottish Government Yearbook.* Edinburgh: Unit for the Study of Government in Scotland, University of Edinburgh.

Eastwood Mental Health Forum (1996) *Mental Health Service Planning and Provision.* Glasgow: Eastwood Mental Health Forum.

Glasgow Association for Mental Health (1996) *Promoting Awareness. Perceptions of Mental Health Needs of Black and Ethnic Minority Communities in Glasgow.* Glasgow: GAMH.

Goldberg, D. and Huxley, P. (1992) *Common Mental Disorders – A Biosocial Model.* London: Routledge.

Health Services Research Unit, University of Aberdeen (1996) *A Survey of Community Mental Health Teams.* Unit Report No. 7. London: HMSO.

Higgins, R. (1994) Working together: lessons for collaboration between health and social services. *Health and Social Care in the Community 2,* 269–328.

Hill, R. and Shepherd, G. (1997) Joint resolutions. *Health Services Journal 107,* 30–31.

House of Commons Health Committee (1997) *Child and Adolescent Mental Health Services.* London: HMSO.

House of Commons Scottish Affairs Committee (1995) *The Future of Scotland's Psychiatric Hospitals.* London: HMSO.

House of Commons Scottish Affairs Committee (1997) *The Implementation of Community Care in Scotland. Vols I and II.* London: HMSO.

Hunter, D. and Wistow, G. (1987) *Community Care in Britain. Variations on a Theme.* London: King's Fund.

JICC (1996) *Study into the Qualifications and Training for Staff and Volunteers Working with Adults of Pre-retirement Age who are Mentally Ill in Residential and Non-residential Services.* London: Mental Health Foundation.

Kendrick, S. (1993) The burdens of illness. Unpublished discussion paper. Information Services Division, Scottish Health Service, Edinburgh.

Knapp, M. (1992) *Care in the Community: Challenge and Demonstration.* Aldershot: Ashgate.

Leff, J. (ed) (1993) The TAPS project: evaluating community placement of long-stay psychiatric patients. *British Journal of Psychiatry 162,* supplement 19.

Martin, F.M. (1984) *Between the Acts. Community Mental Health Services 1959–83.* London: Nuffield Provincial Hospitals Trust.

McCollam, A. (1994) *Training, Employment and Day Activities for People with Mental Health Problems. A Survey of Service Users' Views.* Edinburgh: Scottish Association for Mental Health.

McCollam, A. (1997) *The Challenge of Change. The Training and Support Needs of Mental Health Nurses Moving into Community Settings.* Edinburgh: Scottish Association for Mental Health.

Mental Health Foundation (1993) *Mental Illness: The Fundamental Facts.* London: Mental Health Foundation.

Midwinter, A. (1997) Local government in a devolved Scotland. *Scottish Affairs 18,* 24–35.

National Association of Health Authorities and Trusts (1997) *Mental Health Care. From Problems to Solutions. An NHS Perspective. Research Paper No. 2.* Birmingham: NAHAT.

Nuffield Centre for Community Care Studies, University of Glasgow (1995). *Evaluating the Effectiveness of the Mental Illness Specific Grant: Initial Mapping Exercise.* Glasgow: University of Glasgow.

Office for Population and Census Studies (1995) Report 1. *The Prevalence of Psychiatric Morbidity among Adults Living in Private Households.* London: HMSO.

Petch, A., Hallam, A. and Knapp, P. (1996) *Delivering Community Care. The Initial Implementation of Care Management in Scotland.* The Scottish Office/ HMSO.

Poole, L. and Broderick, A. (1995) *In-Service Training and Support Needs in the New Community Setting: An Exploratory Study of Psychiatric Nurses' Perceptions.* Edinburgh: Department of Social Policy, University of Edinburgh.

Pozner, A. (1996) *Working It Out. Creating Work Opportunities for People with Mental Health Problems.* Brighton: Pavilion Publishing.

Ritchie, J., Dick, D. and Lingham, R. (1994) *Report into the Care and Treatment of Christopher Clunis.* London: HMSO.

Scottish Association for Mental Health (1996a) *Annual Report.* Edinburgh: SAMH.

Scottish Association for Mental Health (1996b) *The Mental Health (Scotland) Act: Consensus for Change? A Report on a Major Conference to Consider the Need for a Fundamental Review of the Mental Health Act.* Edinburgh: SAMH.

Scottish Association for Mental Health (1994–97) *'End of an Era' Briefing Papers.* Edinburgh: SAMH.

Scottish Council for Voluntary Organisations (1997) *Head and Heart. The Report of the Commission on the Future of the Voluntary Sector in Scotland.* Edinburgh: SCVO.

Scottish Health Service, Information and Services Division. Scottish Health Service Costs (1995/96). Edinburgh: Scottish Health Service.

Scottish Health Service, Information and Services Division. Scottish Health Statistics (1996). Edinburgh: Scottish Health Service.

Scottish Home and Health Department (1980) *Scottish Health Priorities for the Eighties. A Report by the Scottish Health Services Planning Council.* Edinburgh: HMSO.

Scottish Home and Health Department (1985) *Mental Health in Focus. Report on the Mental Health Services for Adults in Scotland.* Edinburgh: HMSO.

Scottish Home and Health Department (1988) *Scottish Health Authorities' Priorities for the Eighties and Nineties.* Edinburgh: HMSO.

Scottish Homes (1996) *Scotspen: Supported Accommodation Database for Scotland.* Edinburgh: Scottish Homes.

Scottish Human Services (1996) *Business As Usual? Commissioning for Community Care in Scotland.* Edinburgh: SHS Ltd.

Scottish Needs Assessment Programme (1996) *Mental Health Overview and Programme.* Glasgow: Scottish Forum for Public Health Medicine.

Scottish Needs Assessment Programme (forthcoming) *The Involvement of Users and Carers in Assessing the Need for Commissioning and Monitoring Mental Health Services.* Glasgow: Scottish Forum for Public Health Medicine.

Scottish Office (1991) *Framework for Mental Health Services in Scotland.* Edinburgh: The Stationery Office.

Scottish Office Department of Health (1997) *Draft Framework for Mental Health Services in Scotland.* Edinburgh: SODH.

Scottish Office Statistical Bulletin, Social Work Series (1996)

Social Work Services Group (1997) *Scottish Office Statistical Bulletin.* Edinburgh: The Scottish Office.

Sheppard, M. (1991) *Mental Health Work in the Community: Theory and Practice in Social Work and Community Psychiatric Nursing.* London: Falmer.

Sheppard, M. (1994) Maternal depression, child care and the social work role. British *Journal of Social Work 24,* 33–51.

Shields Report (1996) *Commissioning Better Health. Report of the Short Life Working Group on the Roles and Responsibilities of Health Boards.* Edinburgh: The Scottish Office.

Social Work Services Inspectorate (1996) *Moving Forward with Care. Community Care in Angus, Dundee City and Perth and Kinross.* Edinburgh: The Scottish Office/HMSO.

Tudor, K. (1996) *Mental Health Promotion. Paradigms and Practice.* London: Routledge.

Turner-Crowson, J. (1993) *Reshaping Mental Health Services. Implications for Britain of US Experience.* London: King's Fund Institute.

Watkins, M., Hervey, N., Carson, J. and Ritter, S. (eds) (1996) *Collaborative Community Mental Health Care.* London: Arnold.

White, J. (ed) (1995) *On the Margins. Planning Mental Health Services in Rural Areas.* Edinburgh: Scottish Association for Mental Health.

Further reading

Pickard, L. (1992) *Evaluating the Closure of Cane Hill.* London: Research and Development in Psychiatry.

Schneider, J. and Hallam, A. (1996) *Specialist Work Schemes and Mental Health.* PSSRU Discussion Paper 1178. Canterbury: University of Kent.

Social Work Services Inspectorate (1995) *Time Well Spent. A Report on Day Services for Mentally Ill People.* Edinburgh: The Scottish Office/HMSO.

CHAPTER 3

Community-Based Mental Health Services

Anne Connor[1]

Introduction

One of the main developments in mental health services has been in the range of community-based services providing care and support for people with mental health problems. It is these services with which most of the social workers support-ing people with mental health problems will be in contact most frequently.

People in different situations will, of course, look for, and at, information about community-based mental health services in different ways. The people who are in-volved, and whose interests this chapter seeks to address, include:

- Social workers in case manager roles making an assessment of a service, or type of service, when assessing the needs of a client and identifying a package of services

- managers planning service changes, who have to consider which services to develop and look for objective data to inform decisions about the most effective use of pressured resources

- managers looking at longer-term or strategic planning of mental health services, often as part of a joint strategy

1   The author writes in a personal capacity.

- people in a community development role, looking at what the scope for new forms of service might be in addressing the needs of a local population, and the challenges such projects might encounter.

This chapter reviews the available research evidence on community-based mental health services, and goes on to consider how social workers and other practitioners in contact with these services may apply the findings. The first part of the chapter outlines the context of any consideration of available research about community-based mental health services. The main part of this chapter describes what each service model is and the information that is available about it, and gives an overview of the available research literature. There is then a resumé of the main points which each of the identified audiences needs to consider when looking at the community mental health services with which they are most likely to be in contact.

Context

Range of community-based services

This is an area where clarity about the terms used is important. The concept of a 'community service' in mental health services varies widely. It is influenced partly by the different professional perspectives of the people providing the service, partly by the circumstances of the people using the services (particularly the severity of the illness and the associated disability the person is experiencing) and partly by the intended outcome of the activity.

For the purposes of this chapter, community mental health services are taken as those that exclusively, or very substantially, respond to the emotional, personal support or other needs of people with recognised mental health problems. The services are divided into five broad types:

- overall hospital reprovision programmes or strategic change programmes
- health-based services in a community setting, such as day hospitals, home treatment and community mental health teams
- direct service provision social care services such as supported accommodation and day care

- services which set out to provide an approach which is alternative or complementary to the 'mental health services' delivered by the statutory providers, such as user-led drop-in centres or advocacy
- services which do not set out to have a specific mental health focus, although a significant proportion of their users have a mental health problem or people with a mental health problem find the service has a significant impact.

A useful comprehensive list of the range of possible services which can respond to the needs of people with mental health problems, including those services not targeted specifically at mental health issues, is the Service Elements section of the *Framework for Mental Health Services in Scotland* (Scottish Office 1997).

The chapter does not seek to cover the ways in which people with mental health problems use the full range of other, mainstream social work services, mainly for reasons of space. Feedback from people with mental health problems, and from their families and friends, is that such services are invaluable forms of support, and can be more acceptable by avoiding the stigma associated with mental health and reinforcing the role of people with mental health problems as citizens and members of a local community. Managers and social workers would wish also to consider the ways in which home care, Emergency Duty Teams and the range of other services respond to the needs of people with mental health problems when making decisions about future service provision.

Types of information and how gathered

Another area where care has to be taken is the status of any available 'evidence' about the service. Some innovative services have been well researched and the results are widely published, but these are the exception. Most services have not been evaluated or researched in the sense of an external review against the stated objectives of the service or other explicit policy or practice objectives, using established research methods that are open to outside scrutiny and validation, and the results published.

This does not mean, however, that no information is available about community services. It is also important to remember that community mental health services are subject to much the same type and standards of research and review as other social care services. The information on which this chapter is based has been drawn from:

- research programmes and academic research studies
- reviews by independent external bodies such as the Mental Welfare Commission (see Chapter 4)
- reviews by the provider
- routine statistical health care and social care information, which can provide an important insight into the impact that innovative services have on mainstream services
- reviews by researchers and consultants from outside the provider organisation: these include reports on services funded by Mental Illness Specific Grants
- user feedback and user reviews – both free-standing reports and as a part of a wider review (see Chapter 11).

A fuller discussion of the evaluation of mental health services is given in Chapter 10 of this volume, and a wider discussion of the strengths and limitations of different forms of evaluation and review is in Connor and Black (1994).

Research findings on each service model

Hospital reprovision or strategic change programmes

SCOPE OF THE MODEL

These are usually joint health authority programmes. They comprise many individual services in the categories given below, but with some degree of overall coordination and monitoring of progress.

RESEARCH FINDINGS

The evidence confirms that reprovision programmes and major changes in the pattern of services have been successful in supporting in the community people who were previously receiving long-term hospital care. They have also been successful in supporting people who previously had made frequent use of acute services, often with very high rates of compulsory admissions (see, for example, Leff 1997; Moser and Burti 1994).

Features of the more successful programmes are:

- the focus is on the wider mental health needs of a community, including people with severe and enduring mental health problems, rather than a more narrow focus on hospital reprovision programmes

- a strong emphasis on working with users and the people who care for them: specific aspects include initiatives to deal with difficulties with side effects of medication or concerns about hospital care to avoid compulsory care where possible, through to user and carer involvement in service planning

- a coordinated continuum of care

- sufficient access to housing as well as to social support

- services such as supported employment schemes, and service models within housing-related care and day care, which promote and work towards normalisation, independence and minimising disability, rather than creating a dependence on mental health services: to some extent this is influenced by the welfare benefits system and other social policies, although there are examples of successful schemes across all social systems

- multidisciplinary community mental health teams

- appropriate and accepted response to crises, which is linked to other elements of care

- home treatment and other alternatives to inpatient acute care: these have been particularly important where there was previously a high level of compulsory admissions; for example, among people from minority ethnic communities

- some community services which target the needs of the most vulnerable people: many programmes include an assertive outreach model

- levels of inpatient care which are lower than at the outset, but with ready access for those needing this form of care

- increasingly, the inclusion of dedicated services to respond to the needs of people with alcohol and/or drug problems that are linked to mental health problems.

Health care services based in a community setting

SCOPE OF THE MODEL

These are NHS or joint NHS and social care services delivered from a community, rather than a hospital, setting. Examples would include community mental health teams, day hospitals, resource centres, home treatment teams and some services targeted at the needs of people at times of crisis and/or emergency. The community focus can reflect the location or the principles and values of the service, and often both. Some services have been established as an alternative to inpatient care in an acute or a longer-stay setting, or as a form and location of care that is more convenient for the people using the services. Service users will probably be referred to as patients, and people staying in a service overnight, or for a few days, are likely to have the status of inpatients, even though the 'feel' of the service is that it is not a hospital.

The social work or social services input to these services is often akin to the role of the hospital-based practitioner in the more traditional hospital setting. The level and form of input will vary, although increasingly the social work element is established as an integral part of the service, and there is evidence that this structure is more effective in the outcomes for service users than looser attachments. In some services, there is also access to housing expertise.

RESEARCH FINDINGS

There is a great deal of information now about most of the appropriate models of care for different patient needs. Findings on issues which are likely to be of particular interest to social work managers and practitioners are listed here. Factors associated with the more successful models and outcomes are:

- social work input bedded in from the outset, rather than added later on
- attachment arrangements are also shown to be effective in terms of outcomes for service users, but have less demonstrated impact on the overall workings of the mental health team
- clear arrangements on the relationship with other parts of the social work service such as the hospital-based team, generic team for the local area, the Emergency Duty Team and the Mental Health Officer role; for example, on handover of care and lead responsibility for assessments

- some flexibility around standard operating arrangements may be needed, for example, referral routes, storage of case notes and supervision
- support for the ethos of the multidisciplinary team from senior managers within the local authority
- clarity on the expected balance between direct client contacts, other caseload time and input to the wider activities of the team. This should include 'hidden caseload' work, where the social worker feeds in to the care given by another professional but has no formal contact with the service user, and the expected outcomes of the social work presence. The literature has examples of social work inputs to community mental health teams being judged a 'failure' and withdrawn because the formal caseload was lower than that of social workers in other parts of the department, even though the value attributed to the input by other members of the team and claimed benefits in outcomes for service users were both high.

Direct service provision social care mental health services

SCOPE OF THE MODEL

Included here are the services purchased or delivered by local authority social work or social services departments specifically for people with mental health problems.

RESEARCH FINDINGS

Housing and support

This includes residential care settings with staff living in, visiting support to people living in a group or communal setting and domiciliary support to people living in an ordinary domestic setting. The housing and care arrangements cover many variations in terms of who holds a tenancy and the extent to which the two elements of care are linked.

Overall, these models of care have been established as more effective than institutional models, and especially inpatient care, provided the care levels are adequate for the individual's needs (Petch 1994). More recent studies have looked at the impact of different ways of organising the service and the benefits and limitations of different models within the spectrum. Factors associated with more successful outcomes – including fewer placements breaking down, service user satisfaction and lower proportions of 'voids' or empty places – are:

- good matching of users' individual and specific support needs and the type of support provided, rather than projects being categorised as providing for high/medium/low need: flexibility within a larger project and ready access to a range of projects/types of care are both shown to be effective

- services which are focused on the needs of particular groups of people with mental health problems, including people from black and minority ethnic communities, women, younger people and older people, are in general more successful in supporting these service users than are the general mental health services

- models where housing and support are not linked and where service users can stay in their homes while the support services change to reflect their needs, are particularly successful for users whose needs can be expected to vary over the medium/longer term

- models where support can vary with the needs of the service user while they stay in their home are especially useful for people who have family commitments, and for people who also have needs associated with a physical disability or becoming older which influence their housing needs

- clear liaison arrangements between the housing and social care providers at both service and strategic/planning levels

- clear liaison/back-up arrangements with health care providers

- clarity about the extent to, and ways in which, people who use these services can get access to other support services such as day care services and respite care. The reviews include accounts of situations where the benefits of the main support service were offset by restricted or no access to other services purchased by the local authority on the basis that the central service, and residential care for other groups of service users, was deemed to cover all the users' needs.

Befriending

Befriending services typically match a service user and a volunteer befriender. The befrienders provide companionship and, for many service users, a source of support into eventual use of a wider range of other mental health or mainstream activities. Services are generally delivered to a high standard, with tight management to ensure appropriate recruitment, training, supervision and support of befrienders and sensitive matching of service user and befriender.

These services have been found to be especially effective for:

- people whose needs or circumstances make it difficult for them to use group-based activities such as those provided by most other daytime services, and those who have little in common with the majority of other people using mental health services, for example older people with mental health problems

- complementing the input of other services, such as housing-related support schemes, structured day activities and care from community mental health teams or day hospitals.

Day activities

Daytime services operating on a structured or on a 'drop-in' basis are a long-established form of care for people with mental health problems, and have many positive outcomes for users (Buglass and Dick 1991; Social Work Services Inspectorate for Scotland (SWSIS) 1995). Features highlighted in the research are:

- services which have regularity and continuity of contact are effective for people who need help to establish relationships with other people and for those who need someone to monitor their mental and/or physical well-being and bring in other services when needed

- day services are an effective alternative to hospital inpatient and day hospital care: the outcomes are better when there is a clear and sensitive arrangement about the monitoring role of the day service and the response of the hospital-based or community mental health services when a service user needs additional care

- drop-in centres provide a different range of benefits from those of the more structured facilities

- features such as warmth, a daytime meal and so on are particularly significant to users in some circumstances, including people who live alone and have a tendency to neglect their general well-being

- the ethos and general atmosphere of the services are significant factors in successful outcomes: providing care in a non-stigmatising way in all settings and getting the right balance between the monitoring and supporting roles of structured services for people with higher needs

- services which are able to provide easier or supported access to mainstream activities – such as leisure and sporting facilities, community education, shops and cafés – are likely to have greater throughput as service users move on from, or make less frequent use of, the services

- where there is a range of daytime services in an area, many people make use of more than one service, gaining different forms of support from each: examples include 'packages' which have been put together by the service users.

Aspects of these services that have been identified with less successful outcomes, or as limitations on the service model, are:

- the relative lack of services away from the main centres of population

- general lack of services outside office hours: users particularly value drop-in services and those with less structured activities at evenings, weekends and public holidays, which are often periods of particular difficulty for people with mental health problems

- practical access problems, especially the cost and convenience of transport to centres

- lack of child care facilities, either at the centres or through an associated arrangement with a child care resource

- lack of facilities at the centres to talk to someone in privacy, or just to be quiet and alone for a while

- lack of user involvement in the running and development of the service: some services, more often those which had been operating for many years and those with very strong links to a hospital or local authority service, had limited user involvement. These services were also associated with narrower ranges of activities provided at or through the service, fewer users moving on to other things and generally lower levels of satisfaction among their users.

Even where services are effective and valued by the people who use them, they may fail to meet the needs of other people with mental health problems who wish to use this type of resource. Consistently, the groups who are identified as less likely to use the services are women, single parents or others with caring responsibilities, people from black and minority ethnic communities and younger people (aged under 25). (For a discussion of the needs of older people with mental health problems and service responses, see Chapter 8.) In most cases the response to this has been separate or spin-off services for these groups of service user. There are, however, examples of general projects which appear to have managed to reflect a diversity of users' situations and needs through such means as related child care facilities, sessions for particular groups of users, outreach and follow-up contacts for all people referred to the service who did not return, and a proactive approach to addressing sexism and racism throughout the operation of the project.

A growing sub-set of day activities is the Clubhouse model, which is based on the work-ordered day and a strong emphasis on what each person can contribute, rather than on their disabilities and needs. Members and staff share the day-to-day running of the Clubhouse on an equal basis. Activities typically include the administration of the service, including monitoring and research; snack bars, educational units and other facilities used by members; publishing newsletters; transitional employment; and a social programme that takes place out of office hours. The Clubhouse model was first established in the United States in the 1940s. International expansion has been more recent, but there are now over 300 Clubhouses throughout the world. The model has been well researched – see, for example, MacLean (1997) and reports produced by local Clubhouses in the UK.

The evaluations and reports of these services, as with other innovative projects, seek to highlight the ways in which this model differs from other services which may seem very similar – in this instance, other drop-in or sheltered employment services. The evaluations do confirm that the approach is successful for people with serious mental health problems and a high level of need, as well as for people with a lower level of need.

Supported employment schemes

The reviews note a similar range of benefits to users as those identified for the other day services, plus gaining and/or updating skills and knowledge relevant to the workplace. Benefits identified by users include specific skills related to particular tasks and trades, and the routine and standards expected in employment, including social interactions. Gaining experience and getting references from employment projects and work placements enhanced the chances of continued or subsequent employment. Schemes that negotiate or provide initial support for staff in employment settings are also reported as effective in the short and longer term by staff and employers (Cunningham *et al.* 1996; SWSIS 1995).

Comparisons of the costs of employment and other forms of day activities can be difficult: overall, the cost per user-week is higher in the employment services, especially those providing more tailored support. There are few evaluations which have compared the outcomes for users and costs over longer periods of, say, two to three years and in a way which permits reliable comparison across the characteristics of the users. The information that is available does seem to bear out the claim that the employment projects can be cost-effective in the longer term when there is a clear focus in enabling people to move on to employment or to other activities that reflect their abilities and needs. A complicating factor for many of the employment projects featured in the evaluations reviewed was the form of funding for the project. Those projects which received all or part of their funding from enterprise schemes or economic regeneration programmes were often assessed against the number of trainees moving into paid employment, which could be a strong disincentive to work with users with higher or more complex needs (see, for example, Cunningham *et al.* 1996).

Wider employment support schemes that work with people with a range of circumstances and needs also have to be considered. These tend to be more frequent in areas outwith cities. From the information available, these appear to be as effective as specialised mental health services when the operation of the scheme and the approach taken by the trainers are sensitive to the particular needs of people with mental health problems – such as the fluctuating nature of illnesses, difficulties in relating to other people, and so on. In some cases, users have reported the wider focus as positive in reducing stigma associated with mental health problems.

Respite care

There are very few examples of respite care services focused on the needs of people with mental health problems. One of the rare examples of a report on a mental health respite provision is an evaluation of a residential project in Edinburgh (Petch 1996). There are, however, references in many reports on day services, crisis services and so on of 'respite functions' – some provided explicitly but many more implicitly.

Factors highlighted in the reviews and in more general accounts of user feedback on mental health needs and services as associated with more effective respite care are:

- ease of access, and in particular streamlined assessment arrangements at the time the user seeks respite
- range of responses: opportunities for the person with a mental health problem to be in a different environment and for the person to stay at home while a substitute arrangement is found for the carer's input
- clarity about the nature of the 'respite' and sensitivity to the circumstances of people with mental health problems and their carers: for example, not limiting the scheme to people who live in the same house as their carer
- clarity about the purposes of other services – such as inpatient and crisis care – which are intended to meet a specific care need but can have an important secondary respite benefit, and avoidance of distortions resulting from different access and financial arrangements.

Projects which bridge between hospital discharge and community living

Some of these services are focused on the needs of people leaving long-stay hospital care. Others focus also, or instead, on people leaving acute wards. All aim to ensure fewer readmissions or breakdowns in care arrangements, and fewer demands on social work and health care services in the first few months following discharge.

Factors associated with the more successful services are:

- clear relationship to, and links with, the mainstream health and social work services which will provide ongoing support to the person if needed
- a context of good discharge planning arrangements: from some accounts of services it appeared that the service had been introduced to overcome poorly planned or managed routine discharge planning arrangements
- some flexibility about who could refer to the service and when – in particular, whether the service could take on a case a few days after discharge
- a remit which covered a wide range of practical and emotional support tasks, including referral to services providing ongoing support or guaranteed reassessment of the client's needs

- clear criteria, which enable the service to target appropriately, and timescale for the service's inputs: in these circumstances there were instances of an ongoing service, such as a community mental health team, providing a 'bridging support' as a distinct form of short-term intervention.

Services which set out to provide an alternative or complementary approach
SCOPE OF THE MODEL

For the purposes of this chapter, this set of activities has been taken as services which are focused on the mental health needs of the users and seek to provide an approach to meeting those needs which is significantly different from that of the statutory health or social work services. In practice, this may be a somewhat arbitrary distinction, and many of the notes in the previous section about certain forms of service – such as the discussion of the Clubhouse model and other forms of daytime activity and supported employment – also belong here.

RESEARCH FINDINGS

Self-help groups and user-led drop-in groups

These activities are centred on people with mental health problems coming together with other people who identify themselves as having shared experiences and supporting each other. Many of the self-help groups are based around experience of a particular condition and are linked to national voluntary organisations. Most of the other groups aim to support people with mental health problems who are living in a particular local area: these are frequently found in peripheral urban areas and more rural areas. Common features are that the individual members use the groups in the way that they find helpful in terms of frequency of contact and so on, and that the organisation of the group is member-directed.

The main sources of information about these services are accounts by the projects themselves and reports on specific projects by assessors or outside evaluations in relation to applications for future funding. The common findings are:

- feedback from the users is positive about the benefits they identify from their belonging to the group, which are not gained from other services
- some groups' users include, or are predominantly, people with severe and enduring mental health problems and people with complex social needs: the benefits identified by these users suggest the self-help groups are often used to

complement other forms of support and care and are an important element in the effectiveness of the overall package of support for these individuals

- other groups are mostly providing for the needs of people with less severe mental health problems: in some cases this is the intended and stated aim of the group, but elsewhere groups which were initially set up to provide mutual support to people with higher needs have lost this focus

- some of the external assessments have identified the views of people who do not use the groups: issues raised here include limited awareness about the group, groups with long-standing membership being perceived as unwelcoming, and uncertainty about how the group interacts with the statutory services

- effective models in addressing limitations include an identified member or worker who links with each new member, frequent publicity events and invitations to new members, and established liaison with other health and social care services.

Stress centres

These typically offer a range of therapies and self-help approaches to managing stress and promoting positive ways of preventing or minimising stress. Examples in the literature were run by voluntary sector or private organisations, resourced by core funding and/or charges to users. The contact had to be initiated by the user, although this could stem from a suggestion by a professional or friend.

The types of available report are similar to those on the mutual support and drop-in groups. The main findings are:

- users value the services very highly: positive comments relate to their ability to cope with stressful situations and more general support, contact with other people, and so on.

- fewer reports noted feedback from professionals. Where there was feedback, this was also generally positive in terms of the benefits for clients or patients who had used the project

- aspects such as the physical environment and attitudes and values of those working at the centres (in paid or volunteer roles) are identified as having a strong bearing on the outcomes for individuals

- the more successful interventions had clear and realistic aims, such as working with users to manage their stress and to deal with sources of stress over which the individuals had influence

- where users had complex problems – such as very poor housing, were experiencing violence or other abuse, or were coping with serious illness or disability – the projects had little impact in 'solving' the users' stress. Some projects appear to have been assessed against unrealistic expectations in this regard

- a related issue was how the projects should relate to community development and campaigning activities. The more successful projects appeared to be those which had links with other organisations which worked with service users to address issues which contributed to difficult social circumstances for local people, but limited the effort which the stress centre itself put into the activities.

Advocacy

Accounts of advocacy projects describe the services and report the outcomes as identified by service users, those providing the advocacy services, and professionals in the other – particularly statutory social work and health – services the user is being supported in using. Overall, the feedback confirms that these services contribute to the users receiving more appropriate and more successful care from direct care services and similar outcomes in gaining access to welfare benefits, housing services, and so on (Scottish Health Advisory Service and Scottish Office 1997).

Factors associated with such services being more or less successful consistently relate to:

- clarity about the nature and purpose of the advocacy service

- the organisation of the service, including training, supervision and support for the advocates; there is no evidence of volunteer or paid advocates being the more successful when other factors have been taken into account

- recognition and back-up from senior staff in the social work and health services.

Services run by and for women and people from the black and minority ethnic communities

At first sight, many of the projects aimed exclusively or mainly at the needs of the black and minority ethnic communities, or at the needs of women with mental health problems, may be much the same as the services described in the previous section. The bulk of the activities are day services, residential or domiciliary support, counselling, befriending, and so on. The reason they are considered here lies in the different value base which many of these services seek to embody, rather than an implication that the mainstream services should not appropriately respond to the needs of all their potential users.

The particular needs of people from the black and minority ethnic communities are reviewed in Chapter 7. The reviews of services demonstrate the differences between services which are used extensively by black people, and those which are designed to reflect and respond to the experiences and the needs of this group of service users – even when some of the people who use the latter services are not from the black communities. Features of these services which are identified in the evaluations as contributing to their effectiveness include the greater, and explicit, attention given to:

- a holistic approach, manifested by activities such as Tai Chi and cultural activities, as well as complementary therapies
- concepts of wellness and illness: for example, some services will classify depression separately from mental illness, because this is more meaningful to the users of that service
- the social context in which many service users are living, with activities and 'reasons for referral' including experience of racism, harassment, personal isolation and poverty
- links into activities such as English Language Learning, other education and skills training, and access to services such as Women's Aid, which are intended to assist service users in reducing or avoiding some of the factors contributing to their mental health problems.

Many women have also experienced mental health services as not well suited to their circumstances and needs. Factors in this include:

- the extent to which services focusing on the needs of people with severe and enduring mental health problems are built around the needs of younger men, who are more likely than women to experience psychotic illnesses

- the different experience by women of mental ill-health: more women than men have mental health problems; they are more likely to experience depression and certain other illnesses (Meltzer Gill and Petticrew 1994), and the way in which they use, or are offered care by, the main mental health services tends to involve a more limited range of interventions
- the relatively high extent to which women using mental health services will have experienced sexual abuse or violence
- the particular circumstances of women with mental health problems who are mothers: they are more likely than other women to be single parents, and many women who have received acute psychiatric care, particularly on a compulsory basis, face the loss of custody of their children or periods when their children are taken into care.

Factors in services designed around the needs of women with mental health problems which users particularly value, and which are associated with successful outcomes, have many similarities with those noted for the services developed by the black and minority ethnic communities:

- a range of therapeutic responses to depression, stress and other mental health problems, usually linked to access to a range of complementary therapies and a supportive approach to helping users withdraw from prescribed medication, and reflecting a more holistic approach to physical and emotional well-being
- a women-only environment: this is also a feature of services developed for women from minority ethnic communities
- child care facilities, or easier access to mainstream child care
- support with matters such as coping with violence and abuse and their consequences, personal relationships, and maintaining or regaining custody or access to their children
- activities which promote self-confidence: this ranges from counselling to community education and skills training
- negotiated links with the main mental health services, including ventures such as joint groups with community mental health teams, outreach clinics taking place within the women's project, planned arrangements for the care of

children when their mother becomes unwell, and participation in the crisis plans for users.

Services which do not set out to have a mental health focus

SCOPE OF THE MODEL

This comprises a large and very wide-ranging body of services in the statutory and voluntary sectors. They are not specifically aimed at the needs of people with mental health problems, although a significant proportion of their users have a mental health problem or people with a mental health problem find the service has a significant impact. The descriptions and reviews of these services typically focus on what needs the person has and what the service or project offers – such as help with budgeting skills, companionship, and help with regaining or acquiring confidence and social skills – rather than focusing on the mental health aspects.

For the purposes of this chapter, these activities are taken as including:

- services such as the Samaritans, Rape Crisis and Cruse, which may not regard themselves as 'mental health' services
- activities which provide ongoing support, such as women's groups
- specific services which have a generic focus, such as supported employment services, or which are targeted on other specific social care needs, such as those of young homeless people, where there is a significant overlap.

RESEARCH FINDINGS

The information that is available about this group of activities is similar to that on other services of these types. An additional problem here, however, is that the reviews may not identify separately the 'mental health' elements of the service. The reports are even less likely to have addressed outcomes in terms of the users' mental health and it can be difficult to make a direct comparison of relative effectiveness between these and services with a 'mental health' designation in dealing with mental health problems.

Factors which appear to be associated with effective services, in terms of impact on users' mental health needs, are:

- the service meeting a specific and identified need or issue
- the standards of the service in fulfilling its main aim

- a sensitive and non-labelling approach to people who have mental health problems

- a sympathetic and caring environment: examples highlighted by users include the time given to callers to telephone services as well as the ambience and furnishings of drop-in centres, project offices and other locations

- an awareness of how to respond when someone clearly has a higher level of need, such as relevant suggestions or encouragement to contact other services: this is the area where these services may have difficulties, although there are examples of services being members — sometimes on an 'associate' basis — of local mental health networks, receiving and making referrals to mental health services and linking into mental health services through joint training on specific issues

- high standards of supervision and training of volunteers and staff as a feature underlying the other features.

Summary: what it means for audiences interested in the social work dimension of community mental health services

Social workers in case manager roles

A common finding in most evaluations and reports, and coming through even more strongly when one is taking an overview, is that no service will meet the needs of all users all of the time. The message is that the social worker needs an intelligent and critical questioning of the information about services to determine whether a particular model, and within that a particular service, will meet the needs of a client at that time.

Another central finding is that organisational factors are as important as the type of service. This applies to the management and standards of the direct care service, and also to the standards of practice on the part of those professionals making the assessment and referrals.

In this, factors associated with successful selection of services — across all types — include:

- clarity about which needs that service is expected to address

- services having access to relevant information about the service user's needs or circumstances

- care arrangements being updated to reflect users' changing needs (both when people have increasing needs and are insufficiently supported and when people have decreasing needs and find the service restricting)
- services and enduring mental illness, particularly in the earlier phases of the illness: problems are more frequently noted in services which were designed to deal with a fairly static type and level of need, sometimes based on provision for frail older people or people with learning disabilities
- single-sex facilities, or space within services
- services which take account of users' wider needs, rather than focusing only on the mental health needs (although not necessarily providing for these wider needs): the research studies and reviews highlight that to many people their financial, housing, work or relationship problems have much greater significance for them than their mental health problems
- services that take account of users sometimes being unable to, or reluctant to, initiate or maintain contact: this can be an 'assertive outreach' approach or a more flexible way of interacting with users, especially with those with severe and enduring mental health problems
- services which plan with service users for their moving on.

Managers planning service changes

Research-based reviews of services tend not to offer simple answers to managers considering which services to develop or reduce. However, if one reads the reports widely and carefully, there is a lot of useful material which can inform decisions about the most effective use of pressured resources.

One important aspect is in identifying needs for services and gaps in service patterns. For example, in a way typical of many of the reports reviewed for this chapter, one review of day services identified evening and weekend services and access to services in rural areas as unmet needs. It also highlighted the extent to which service users valued befriending, counselling and crisis responses, which were at that time largely undeveloped (Buglass and Dick 1991). But the limits of accounts of unmet needs based on existing patterns of service and perceived demand are well established. The report by SWSIS (1996), for example, identifies the strengths and limitations of a range of sources of apparent information about need and demand for services, including statistical data, prevalence of mental health conditions, and user-identified needs and preferred responses.

Factors identified from the research which managers would wish to consider in planning any mental health services are:

- the extent to which service users feel empowered and a lack of stigma: this is not limited to mental health but is particularly important here, in light both of features of the impact of these illnesses and our society's attitudes to mental illness

- users, carers and professionals having information about what services are available, and users and carers having ready access to information about their mental illness and its treatment

- services where the staffing levels and skills continue to reflect the scale of activity and needs of the users. There are innumerable accounts in the literature of services that gradually expanded beyond the initial client group or format until they hit an apparent 'crisis' requiring additional funding and/or considerable internal restructuring

- general projects that cut across client groups but focus on a specific need or activity can be very effective if structured to take account of the particular needs of people with severe and enduring mental health problems. The more successful projects usually tailor the package to the needs of each individual user. Examples include supported employment and community education projects.

Managers looking at longer-term or strategic planning of mental health services

The research findings are brought together in a more manageable form by the main policy and practice reviews – for example, on the contribution of social work services as part of a joint strategy. They are also borne out by the studies of individual local services.

The successful outcomes which many managers are seeking reassurance on are those relating to the care of people with severe and enduring mental health problems in community settings. Factors which elected members and senior staff in local authorities, like their counterparts in the health service, will often have in mind are:

- making sure relatively few people lose contact with the service
- preventing suicides and serious acts of violence towards other people
- avoiding undue delayed discharge or bed blocking on acute wards
- assessing whether the programme works over a lengthy period
- ensuring the costs are not escalating over time.

Factors associated with more successful developments are:

- continuum of services, with no significant gaps between those offering extensive and lower levels of care
- services which interact with each other to provide an effective continuity for the individual service user. There are examples of this being achieved through central coordination and through good links between the individual services. The research does not appear to be conclusive about which model is the more effective, but is clear that effective links are essential
- social work input bedded into community mental health teams from the outset, rather than added on as a later development.

People in a community development role

These groups of staff are often looking at what new forms of service they might bring to address the needs of a local population, and the challenges such projects might encounter.

Outcomes in which this audience may be particularly interested include:

- the extent to which the project leads to the development of other projects, in the local area or for the district
- balance between expanding to meet growing demand from users and/or those commissioning the service, and having a 'homely' or 'family' focus
- types of funding: tension between security of service-level agreements for a certain level and type of service, and less secure funding for a more flexible range of activities to reflect emerging and user- or community-identified needs
- difficulties in explaining the ethos or form of innovative community services to decision makers who are more familiar with traditional forms of service.

Findings from studies are that:

- community development projects can be successful in direct service delivery, including meeting the needs of people with a high level of mental health need. Not all services set out to provide this kind of support, however

- effectiveness of general projects in addressing specific mental health needs: examples include women's projects, carer support services and support for people from minority ethnic groups. All of these are likely to be used by a significant number of people with mental health problems and to be effective in meeting some of these users' needs.

Case example: a community mental health resource

As a case example, it is useful to look at the experience of a local mental health project which arose out of a generic health promotion project in an inner-city area with high levels of social deprivation. The project was jointly funded by the local authority and the health authority, with additional short-term funding at the outset as part of an urban regeneration programme. Over ten years the spin-off projects were:

- a drop-in café for women, which in turn led to a post-natal depression support group and another, more structured, women's group

- an unemployed workers' project

- a support service for carers, primarily of older people, with a strong emphasis on stress management

- a city-wide project for women from black and minority ethnic communities, and latterly a partnership project for men from the black communities

- a city-wide young carers project

- a support group for carers of people with mental health problems

- a stress centre

- a counselling project

- a youth project with a strong counselling focus which later became a young men's mental health project

- a user-led drop-in centre mostly for people with severe and enduring mental health problems which in turn led to a small supported employment scheme
- an advocacy project, originally linked to the user-led drop-in centre but now an independent group
- a partnership project for supported access into community education.

Not all of these projects survived beyond the first two to three years, and perceived 'failures' have been cited against the project. The project has also been criticised for stimulating additional demands at a time of budget pressures.

Issues for the core project, as for many other community development projects, have been:

- the balance between meeting the needs of the current users of services and the wider community
- the balance between very local services and issues of service models which would be more effective when delivered on a larger basis
- the balance between obtaining core funding for the central service – which now has little direct service activity – and for new developments in direct services
- how far, and for how long, the core project continues to support and manage the spin-off projects
- responding to the by now sometimes strongly conflicting expectations and views of the users of services and people within the local community.

References

Buglass, D. and Dick, S. (1991) *Not Just Somewhere To Go.* Edinburgh: Scottish Association for Mental Health.

Connor, A. and Black, S. (eds) (1994) *Performance Review and Quality in Social Care. Research Highlights in Social Work 20.* London: Jessica Kingsley Publishers.

Cunningham, G., Dick, S., Temple, M. and Whiteley, S. (1996) *Work at Your Own Pace: An Evaluation of SAMH Training Projects.* Edinburgh: Scottish Association of Mental Health.

Leff, J. (ed) (1997) *Care in the Community – Illusion or Reality?* Chichester: Wiley.

MacLean, C. (1997) *The Clubhouse Model in the UK: A Personal Overview; the Mental Health Review 2:2.* Brighton: Pavilion Publishing.

Meltzer, H., Gill, B. and Petticrew, M. (1994) *The Prevalence of Psychiatric Morbidity among Adults Aged 16–64, Living in Private Households in Great Britain; in Number 1.* London: Office of Population Censuses and Surveys.

Moser, L. and Burti, L. (1994) *Community Mental Health: A Practical Guide.* New York and London: Norton and Co.

Petch, A. (1994) Heaven compared to a hospital ward. In M. Titterton (ed) *The New Welfare.* London: Jessica Kingsley Publishers.

Petch, A. (1996) Cairdeas House: Developing good practice in short breaks for individuals with mental health problems. In K. Stalker (ed) *Developments in Short-Term Care. Research Highlights in Social Work 25.* London: Jessica Kingsley Publishers.

Scottish Health Advisory Service and Scottish Office (1997) *Advocacy – A Guide to Good Practice.* Edinburgh: Scottish Office.

Scottish Office (1997) *Framework for Mental Health Services in Scotland.* Edinburgh: Scottish Office.

Social Work Services Inspectorate for Scotland (1995) *Time Well Spent: A Report on Day Services for People with Mental Illness.* Edinburgh: HMSO.

Social Work Services Inspectorate for Scotland (1996) *Population Needs Assessment in Community Care, A Handbook for Planners and Practitioners.* Edinburgh: HMSO.

The sources reviewed for this chapter also included a large number of reports on local projects: local projects in Glasgow and Lothian; other Scottish projects identified through the Community Care Works database, Nuffield Centre, University of Glasgow; and published accounts in the professional journals.

CHAPTER 4

Policy and Management of Social Work Services

The Mental Welfare Commission in the Context of Inspection

Christine E. McGregor

Introduction

The crucial role of organisations which undertake inspection or review of services for vulnerable people has received increasing recognition in recent years (Connor and Black 1993; Henkel 1991). Models include:

- independent organisations with a range of functions which overlap with inspection, such as the Mental Welfare Commission described in this chapter
- visits within government departments, such as the Social Services Inspectorate described by Mitchell and Tolan and by Henkel (both in Connor and Black 1993)
- visits within organisations providing services, such as the Registration and Inspection Units in local government.

These functions are relatively recent in origin, having been established within the last 20 years or so. A notable exception is the statutory oversight of services for people with a mental disorder, where such a function has existed in various forms since the nineteenth century. From the accounts of the early bodies, the factors which influenced their establishment included:

- potential for abuse when people were cared for in closed institutions
- the needs of individuals whose mental illness or disability made them dependent on others but also prevented their taking action to protect their own interests
- society's concern for both the care and control of vulnerable individuals and for the well-being of the wider population
- cost-effective management.

The Mental Welfare Commission is not an inspection body as such, but it does in the course of its duties carry out functions which overlap with those of inspection. The Commission can comment on the standard of services for people with mental disorder but only through individual cases being brought to its attention. This chapter describes the role of the Commission, some of the work it does in relation to the services provided by local authority social work departments, and the interface with inspection.

History and background of the Mental Welfare Commission

There has been a body charged with the responsibility for supervising the care and treatment of persons suffering from mental disorder since 1859, when mental health legislation was first enacted. A General Board of Commissioners for Lunacy for Scotland was in operation until 1913, followed by the General Board of Control until 1960, when the Mental Welfare Commission was brought into being.

The Commission is independent of the National Health Service and local authority. It operates only in Scotland, though there are sister Commissions in England and Wales and in Northern Ireland, albeit with slightly different duties and powers. Each year the Commission submits a report on its activities to the Secretary of State for laying before Parliament.

Commissioners and staff

Commissioners are appointed by Her Majesty the Queen on recommendations from the Secretary of State. Under the terms of the Mental Health (Scotland) Act 1984, the Secretary of State has to consult with persons or bodies with an interest or concern in the appointment of Commissioners. At present there are three full-time Commissioners, including the Director (two medical and one social work), and 16 part-time Commissioners. The Commissioners come from a variety of relevant backgrounds – medical, nursing, social work, occupational therapy, and legal and voluntary organisations. The Commission also employs a group of professional staff – psychiatrists, social workers and a nurse – and in addition has an administrative team headed by the Secretary to the Commission.

General functions

The Commission has a statutory duty to protect persons who by reason of mental disorder (defined in the Act as mental illness or mental handicap) may be incapable of adequately protecting themselves or their interests. This duty extends to all mentally disordered persons irrespective of whether they are in hospital, in local authority or privately run accommodation or in their own homes. In appropriate cases, where mentally disordered persons are liable to detention in hospital or subject to guardianship or a community care order, the Commission may order discharge.

Duty to visit and to make inquiries

The Commission is specifically required to inquire into any case where it appears that there may be ill-treatment, deficiency in care of treatment, or improper detention of any person who may be suffering from mental disorder or where the property of any such person may be exposed to loss or damage. It also has to visit regularly people who have been liable to detention in hospital or who have been made subject to guardianship. In 1996 the Commission's duties were extended to include those subject to community care orders.

The interface with social work services in general

The Commission carries out its functions in different ways which bring it into contact with individual people suffering from mental disorder, their families and carers, health boards and NHS trusts, voluntary organisations, private services and local authority social work departments.

The Mental Health Act, either by implementation of its direct terms or by the formulation of practice based on its terms, defines much of the activity the Commission has in relation to social work services. The Commission has to bring to the attention of the local authority the facts of any case in which the Commission thinks that the local authority should exercise any of its functions to secure the welfare of a person suffering from mental disorder. In so doing, the Commission is guided by its remit of preventing ill-treatment, remedying any deficiency in care or treatment, terminating improper detention, or preventing or redressing loss of damage to property. The Commission has also to give advice to local authorities when they have referred any relevant matter to the Commission.

As can be seen, this is a wide remit which has potential for frequent interaction between the Commission and many of the services which social work departments provide, commission and deliver. There are, however, main areas of activity which regularly keep channels of communication going between the Commission and social work departments: the role carried out by Mental Health Officers, the Commission's visiting programme, guardianship, leave of absence, community care orders, inquiries into complaints and deficiency in care.

Mental Health Officers are social workers within local authorities who are specially trained to carry out social work in relation to the Mental Health Act. The Commission has regular contact with them as they discharge their various duties. For example, the Commission receives Social Circumstance Reports (SCRs), prepared and submitted by Mental Health Officers in respect of those who are detained under the Act. The SCR is valued by the Commission because the context of the patient's detention is described and aspects which coincide with the Commission's core remit are revealed. The Mental Health Officer is also a key contact person in relation to what is happening to the patient, his or her family, the future care plan and any irregularities which may disadvantage him or her (Ulas, Myers and Whyte 1994).

The Mental Welfare Commission recognises the important contribution of Mental Health Officers up and down Scotland and confirms this by participating in the training of Mental Health Officers, both by teaching on courses and supervising short placements at the Commission.

Case example

A Mental Health Officer, in writing an SCR, described the background of a patient detained in a psychiatric hospital and revealed a worrying domestic situation. The woman had been living alone in a large owner-occupied house which had deteriorated in fabric to such an extent that there were holes in the roof with tree life sprouting, an absence of water and electricity services, and primitive conditions in the one room she used. It appeared that she had been suffering from a mental illness for a number of years but because she was resistant to any help and a past master at avoidance, she had not been actively followed up by GP, social work or psychiatric services until the situation had become almost irretrievable. It emerged that she had literally abandoned another property because of its neglected disintegration, and the house in which she was living was rapidly going the same way. The Commission mounted inquiries and reached the opinion that over the years there had been deficiency in care in relation to this person suffering from mental disorder. Without the SCR, the Commission would have been unaware of this woman's history of untreated illness and loss sustained by her in deterioration of her property.

The Commission regularly visits all psychiatric and mental handicap hospitals in Scotland on a rolling programme basis. As might be expected in these times, it has also developed a programme of visiting establishments in the community. The purpose of visiting is mainly to offer individual people suffering from mental disorder an opportunity to raise any matter with an independent body which has powers to effect change in their circumstances.

The task in relation to those who are detained under the Act or on guardianship or leave of absence or community care orders, is more precisely targeted as one of reviewing the person's status and the services being given. As has been stated, the person detained in hospital under the Mental Health Act may seek discharge by the Commission and this is also true of those who continue to be liable to detention although in the community on leave of absence and those on guardianship and community care orders. Assessing for a possible discharge, however, is not the only purpose served by regular visits from the Commission. Many of those visited may benefit from an independent appraisal of their situation and the services being provided.

Case example

A young woman with learning disabilities was living in residential accommodation run by the Social Work Department. She was subject to guardianship because over a period of time it had been established that she was being sexually and financially exploited in the family home. Good assessment and sensitive management of the case settled Miss A in a residential situation, independent of her family and yet permitting some contact with them on a regular basis. The Commission, in accordance with the terms of the Act, visited Miss A regularly and liaised with the Social Work Department about the management of the case under guardianship.

After a year or so of a settled routine, the Social Work Department agreed to the family requests that Miss A should have regular weekend visits to them, including overnight stays. In view of the history, the Commission suggested that it would be in the interests of Miss A's welfare that unannounced visits should be made to the family home when she was there for visits. This was accepted and carried out by the Social Work Department, resulting in less than satisfactory arrangements being revealed and changes in the care plan being effected.

The Commission, with its experience of visiting many people suffering from mental disorder throughout Scotland, has built up a body of knowledge and a view of practice which can lead to suggestions being passed on in local situations. Social work departments and individual workers may have very little experience of working with people on leave of absence or on guardianship or community care orders because the overall national figures are small and therefore, expertise may not get a chance to develop in any sustained way (Mental Welfare Commission for Scotland 1995, 1996, 1997). Advice giving, however, is at the softer end of the Commission's sphere of responsibility.

Getting nearer inspection

It could be argued that by appraising the services being given to people on leave of absence, guardianship and community care orders, the Commission is inspecting the work of health and social work professionals and some view the Commission's role in this way. In fact, this has to be resisted – the Commission is not an Inspectorate, its protective duty is to individuals with mental disorder. It does not inspect services and establishments but looks at the care needs of the person who is ill and vulnerable as a result of mental illness, learning disabilities or dementia. Inevitably the line gets blurred because such persons use services and establishments – how does one separate what help someone needs from what he/she actually gets? How he/she is treated, what accommodation, finances, day programmes and respite care are available, and what respect, dignity and attention are accorded, add up to services, professional practice, resources and the running of establishments – all the essentials of inspection functions. The truth is that the line is hard to hold and there is some inevitable overlap with the work of Social Work Department Inspection Units, the Scottish Office Social Work Services Inspectorate, and the Scottish Health Advisory Service and Registration Teams (for an overview see Connor and Black 1993; Henkel 1991). The Commission does, however, have to remind itself and others regularly that its work is with the individual.

Case example

Mrs B, a 75-year-old lady with dementia, could no longer be managed in the residential home where she had lived for some years. Acknowledging that she had no capacity to agree to her transfer to a nursing home, the Social Work Department applied successfully for guardianship. Mrs B was transferred to a large nursing home with units on three floors. In accordance with its practice of seeing all people on guardianship within a few weeks of court approval, the Commission visited Mrs B. On arrival at her third-floor unit, the Commission's representative immediately encountered an overwhelming smell of urine, and as the visit continued, noted that the level of staff attention being given to the very confused group of elderly patients was poor.

   The Commission immediately drew the matter to the attention of the Social Work Department and wrote directly to the proprietor of the nursing home indicating dissatisfaction with the conditions in which Mrs B was living. It emerged that the social worker had visited only the matron's office in the nursing home and had not inspected the third-floor unit where he was going to require Mrs B to reside through the powers of guardianship. Although the Commission could address the situation of Mrs B, the wider issue of improving general standards and ensuring that the problems were tackled had to be passed to the Registration Department of the Health Board. The deficiencies of the service in matching resources with Mrs B's needs was followed through with the Social Work Department.

There can be considerable difficulties in sorting out the Commission's sphere of responsibility in relation to people in establishments. A home may cater for the frail elderly (not the Commission's responsibility) alongside those becoming confused (questionably the Commission's responsibility) and those who are dementing (definitely the Commission's responsibility). Ongoing action may be being pursued by Inspection and Registration Teams to improve standards of care and physical conditions in establishments which are regarded as below standard. In situations where poor standards are giving concern, effecting change can take time and applying registration regulations can be ponderous. Meanwhile the focus may not be on the individual but on the proprietor, manager and physical conditions. More attention requires to be given to how the Commission works with various bodies which regulate the standards of services given in care establishments.

Complaints

Complaints are a growing business. Citizens' and Patients' Charters have properly encouraged people to know their rights in relation to services. Local authority social work departments are required to have formal complaints procedures under the terms of the NHS and Community Care Act 1990. National Health Service Complaints Procedures have just been reviewed with the aim of achieving a simplified and more user-friendly system. The Commission too has had to formulate and introduce a complaints system and in so doing has had to think out how it relates to other systems.

The Commission is in a position akin to the Health Service Commissioner and Local Government Ombudsman in that most complaints brought to its attention are in respect of services provided by other bodies, and this of course includes the local authority. The Commission therefore encourages the use of primary complaints systems and tries to facilitate individual access to them. People can be frustrated by the Commission taking such a position, however, not trusting that the body complained about can be dispassionate and fair in the examination of its own performance. In many instances complaints are pursued because the complainant wishes to obtain information or an apology which has not been forthcoming from the service provider. Often it appears that the body which is subject to complaint is inhibited from acting in a straightforward spontaneous way as though any admission of error has to be avoided. No doubt this is because of fear of litigation or personal consequences. Indeed, it is known that defence organisations, for example, advise doctors not to say anything which might imply culpability. While this is to some extent understandable, it leads to individuals feeling that they have not had a fair hearing, which in turn fosters dissatisfaction.

Most bodies which give a public service, including the Commission, are learning how to deal with complaints in a way which most fair-minded people will find acceptable. The Commission in carrying out a role as broker for complainants and service deliverers has to enlarge its knowledge of how primary systems work. Obviously this includes the social work department, and one of the complicating factors in our experience is that there was regional variation, and there still is district variation, in how complaints procedures have been written up and implemented. With the larger number of unitary authorities in Scotland since local authority reorganisation, the task of liaison has become more complex.

Case example

A family complained that the Social Work Department would not institute a guardianship application in respect of their elderly mother in order to compel her to remain in a nursing home. She had agreed to go there for a period of convalescence, as she saw it, and wished to return to her own home. Careful assessment of the elderly lady over a number of weeks led to the decision that she could be supported in her own home with a care plan, not necessarily involving the family.

The complaint against this decision was investigated by the quality assurance section of this particular district – the normal arrangement in that area. The family would not accept that this was an independent inquiry into their complaint and expressed their dissatisfaction with the outcome. At this point the Commission was brought in and after careful investigation upheld the local authority's decision not to go for guardianship in this particular instance. Although this case can be summed up in just a few lines, the actual work took a considerable number of weeks on the part of both the Social Work Department and the Commission.

Inquiries concerning accidents and incidents

The final area of work where there is an interface between the Commission and social work departments is that of accidents and incidents. As has been seen, the Mental Health (Scotland) Act (1984) gives the Commission a duty to make inquiries into any case where it appears there may be ill-treatment or deficiency in care, or where the property of a person by reason of mental disorder may be exposed to loss or damage. Clearly, before the Commission can make inquiries into such cases, it has to be made aware of individual situations. This happens through the Commission being alerted by patients or relatives or others, but the Commission also has to depend on being informed by those responsible for the services in question. Circulars from the Scottish Office Home and Health Department instruct NHS authorities to report to the Commission (NHS Circular NHS 1977 (Gen) 4 and Circular NHS 1977 (Gen) 13). Up until now there has been no similar requirement to report serious cases of accidents and incidents happening in the community to the Commission. The Social Work (Representations Procedure) (Scotland) Directions 1990 and Circular number SW5/1991, which deals with local authorities' complaints procedures, do not specifically cover the matter of reporting accidents and incidents. The Commission, supported by discussion with the Association of Directors of Social Work, has called upon the Scottish Office to issue specific guidance.

There are two main benefits in the Commission being aware of serious happenings to individuals with mental disorders. The first is that if relatives report the matter to the Commission then it is of advantage to the Social Work Department for the Commission to be able to say that a report has already been lodged. It enhances the light in which the Social Work Department may be regarded and projects a fair-minded and open image. The second benefit is that the Commission, by carefully logging incidents and accidents, can establish whether any patterns of events are occurring and, if so, comment on possible changes in practice and the necessity for special vigilance.

With the move towards community care and the increasing numbers of people vulnerable through mental disorder living in the community, the Commission does not see any good reason for a discrepancy in reporting requirements between the NHS services and local authority and independent services. This is not to suggest that the local authority cannot keep its own house in order or that there is anything suspect in the way investigations are carried out in relation to accidents or incidents. It is simply to put the Commission in a position of knowing what has happened to individual people and for users, carers and the public to be able to rely on the Commission discharging its duty to inquire, irrespective of the setting.

Case example

A young man died suddenly in supported accommodation after having lived there for only five weeks. The Social Work Manager reported the incident to the Commission within 24 hours, and indicated that internal inquiries had already been started and that the Commission would be given a copy of the eventual report. Three days later the Commission received a distressed and very angry letter of complaint from the parents and it was conciliatory to be able to assure them that a report on the tragedy had already been submitted to the Commission.

Conclusion

The Commission has been steadily building up its liaison with social work departments over the past ten years or so. Prior to the 1984 Mental Health (Scotland) Act the relationship between both bodies was intermittent and not always based on mutual understanding. The enhanced role for social work in mental health, brought about by the Act, meant that the Commission had to be much better informed about the duties and activities of professional social work and had to build bridges of contact throughout Scotland.

In recognition of the work that had to be done, the Commission appointed its first professional social worker in 1984 and, as a recognition of the effectiveness of that appointment, negotiated and achieved a full-time Social Work Commissioner on the staff in 1988. Since then a further part-time social work post has been created. Among the part-time Commissioners there are two social work-derived appointments, both former Directors of Social Work in Scotland. The full-time Social Work Commissioner has close links with the Association of Directors of Social Work. The Commission enjoys good relationships with all the 32 unitary authority social work departments in Scotland over individual case matters and the exchange of information. The challenge for the future is to build on the strength of the present position and to carry that forward.

References

Connor, A. and Black, S. (eds) (1993) *Performance Review and Quality in Social Care. Research Highlights in Social Work 20.* London: Jessica Kingsley Publishers.

Henkel, M. (1991) *Government, Evaluation and Change.* London: Jessica Kingsley Publishers.

Mental Welfare Commission for Scotland (1995) Annual Report 1994–95. Edinburgh: Mental Welfare Commission.

Mental Welfare Commission for Scotland (1996) Annual Report 1995–96. Edinburgh: Mental Welfare Commission.

Mental Welfare Commission for Scotland (1997) Annual Report 1996–97. Edinburgh: Mental Welfare Commission.

Ulas, M., Myers, F. and Whyte, B. (1994) *The Role of the Mental Health Officer.* Edinburgh: Central Research Unit, Scottish Office.

CHAPTER 5

Research Issues in Mental Health Social Work
The Problem of Continuity of Care and a Consistent Role

Marion Ulas

Since the publication of the previous Research Highlights volume, there have been major changes in the way mental health social work is conceived, delivered and organised. Research on policy and practice in this field has added new perspectives, for example on the deployment of Mental Health Officers (MHOs) or the quantity of 'actions' carried out under the Mental Health Act 1983 and the Mental Health (Scotland) Act 1984 (Barnes, Bowl and Fisher 1990; Smith 1991), but in a number of ways the research carried out has been limited. Other studies undertaken over the last 20 years describe the services deployed (Tibbitt 1978; Tibbitt, Ulas and Connor 1984) or describe variations in practice (Barnes, Bowl and Fisher 1986; Fisher, Newton and Sainsbury 1984; Sheppard 1990). It is argued here that because of limitations in the research, it is difficult to provide a picture of mental health social work in Britain.

In particular, there are gaps in areas which are also increasingly of interest to service users, managers and practitioners – the extent of professional accountability and implications for the individual service user's rights in the way both the social work role and the more formal MHO and Approved Social Worker (ASW) roles operate. Until recently, this area of service was under-researched. Moreover, the public perception of risks attributed to the discharge from hospital of vulnerable and potentially unpredictable patients has also raised the profile of the social work role and how it is managed (Blom-Cooper, Hally and Murphy 1995). The discussion of some of these issues, specifically the overlaps and tensions inherent in social work roles, is described in more detail in Chapter 6.

This chapter highlights some research findings from six studies which address aspects of the social work role in mental health. Particular emphasis is placed on those which explore compulsory detention under the Mental Health Act 1983 and the Mental Health (Scotland) Act 1984.

Policy changes influencing the research studies

The most significant changes in the organisation of statutory social work in the last 20 years relate to the service provision and professional roles which have been affected directly by legislation.

Some of the main changes in the provision of mental health services which have affected both professional social work practice and service user experience are:

1.   The changing policy and practice resulting in a shift from hospital to community provision and from health to social care. As a result, people with severe and enduring mental health problems who would have been hospitalised for longer periods in the past are now living in the community following short hospital admissions. (Chapter 2 addresses these implications in detail.)

2.   Following the implementation of community care legislation which instituted the purchaser/provider split, there was an increase in models of care and in the range of providers, for example Community Health Service Teams and Crisis Teams. The introduction of the Mental Illness Specific Grant has encouraged the establishment of successful innovative projects of all kinds, sponsored by the voluntary sector and by the provider arm of local authorities.

3.   The Mental Health Act 1983 and Mental Health (Scotland) Act 1984 created new roles for social workers, giving them new powers and responsibilities in the roles of the ASW and MHO. The Mental Health (Patients in the Community) Act 1995 similarly created another formal statutory role, the Aftercare Officer, a role which has specific responsibilities related to

community care orders in Scotland, and the equivalent officer under supervised discharge orders in England and Wales.

4. Under the NHS and Community Care Act 1990, which instituted care
    management and the care programme approach, the role of purchasing,
    providing and planning care became more formally integrated into social
    work practice.

Because of the nature of the research studies discussed here, which explore local
authority social work practice and the implementation of policy following legislative changes, most of the research has been funded centrally or by a combination of
local authority and pump priming by central government (and in one case seed
money from the ESRC).

The following sections address the following six research studies: Tibbitt *et al.*
1984; Tibbitt 1978; Barnes *et al.* 1986; Smith 1991; Social Services Inspectorate
(SSI) 1991; and Ulas, Myers and Whyte 1994.

Tibbitt *et al.* (1984): hospital social work deployment

Background

Until 1974, psychiatric social workers employed within the NHS in Scotland were
the main source of social work provision in adult psychiatry and were all based in a
hospital setting. By 1974, the last year health boards were responsible for the social work service, there were 305 whole-time equivalent posts in hospitals. Following the recommendation of the Mitchell Report (1976) that more information
on the numbers and reasons for deployment of hospital social workers was required, the deployment of social workers was researched by the Scottish Office
(Tibbitt *et al.* 1984).

The above study by Tibbitt *et al.* was undertaken in 1982 to describe hospital
social work provision after 1976. It was found that there was very little guidance
on the way psychiatric social work services should be developed throughout the
health service and none was available in relation to social work duties involving
compulsory detention assessment. Across all categories of hospital, estimates were
made based on hospital bed numbers, but the increasing use of day hospital, day
care and out-patient treatment, as well as reorganisation of social work services in
the community, made such estimates outdated by 1982. Within the social work

profession there was also awareness of the different needs of different individuals according to their acute or chronic condition and these factors influenced the types of service offered within and outwith the hospital setting. It was found that there were few consistent factors in the way individual workers were deployed or in the size of potential workload. Provision varied between districts, regions and types of hospital, as well as within hospitals of the same category.

The limitations of the research and published statistics available were such that there was no comprehensive picture of the deployment patterns of social workers based in and outwith psychiatric hospital. There was an illusion of rational decision making in the planning of mental health social work resources.

Themes arising in the data from this study undertaken in 1982 were also salient in subsequent studies which explored tensions in mental health social work across settings (Ulas *et al.* 1994). In Tibbitt *et al.* (1984) some factors affecting the deployment of workers concerned the model of attachment to wards and multidisciplinary teams; whether there were effective links from the staff in the setting to those based in the community; and the types of resource in the community influencing all the arrangements of coordinated through-care for people entering and leaving hospital care. All of these characteristics are central to informing service planning today.

Tibbitt (1978): social workers as MHOs

Deployment patterns of those social workers dealing with psychiatric assessment and detention under the Mental Health (Scotland) Act 1960 as MHOs based either in hospitals or in the community were not systematically collected. The only study in which the training and role of MHOs under the 1960 legislation were explored found that there was confusion over roles and responsibilities, lack of experience and inadequate training (Tibbitt 1978).

In Tibbitt's study, 64 workers (including area managers, community-based seniors, and social workers and hospital social workers) were interviewed in four regions in Scotland. It was found that the average number of cases held under the mental health legislation was 1.5 per year, with hospital workers dealing with three times as many cases as community-based workers. Tibbitt found that there was a major issue to be addressed concerning the development of expertise and confidence to practise.

The social workers' views of their role were described, together with the diffi-culties they experienced in carrying out their duties (Tibbitt 1978, p.1). There was variable practice in terms of the procedures applied to designate MHOs. In some areas all staff were designated, in others only qualified staff were, and in one partic-ular area all staff employed in 1974 were designated but no more were until the Mental Health (Scotland) Act 1984 was introduced. Another unusual situation arose where recently appointed qualified staff were not designated but long-serving unqualified staff were (Tibbitt 1978, p.5).

Tibbitt documented that the social workers themselves were 'unclear' about the MHO role and they thought that others working with them would also be unsure. One social worker described the view held by other professionals: 'the social worker is often considered to be a person to assist in a compulsory admission, in containment, rather than in a positive role' (Tibbitt 1978, p.24). Nearly half the sample (40%) saw their role as 'extremely limited', especially in emergency admis-sions, although several suggested that this depended on the stage at which the worker became involved. There was great individual variation in views held about the role. Some held a more sophisticated view, where their role was to protect the client, to negotiate and to coordinate action to be taken, while others thought that they were simply acting as a medical auxiliary. The significant finding was that the most common role was one where the MHO, in partnership with the medical pro-fessionals, had a continuing role through detention and afterwards.

New directions in practice and research:
the Mental Health Acts 1983 and 1984

The only social work post-qualifying training that is stipulated in legislation is that concerned with compulsory assessment of people with severe mental illness. Un-der the Mental Health Act 1983 in England and Wales and the Mental Health (Scotland) Act 1984, for the first time specialist training for social workers dealing with compulsory detention was mandated in legislation and new powers were given to social workers fulfilling these roles. Under both Acts local authorities are empowered to appoint social workers as ASWs and as MHOs. Both the MHO role and the ASW role are shaped by the legislation, which lays out the parameters of their powers and obligations. The legislation does not define in detail the profes-sional practice involved and circulars and notes of guidance only outline some parameters of practice. A distinction must be made between the role in law and in practice – the law shapes but does not directly define practice (Ulas 1992).

Before starting their training, qualified social workers are expected to have had two years' experience in mental health work. This post-qualifying training is now accredited by the Central Council for Education and Training in Social Work through the submission of portfolio work to demonstrate a wide range of competence in the knowledge, skills and values underpinning social work practice in mental health.

Issues in the practice of the statutory role

MHOs and ASWs are expected to provide a check on the power of the Responsible Medical Officer (RMO) in the process of decision making in compulsory detention. In practice, these social workers combine their knowledge of working with crisis and of the impact of both acute and chronic mental illness with skills in the assessment of risk. They take account of the person being assessed and the social context, particularly the availability of alternatives to hospital in-patient care at the time of assessment. Following a full assessment, they offer to organise and possibly provide day care, respite, accommodation, counselling and advice. With the introduction of the NHS and Community Care Act 1990, some of the above tasks would be available according to the team to which the MHO or ASW was attached, either purchasing or providing services.

Smith (1991), Barnes *et al.* (1986): quantitative research and monitoring the Mental Health Acts

Research which monitored the actions by MHOs and ASWs was required to give an estimate of the volume of work carried out to inform managers and policy makers about the way staff are used.

The Mental Health Monitoring Project was carried out in all the 12 Regional and Island authorities in Scotland for a year, starting 1 March 1989 (Smith 1991). This was modelled on the same exercise in England and Wales conducted during 1985/86 and initiated by the national Social Services Research Group (SSRG). Many of the researchers in local authorities in Scotland and England and Wales who carried out the research exercise were SSRG members. The collection of this type of descriptive data provided those managing the service with reliable information on how the Mental Health Act(s) were operating with respect to the actions of social workers.

The findings from the Scottish project can be summarised in terms of:

- *the quantitative description of the work:* 405 MHOs carried out duties under the Act relating to nearly 2000 clients. Most of the clients (60%) were not already known to the MHOs and fewer than half were retained as cases by the MHOs. Half of all the assessments related to people who had been detained previously. The use of compulsory powers was avoided in 15 per cent of all assessments

- *frequency:* it was found that 75 per cent of the total number of MHOs practised at least once during the 12 month period and those based in psychiatric hospitals were called upon more often than community-based workers or out of hours workers

- *range:* MHO work 'tends to be concentrated in the hands of a few. More than half of the practising MHO workforce use their MHO skills infrequently... 100 did between ten to twenty actions, while at the other end of the scale 1 MHO was involved in 105 actions' (Smith 1991, p.55).

Barnes *et al.* (1986) summarised the findings from the initial major collaborative quantitative research study undertaken in 42 social service departments in England and Wales on the numbers of actions under the Mental Health Act 1983. They noted the tendency for statutory mental health social work arising under the Act to be regarded as a 'one-off service' (Barnes *et al.* 1986, p.33). For 30 per cent of the ASWs the mean number of assessments undertaken in the year was 1.

Overall, the monitoring studies provided important national data on the volume of work generated under the Acts in the course of one year, which would be useful for managers to plan the service and would provide baseline information for future evaluation.

SSI (1991): inspection of approved social work

In reviewing a study of the profile of approved social work arising out of an inspection of the service it was evident that this surveillance of practice differed from the research studies described above. Key aspects of approved social work were inspected to give basic information on activity in 60 local authorities (over half the total authorities in England) and follow-up visits were made to interview staff on topics ranging from policies and organisation to management, supervision and monitoring. The monitoring was specifically designed to check that 'service activity remains in line with the Code of Practice, Mental Health Act Commission or Hospital Advisory Service recommendations' (SSI 1991, p.2).

Most ASWs worked as generic social workers in generic teams. In a quarter of the authorities the ASWs were specialist workers in generic teams, hospital teams or other specialist teams, and in a minority of authorities ASWs were situated in multidisciplinary teams.

In summary, the inspectors found that in most of the authorities there was no evidence of systematic review. There was large variation in the numbers of ASWs in different authorities, ranging from a ratio of 1 per 5713 population to 1 per 24,444 population, with no obvious logic or pattern to the differences observed. Thus it is not surprising that the inspectors found that deployment was based on factors unique to each individual authority and that there was no common pattern of deployment. Most important, with regard to the development of competence and confidence, the management of statutory duties by managers qualified and experienced in approved social work, did present problems for many authorities, but this was less so where ASWs were based in specialist teams with specialist managers (SSI 1991). This last point was echoed in the findings of research carried out in Scotland (Ulas *et al.* 1994).

Management and supervision: findings from inspection

A key issue for practitioners was getting supervision appropriate to their role. The inspectors found that this was a major problem in the service: 'A common problem in non-specialist teams was how managers without mental health knowledge were able to supervise [approved social work] activity' (SSI 1991, p.12). Training for seniors, joint supervision with an approved social work specialist, cross-team supervision and involvement of specialist higher management were introduced to meet this need. Peer support was seen as an important feature where there were other ASWs available for consultation. The inspectors noted that peer group support played a part in developing the professional identity of all the ASWs as consultants for other social workers, but that the managers did not acknowledge the value of these supports. Because ASWs did not use supervision to debrief and reflect on episodes of compulsory admission and the implications for the client and their family, most specialist mental health consultation was obtained from clinical team members and colleagues in hospital settings.

Alternatives to hospital admission: findings from inspection

Since preventive work and diversion from hospital did not occur, the inspectors viewed this as a worrying trend in practice. They argued that in order for a proper assessment to be made and for an examination of the full range of options, more information than was usually obtained was required. In particular ASWs needed time, skill and a 'predisposition to think of ways of making these options realistic' (SSI 1991, p.104). Thus the inspectors found that 'opportunities and organisational incentives for ASWs to intervene and act preventively towards clients with sub-acute or incipient mental illness appeared to inspectors to be few and far between' (SSI 1991, p.105). Overall this report provided useful information about the difficulties facing ASWs, and essential information was produced for service planners on the use of valuable resources.

Ulas *et al.* (1994): the MHO role

This study used mainly qualitative methods to examine issues for social workers operating as MHOs which could not be explored through the methods of a national quantitative monitoring study. This chapter focuses on MHO deployment and management and the implications of structural changes, as these were identified as important in Tibbitt (1978) (under previous legislation) and remain as problematic for MHOs and ASWs (SSI 1991). The study by Ulas *et al.* (1994) is part of a tradition of centrally funded research exploring practice in the context of legislative changes.

The study, which was funded by the Scottish Office, was designed to examine the role and responsibilities of MHOs in three regions in Scotland; describe how MHOs interpret their practice in relation to compulsory detention and the care of people with severe mental health problems; collect managers' and consultant psychiatrists' views on the MHO service; and examine the outcomes following MHO intervention (Ulas *et al.* 1994).

The study had five phases:

- 60 MHOs kept diaries of their mental health-related work and statutory mental health work, providing data for a quantitative workload review

- in-depth interviews with 46 MHOs were undertaken to explore practice issues and MHO perceptions of their role, focusing on their most recent case

- follow-up schedules were given to these 46 MHOs to obtain a description of the range of outcomes following MHO intervention

- 14 psychiatrists, 6 service users and 1 relative were interviewed to obtain their views on the MHO service

- interviews with 19 managers of MHOs were carried out to provide information on the service, on how MHOs were managed and on operational links with the rest of the department.

Although the research was completed prior to the implementation of the care assessment phase of the NHS and Community Care Act 1990, data were collected from the managers at the transitional stage which enabled some conclusions to be drawn of the potential impact of community care on MHO practice and the service. The research study was concerned with MHO activity in relation to Sections 18, 24, 25 and 26 of the Mental Health (Scotland) Act 1984. In Chapter 6 of this volume, the practice aspects of the role of the MHO are discussed in detail.

Organisation and deployment of MHOs

Statutory mental health work comprised only a small part of MHOs' total workload. This was true even for MHOs based in psychiatric hospitals. The workload review which registered caseload and workload information for the MHOs across three regions over a ten day period, indicated that events with a statutory mental health component comprised 4 per cent and 7 per cent, respectively of the working time of area-based and hospital-based MHOs (Ulas, Myers and Whyte 1991). Mental health-related activities took up 20 per cent of the total hours worked by area-based MHOs, and 75 per cent of the total hours for (psychiatric) hospital-based MHOs. Direct client-related work, other duties and responsibilities such as intake duty work, and attendance at meetings which had a mental health component counted as mental health-related activities.

Sixteen per cent of clients in the caseloads of area-based MHOs were identified as having a 'mental health problem'. Another 3 per cent were categorised jointly as 'child and family' and 'mental health problem'. While half the clients of area-based MHOs were under the 'child and family' category, slightly more than 5 per cent of all clients were subject to statutory activity under the Mental Health (Scotland) Act 1984. Perhaps most surprising, and indicative of the pervasiveness of mental health problems in the community, was the finding that area-based MHOs reported that nearly 60 per cent of their other duties and responsibilities had a mental health component.

For hospital-based MHOs, 75 per cent of clients were categorised under 'mental health problem' and a further 5 per cent were reported under the joint categories of 'child and family' and 'mental health problem'. Only 2 per cent were of the 'child and family' group alone. During the period of the research, 13 per cent of the clients were subject to statutory mental health procedures. Over 80 per cent of the MHOs' other duties and responsibilities had a mental health component.

These findings indicate that area-based workers who are MHOs tend to spend more of their time working with clients with a 'mental health problem' than was suggested in previous studies which examined workload of all types of social workers (Newland 1989; Tibbitt *et al.* 1984).

How were the MHOs deployed?

There were three ways that MHOs received referrals: referrals came into the office in an ad hoc way, while they were on duty or by direct allocation. A combination of all three systems could be in operation. Organisational features, in particular other workload pressures, had an impact on how much time was available to undertake statutory work. Moreover, MHOs often dealt with cases outwith the team's area, adding to travelling time as well as tensions in crossing team boundaries.

For both hospital- and area-based MHOs, statutory mental health work was not counted as part of their normal workload. This meant that practitioners had to 'juggle' or 'squeeze' time to accommodate these time consuming and often professionally and personally demanding pieces of work. For hospital-based MHOs this meant managing the competing demands of mental health-related work, statutory mental health work and child care work. For community-based MHOs, child care work in particular was given greater priority and legitimacy in comparison with mental health work.

Experience and levels of skill

There was a division of labour between hospital-based MHOs and area-based MHOs. Mainly hospital and Emergency Duty Team workers were involved in giving 'consents' to detentions under Sections 24/25 of the 1984 Act, the 72 hour emergency detentions, while area-based workers were more involved in the later stages of writing assessment reports.

The different ways of allocating referrals for statutory work adopted in different localities had major implications for the frequency with which MHOs carried out their tasks, and therefore for the extent to which MHOs could build up experience and competence in their practice. Studies carried out both prior to and following the introduction of the 1983 and 1984 Acts illustrated that receiving only infrequent referrals undermined confidence, especially for community-based workers (Smith 1991; Tibbitt 1978; Ulas *et al.* 1994). While infrequent referrals limited their ability to develop expertise, MHOs commented that even if more referrals were received, it would be difficult to find the time to fit in the work, due to workload problems.

The management of MHOs

Management of the social workers in their roles as MHOs or ASWs was controversial both in Scotland and in England and Wales (SSI 1991; Ulas *et al.* 1994). As social workers, MHOs received support and supervision through the line management system. However, in matters related to MHO work, all types of MHO looked to other MHOs for support, rather than to their line managers simply because the latter were not MHOs and had little appreciation of what the role involved. Indeed, MHOs resisted perceived management 'interference' and threats to the semi-autonomy in the role.

In interviews managers indicated that the organisation and practice of MHOs were being addressed, following the introduction of community care. They were concerned to ensure that MHOs had sufficient practice experience to retain or develop their skills. They argued for this on grounds of both cost-effectiveness, that is, getting a return on investment in training, and concern to maintain practice standards.

Aftercare models

According to findings on outcomes of interventions, the MHO and/or another social worker provided a social work service in over half the cases examined. As expected, individuals who were already clients of social workers were the clients likely to receive a follow-up service.

Data from the practitioner interviews suggested varied patterns of response to aftercare, reflecting different interpretations of the MHO role itself. Some saw their role simply as a narrowly defined legal function, while others saw it as a broad role taking in both legal and welfare elements. Those who held a narrower perspective did not ignore other immediate or longer-term needs; rather, they thought that the planning and coordination of provision were beyond the parameters of the MHO role. This difference in approach to the role did not depend on the work base, as often there were more similarities between MHOs in hospitals and in the community with regard to interpretation of role than among MHOs within each base. Only in Emergency Duty or Out of Hours Teams did MHOs agree in descriptions of their limited role.

Four different models of roles of aftercare were identified:

1. *An extended social work role:* follow-up was an extension of the MHO's existing social work involvement with the client.

2. *A referring-on role:* MHOs would identify social care needs in a Social Circumstances Report or refer the case to another social work colleague, but not keep the case.

3. *A planning role:* MHOs set up and coordinated a service but did not directly provide it.

4. *A providing role:* an MHO both planned and provided the service needed beyond detention.

The models developed through custom and practice, personal choice and expediency. The diversity of roles even within teams raises questions about both continu-

ity of care, especially if a number of different MHOs or ASWs were involved at
different stages of the same case, and standards of practice across the country.

Community care and the MHO role

The implementation of community care has forced planning of social care for mentally ill people to the top of the management agenda. Where the MHO role fits in
the new organisational structures is debatable. The main determinant of the position of the MHO was the type of team to which the MHO was attached: whether
the MHO was in a community care team and, if so, whether the MHO was in an assessment or a resource provider team. Managers thought that MHOs outwith community care teams, and attached to Criminal Justice or Children and Families
Teams, would have difficulty in continuing their statutory role and in providing
aftercare. For those in assessment teams, aftercare would also be excluded: their
role would be more one of gatekeeper to services. MHOs in resource provision
would be responding to the assessment made by another and strict limits would be

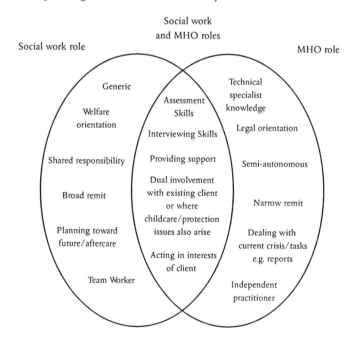

Figure 5.1 Social work and MHO roles, and their overlap

placed on the service provided. The findings concerning the overlap and convergences between the social work and MHO roles, regardless of team, are illustrated in Figure 5.1.

Implications of the research findings from Ulas *et al.* (1994)

- Over half of the qualified MHOs use their skills infrequently. Confidence and expertise would develop for them with a more even spread of work.

- The balance of time within total workload is uneven and the MHOs do not have enough time to devote to statutory demands.

- Refresher training is required because of a lack of confidence.

- Since MHOs rely on each other and not on supervisors to discuss statutory work, issues of accountability exist.

- Employers wish to have a sufficient number of MHOs to meet the demands of legislation and it is good practice to have an MHO involved in every assessment. However, it is often difficult to achieve this goal because the skills and expertise lie with a small number of MHOs.

- Carers and users requested a more consistent service, that is one individual helping through the crisis and afterwards helping them manage in the longer term. How far MHOs should contribute to continuity of care and link with local mental health professionals and the voluntary sector to offer a preventive approach to hospital admission in the community is a question for managers to debate.

Conclusion and future direction

There has been public concern about the frequency of tragic fatalities arising as a result of previously detained patients, either being assessed as ready to live freely in the community or doing so by default, without professional and/or other support and continuity of care (Blom-Cooper *et al.* 1995; Robbins 1993; Mental Welfare Commission for Scotland 1995; Ritchie, Dick and Lingham 1994; Sheppard 1995).

The role of the MHO and ASW in the new local authority structures impacts on both the protection of the community and the civil rights of people suffering from mental illness. However, with the fragmentation of social work services following local government reorganisation, MHO training is not now provided in every authority (Association of Directors of Social Work (ADSW) 1996). For the future, the ADSW recommended considering the use of specialist mental health social workers who would concentrate on mental health work and statutory MHO work (ADSW 1996, p.5).

If the compulsory detention legislation is used in a positive way, to prevent admission, seek alternatives and provide continuity in aftercare, then this would be in keeping with the spirit of the NHS and Community Care Act 1990. In light of the research reviewed in this chapter, it is clear that more care and attention are required to resolve the structural and organisational tensions affecting and limiting the operation of the role of the MHO and ASW. More discussion is needed to find the best ways to develop a partnership with other professionals, statutory, private and voluntary as well as user-led services, and to add to the existing knowledge about professional roles providing specialist input in compulsory admission to hospital and to aftercare (Huxley and Kerfoot 1994; Sheppard 1995; Smith 1991; SSI 1991).

Similarly, more evaluation is required to improve the planning for the transition from hospital to the community. Little is known about how different organisational models affect clients in terms of the outcome and the quality of service. It may be the case that alternatives to detention could be found if links to other professional resources and community supports were made earlier (Audit Commission 1994; Robbins 1993).

Research carried out to date and summarised above indicates the potential value of further research to inform managers, policy makers and funders.

To plan MHO services effectively, managers need data from monitoring and evaluation studies, describing, for example, the balance and volume of work and the consequences of different patterns of working.

To plan, and argue for funds for the MHO service that meets the requirements of the legislation and provides sufficient cover, research is needed on deployment patterns and where cover is not achieved.

It is important to have sound information in order to justify the use of resources for this client group within social work and to inform participation with other professionals with a shared interest in the care of people with mental health problems.

Research on both service users' and professional providers' experiences of the processes of compulsory detention and aftercare are necessary as part of an evaluation of the service and policy.

Dissemination of research findings, for example of the monitoring of actions, is essential if practice is to benefit from research. Staff will contribute to research more readily if its use to them is made clear and if research findings are acted on by line managers.

Research will not resolve the tensions in the system, but has contributed to an understanding of practice and of outcomes of the service following legislative change. Further monitoring and evaluative studies drawing on the findings and methods of the studies described in this chapter would clarify the value of the service to users and the public at large.

References

Association of Directors of Social Work (1996) 'The Development of Mental Health Services with Particular Reference to the Role of Mental Health Officers.' Unpublished report.

Audit Commission (1994) *Finding a Place. A Review of Mental Health Services for Adults.* London: HMSO.

Barnes, M., Bowl, R. and Fisher, M. (1986) The Mental Health Act and Social Services. *Research, Policy and Practice 4,* 1&2.

Barnes, M., Bowl, R. and Fisher, M. (1990) *Sectioned: Social Services and the 1983 Mental Health Act.* London: Routledge.

Blom-Cooper, L., Hally, H. and Murphy, E. (1995) *The Falling Shadow: One Patient's Mental Health Care 1978–1993.* London: Duckworth.

Fisher, M., Newton, C. and Sainsbury, E. (1984) *Mental Health Social Work Observed.* London: Allen and Unwin.

Huxley, P. and Kerfoot, M. (1994) A survey of approved social work in England and Wales. *British Journal of Social Work 24,* 311–324.

Mental Welfare Commission for Scotland (1995) *Report of the Inquiry into the Care and Treatment of Philip McFadden.* Edinburgh: Mental Welfare Commission.

Mitchell Report (1976) *Social Work Services in the Scottish Health Service: Report of the Working Party.* Edinburgh: HMSO.

Newland, C. (1989) *Area/Health Workloads and Need Study: Time Sample Diary.* Winchester: Hampshire County Council, Research Section Social Services Department.

Ritchie, J., Dick, D. and Lingham, R. (1994) *Report of the Inquiry into the Care and Treatment of Christopher Clunis.* London: HMSO.

Robbins, D. (ed.) (1993) *Community Care: Findings from Department of Health Funded Research 1988–1992.* London: HMSO.

Sheppard, M. (1990) *Mental Health – The Role of the Approved Social Worker.* Sheffield: University of Sheffield, Joint Unit for Social Services Research.

Sheppard, M. (1995) *Care Management and the New Social Work: A Critical Analysis.* London: Whiting and Birch.

Smith, R. (1991) *A Study of Mental Health Officer Work in Scotland.* Stirling: University of Stirling, Social Work Research Centre.

Social Services Inspectorate (1991) *Approved Social Workers Developing a Service.* London: Department of Health.

Tibbitt, J. (1978) *Social Workers as Mental Health Officers.* Edinburgh: HMSO.

Tibbitt, J., Ulas, M. and Connor, A. (1984) *Features in the Deployment of Social Workers in Scottish Hospitals in 1982.* Edinburgh: Central Research Unit, Scottish Office.

Ulas, M. (1992) Detention, diversion and dissent: Mental Health Officers and the Mental Health (Scotland) Act 1984. In D. McCrone and L. Paterson (eds) *Scottish Government Yearbook Jan. 1992.* Edinburgh: Edinburgh University Press.

Ulas, M., Myers, F. and Whyte, B. (1991) *The Role of Mental Health Officers. Interim Report: MHO Workload Review.* Edinburgh: University of Edinburgh, Department of Social Policy and Social Work.

Ulas, M., Myers, F. and Whyte, B. (1994) *The Role of the Mental Health Officer.* Edinburgh: HMSO.

Further reading

Boyd, W. (1996) *Report of the Confidential Inquiry into Homicides and Suicides by Mentally Ill People.* London: Department of Health.

Mental Health Act Commission (1993) *Fifth Bicentennial Report of the Mental Health Act Commission.* London: HMSO.

CHAPTER 6

Social Workers as Mental Health Officers
Different Hats, Different Roles?

Fiona Myers

Introduction

In Chapter 5 the impact of organisational features on service response is illustrated with reference to the role of the Mental Health Officer (MHO) in Scotland. The author draws attention to the implications of the support and management infrastructure within which MHOs operate. Based on findings from the study by Ulas, Myers and Whyte (1994), this chapter focuses on the implications of the social work context for MHO *practice*. Although organisational and practice issues are treated here as distinct, this is not to deny the overlaps: grey areas where the organisational structure within which MHOs are located both contribute to, and are affected by, issues of practice. For example, the worker's role as an advocate for an individual being assessed under mental health legislation may be at risk of being compromised not only by the need, on occasion, to act against the individual's expressed wishes to ensure their own and others' safety, but also by the worker's role within a 'provider' organisation with limited financial and service resources.

By describing some of the implications for practitioners of wearing both a social work and an MHO 'hat', it is hoped to make explicit some of the tensions which may, at the level of day-to-day practice, be present but unrecognised. Although of immediate relevance to those directly or indirectly involved in the detention process, whether as social workers, other professionals, users or informal carers, these tensions may have their parallels in other areas of social work in mental health.

Following a summary of the legislative context, this chapter provides a brief overview of studies focusing on the operation of mental health legislation and the role of social workers within the detention process. A brief description of a Scottish study of an MHO organisation and practice provides the context for the subsequent analysis of some of the continuities and discontinuities between roles which emerged from the research. This is followed by a discussion of some of the implications of 'wearing two hats'. The final section highlights the dynamic nature of the role of the local authority representative in the statutory mental health context and suggests areas for further research.

Legislative context

In Scotland, as in England and Wales and Northern Ireland, mental health legislation determines the criteria and means by which it is lawful compulsorily to detain and treat someone deemed to be suffering from a mental disorder. The legislation sets out both the rights of people at risk of being detained and the roles and responsibilities of agencies and individuals involved in the process. These others include not just medical personnel but also local authority and legal representatives, as well as the individual's 'nearest relative'. Focusing specifically on the role of the local authority representative, McGregor (1983) has pointed out that under Scottish legislation there has been a 'non family, non legal, non medical figure' involved in compulsory detention since poor law times.

The role of this third party has evolved with successive revisions of mental health legislation, its most recent incarnation emerging from legislative changes introduced in the mid-1980s. In England and Wales the role of the local authority Mental Welfare Officer was reconstituted as the Approved Social Worker (ASW) under the Mental Health Act 1983. In Scotland, the Mental Health (Scotland) Act 1984 revised the role of the MHO, first introduced under the Mental Health (Scotland) Act 1960 to replace the post of the Duly Authorised Officer. The different sections of the Mental Health (Scotland) Act 1984 have different procedural requirements and imply different outcomes for the person detained, but in all cases it is the MHO's responsibility to: 'Satisfy himself that detention in hospital is, in all circumstances of the case, the most appropriate way of providing the care and medical treatment the patient needs' (Mental Health (Scotland) Act 1984, Section 18(5)).

Compulsory detention and the social work role: underlying issues

The subject of compulsory detention in hospital and the role of social work and social workers in the process have been approached from a number of perspectives. At a very fundamental level, there is a burgeoning literature focusing on issues of ethics, morality and jurisprudence, as they appertain to the detention of someone against their will (see, for example, Bean 1986; Unsworth 1987). Chodoff (1984), writing in an American context, counterposes a 'utilitarian' approach to involuntary admission with a civil liberties or 'deontological' approach. The former argues that detention may be a regretful but essential last resort, justifiable to the extent to which it serves the good of the individual or society. The civil liberties approach argues that whether an act has good consequences should not be the only factor determining rightness or wrongness, fundamental principles such as liberty, fairness and justice must also enter into the judgement. This surfaces within mental health legislation as the tension between the 'police powers' of the state to protect individuals from the harm caused by others, and the *parens patriae* power by which the state as 'good parent' protects people unable to protect themselves.

Bean (1980), in his study in England of compulsory admissions under the 1959 Mental Health Act, takes up this theme in his account of what he calls the 'drift from legalism'. Bean argues that while the 1930 Lunacy Act emphasised legal procedures and judicial authority, the 1959 Act, following the Royal Commission, stressed therapy/treatment and the exercise of professional, that is, medical, judgement. The role of the Mental Welfare Officer under the 1959 Act remained procedural, to make the application when a relative was unwilling or unable to make it, and was responsive to the medical assessment. According to Bean, there was no expectation on the part of the Royal Commission that the relative or Mental Welfare Officer would lightly disregard or dissent from medical advice.

Focusing specifically on the role of social work practitioners, Tibbitt's study of MHOs in the context of the Mental Health (Scotland) Act 1960, draws attention to what he describes as 'the uncertain position of the social worker acting as MHO' (1978, p.1). Tibbitt identifies the sources of this tension within the legislative and organisational frameworks in which MHOs operate and the dilemmas arising from practice. First, in making an application where there is no nearest relative or where the nearest relative is unwilling to do so, the MHO is required to use professional discretion to satisfy herself or himself that the application is appropriate. Tibbitt argues that ambiguity arises over the criteria upon which this discretion is based and the relationship between these criteria and medical judgements about the need for compulsory admission. Organisationally, Tibbitt suggests that the then recent move away from specialist teams had implications for the experience of workers designated but not necessarily trained as MHOs. Third, Tibbitt identifies the tensions between statutory and therapeutic roles which can emerge in specific cases, for example relatives may view the MHO negatively as an authority figure such as a 'policeman'.

The core tensions identified by Tibbitt have their echoes in Fisher, Newton and Sainsbury's (1984) study undertaken in England under the 1959 Mental Health Act. In Fisher *et al.*'s analysis the ambiguities and tensions pull the Mental Welfare Officer between being a substitute relative performing an administrative or procedural function, and an independent professional making a judgement based on professional skills. In addition, organisational issues affect the training and expertise of the practitioner. Third, for Fisher *et al.,* issues of practice arise from the circumscribed nature of the worker's involvement. In their study they found that assessments for compulsory admission were regarded by practitioners as 'a distinct category of social work practice in which they tended to set aside their wider professional concerns in favour of the more limited role of legal applicant' (1984, p.170). Further, among the workers in their study the authors identified an apparently uncritical attitude towards risk, to the effect that if a client was mentally disordered then any risk-taking behaviours were perceived to be the product of mental disorder.

Studies undertaken since the introduction of the Mental Health Act 1983 and the Mental Health (Scotland) Act 1984 suggest that some of these issues remain unresolved. Prior, for example, writing in 1992, argues that legislation in England and Wales, Scotland and Northern Ireland continues to give similar powers of application to the professionally unqualified nearest relative and the professionally trained social worker, thereby undermining the value of specialist expertise.

A study in Scotland (Ulas, *et al.* 1994) also suggests that the ambiguities alluded to by Tibbitt (1978) and Fisher *et al.* (1984) in respect of the criteria upon which the MHOs make their assessment of the appropriateness of detention in hospital are also still evident. For example, in relation to the requirement for the individual to be suffering from a mental disorder, MHOs may find themselves on the horns of a dilemma. On the one hand practitioners recognise that they are neither qualified nor licensed to diagnose mental illness. On the other hand, in order to establish appropriateness they need not only to identify the potential risks arising from someone's behaviour, but also to establish that these risks arise from the individual's mental state. Further, the requirement to establish that detention in hospital is the most appropriate action implies the exploration of alternative sources of care. However, in the monitoring studies of the mental health legislation in Scotland (Smith 1991) and in England and Wales (Barnes, Bowl and Fisher 1990), it was found that in a high proportion of cases, assessments resulted in detention, particularly where the assessment actually took place in hospital. This has to be understood not only in terms of the severity of the illness among the people assessed, but also in terms of the existence or otherwise of opportunities for 'diversion'. From interviews with MHOs in Scotland (Ulas *et al.* 1994) it became apparent that, in the absence of alternative options, hospital may not be the *best* way, but the *only* way of providing care. As such, the 'alternative' may be to persuade the individual to remain in hospital voluntarily.

In negotiating these potential minefields, since 1984 workers have had the advantage of specialised training, but this needs to be built upon with practice experience. The two national monitoring exercises (Barnes *et al.* 1990; Smith 1991) revealed how infrequently ASWs and MHOs had the opportunity to put their training into practice. Although the average number of pieces of statutory mental health work per year was higher in Scotland than in England (8.5 and 4.3 pieces of work, respectively), nonetheless both studies found that some workers, particularly those in generic settings, were undertaking very few pieces of work. Ulas *et al.* (1994) found in their study that, on the basis of the MHOs' own estimates, those who were based in psychiatric hospitals appeared to undertake more pieces of statutory mental health work during one period of MHO duty than some community-based workers completed over a 12 month period. Such low levels of activity inevitably left some workers questioning their own competence to practise.

What the different studies suggest is that while workers have gained in terms of training, the role itself is still threaded through with potential conflicts, contradictions and traps for the unwary. Under Scottish legislation, for example, there remains the ambiguity of the role of the MHO in relation to the nearest relative; the problematic nature of the criteria for determining the appropriateness of detention in hospital; and the enduring tension highlighted by both Tibbitt (1978) and Prior (1992) between care and control. How practitioners, as *social workers*, negotiate their way through the process is the focus of the remainder of the chapter.

The study

The findings are drawn from a four year study exploring the organisation and practice of the MHO role (for a more detailed discussion of the approach and research findings see Ulas *et al.* 1994). The study, which commenced in November 1989, comprised a number of elements:

- a workload review across a sample of 60 MHOs
- a study of client and service outcomes in relation to 46 individuals following MHO assessment under the Mental Health (Scotland) Act 1984
- in-depth interviews with 46 MHOs, 14 psychiatrists, 6 service users and 1 relative, and 19 social work service managers.

The selection of MHOs included those working in urban and rural areas and workers based in psychiatric hospital teams, generic teams and Emergency Duty

Table 6.1 In-depth interview sample of MHOs by region and type of team

Team	Region 1	Region 2	Region 3	Total
Area	3	9	6	18
Hospital	14	3	5	22
EDT	2	2	2	6
Total	19	14	13	46

Table 6.2 Legal requirements under Sections 24, 25, 26 and 18 of the Mental Health (Scotland) Act 1984

Section	Maximum period of detention	Legal requirements
Section 24	72 hours	Recommendation by medical practitioner following personal examination of the individual
Emergency recommendation		Where 'practicable', consent of a relative or of an MHO to be obtained
Section 25	72 hours	As for Section 24
Emergency recommendation in respect of a patient already in hospital		
Section 26	28 days from the expiry of the Section 24/25	Approved medical officer to provide report to the hospital managers on the condition of the patient
Short-term detention		'Where practicable', consent to the continued detention is given by the nearest relative of the patient or by an MHO
		Where a relative has given consent to a Section 26, it is the duty of the hospital managers to inform the local authority, which arranges for an MHO to interview the patient and to provide a report for the RMO and the Mental Welfare Commission on the patient's social circumstances
Section 18	6 months	Application for admission to be made to the sheriff by either the nearest relative or by an MHO
Application for admission. This may follow on from a Section 26 or be an admission straight from the community		Application to be founded on and accompanied by two medical recommendations

teams (EDTs). The study was undertaken prior to the reorganisation of local government in Scotland in April 1996, at a time when social work services were organised on a region-wide basis. The sample was drawn from three regions. Table 6.1 summarises the interview sample by region and type of team.

The study focused on MHO activity in relation to Sections 24, 25, 26 and 18 of the Mental Health (Scotland) Act 1984. Sections 24 and 25 cover detention in hospital for up to 72 hours, Section 26 allows for detention in hospital for up to 28 days, and Section 18 enables someone to be detained for up to 6 months. Table 6.2 sets out the legal requirements for each of these sections of the Act.

Data collected in the course of the Scottish Mental Health Monitoring Study (Smith 1991) indicate the scale of statutory mental health activity by MHOs. Of the 3428 requests made of MHOs, one-quarter were for assessments under Sections 24 and 25. Just over one-quarter (27%) were for Section 26 assessments. Section 18 applications accounted for just over 11 per cent (11.4%) of requests.

Of the 46 cases included in the study, all but 3 people were detained in hospital following assessment. Of the three not detained initially, two were subsequently detained during the following six months and the third was admitted to hospital as an informal patient.

Social work and MHO roles: wearing different hats

Following their accreditation, the majority of practitioners will not function as full-time MHOs, but undertake the role within their day-to-day social work responsibilities. As statistics have shown (Barnes *et al.* 1990; Smith 1991; Ulas *et al.* 1994), statutory mental health work comprises only a small proportion of total activity, even for workers based in psychiatric hospitals. A frequently encountered metaphor used by workers to describe the need to combine different roles was of wearing a different hat, for example one worker described 'taking off the MHO hat and putting on the social work hat'. What this suggests is that for some practitioners the adoption of the MHO role necessitates the taking on of a different persona: the wearing of a social work hat implies one set of procedures, approaches and attitudes; that of the MHO another set. This sense of adopting a different identity is further underlined by the responses of the workers when asked how they saw themselves when undertaking the tasks of an MHO. While some described themselves as 'first and foremost a social worker', others perceived themselves specifically as MHOs: 'I just wear the Mental Health Officer's hat when I'm dealing with sections, never a social worker's.'

Before looking at the implications of this adoption of different professional identities, it is worth exploring further the overlaps and disjunctures which appear to inform these different perceptions. It should be stressed that what are described are the practitioners' perspectives of their roles as social workers and MHOs, not descriptions of practice.

Social work and MHO roles: continuities

Focusing first on the perceived continuities, irrespective of whether workers regarded themselves in these contexts as a 'social worker who happens to be an MHO' or 'first and foremost an MHO', the skills, sensibilities and values they felt they brought to bear on the assessment process were those of a social worker. For example, the ability to relate to people to obtain and interpret information was felt to be one of the core skills transferable to the statutory context, as were decision-making skills, notably risk assessment.

Additionally, what workers felt they brought was a specifically *social* perspective: a view of the individual as part of a social network, as a member of a family and a community. Sensitivity to issues beyond the specific assessment tasks was also felt to reflect a social work sensibility. For example, one worker remarked in relation to a client who had been sexually abused as a child: 'I think what bothers the social worker in me is that because it was never dealt with through the courts or the female and child unit...I'm never convinced that for A it's been resolved.' This skill base was felt to be underpinned by a knowledge of both resources within the community and of processes such as the children's panel system, and criminal justice and benefits systems.

A number of workers also alluded to employing a value system which sought to maximise client self-determination. At the same time, workers acknowledged what they described as the 'authoritarian' nature of the MHO role. Some workers felt able to accommodate this shift in values, recognising that there were similar issues around other pieces of social work activity; for example, one hospital-based MHO remarked:

> I think [if] people are so ill that they need to be detained...there is a reality there just the same as if you've got to take a child into care under a place of

safety order, and part of your social work working is to acknowledge that
there are these realities around.

Other MHOs appeared to be struggling, seeking to distance themselves in the way
that workers in Emerson and Pollner's (1975) study employed 'dirty work designations' as a way of re-affirming their own integrity. As another psychiatric hospital-based worker commented: 'I don't like my Mental Health Officer's role. I don't
like taking people's freedom away from them.'

Social work and MHO roles: discontinuities

The tensions between a value system predicated on client self-determination and a
role which gives the practitioner the power and authority to contribute to the deprivation of someone's liberty may open up a gulf between principles and practice.
For example, the sense among MHOs of their personal responsibility and of the responsibility vested in them by society, together with the unpredictability of the individuals being assessed, may tend not towards an emphasis on client
determination, but to a presumption of risk. In effect, MHOs may adopt the approach that the consequences of not detaining someone who subsequently causes
harm to themselves or another person would be far greater than to deprive someone of their liberty who may pose no threat. As one MHO remarked: 'There can be
cases where you could be in a situation where you're living with the thought "God,
have I done the right thing?"...I mean, if you get into a decision between protecting somebody's liberty and somebody's life you have to err on the side that protects their life.'

Further, despite the emphasis among practitioners on bringing a specifically
social work sensibility to these pieces of work, there was evidence of some of the
MHOs adopting what Sheppard (1990) has described as a mental health, rather
than a social work, orientation. As a result, the mental health status of the individual takes precedence, and the health and safety of the individual and the protection
of others are seen as dependent upon this, rather than subject to separate assessment. This is illustrated by one MHO who commented: 'If anybody suffers from
mental illness there's always an element of risk, either to self or others. In most
cases it's usually self.'

The discontinuities, however, extend beyond the disjuncture between accounts
of principles and accounts of practice. For MHOs in the study, the role itself was

distinguished, first, by the statutory requirements which structured the process, second, by the focus of the task itself, and third, by their 'semi-autonomous' function.

For the majority of workers in the study, the MHO remit itself was quite narrowly defined: it was about making a decision based on the 'here and now', as summarised by one worker:

> Going in as a social worker [you] would look at it more long-term saying 'right, we'll do an assessment, what needs to be done?', so in that you're looking forward, and as an MHO you're going in very much to see…just at this point in time, is this the right course of action?

In other words the 'MHO bit' is about making a decision on the appropriateness of detention in hospital, as opposed to a more general assessment. What distinguished the MHOs was the extent to which during, or on completion of, the 'legal bits' they also responded to the 'social work bits', that is, whether they adopted a welfare function over and above their statutory role.

For some of the workers interviewed, the MHO task was a 'discrete piece of work', structured by statutory requirements but circumscribed in breadth beyond assessment. As one psychiatric hospital-based MHO explained: 'I think once I've done my legal bits, that's it, I pass it on to the social worker then, because it's social work issues we're really addressing here, rather than further detentions.'

For others, however, the statutory requirements which defined the tasks were only part of a potentially wider remit, as illustrated by the following comment:

> I pick that up as a role of the MHO, to ensure the patient's rights and the patient's welfare…I otherwise wouldn't see the need for it to be a social work[er]…I think the whole obligation of a social worker's role in mental health…is to ensure there's reasonable long-term plans, relationship plans.

What this suggests, in a very simplified form, is two different models of practice. In one model the MHO role is perceived as a discrete function separate from the social work function. In the second model the MHO function is absorbed into a broader social work role. In this latter model there is less sense of a disjuncture. In relation to those workers adopting the 'discrete' approach, it was not that they were unaware of other immediate or longer-term needs, but that the detailed planning, coordination and implementation was felt to be beyond the boundaries of their MHO role. The difference in the approach adopted was not something which reflected the type of team of which the worker was a part: only EDT-based MHOs were consistent in describing the limited nature of their involvement.

Beyond practice it was the issue of personal autonomy which was identified as distinguishing the MHO role from other social work functions. As described in Chapter 5, under the Mental Health (Scotland) Act 1984 the tasks that the MHO carries out are not the delegated functions of the employing authority, but the functions of a specified officer. This was interpreted by the practitioners in the study as implying that they were personally responsible for the decisions they made as MHOs. Many workers in the study felt it was this which distinguished this role from their way of working as social workers, that is, it was not just what they did, or the skills they applied, but the structure of accountability within which they operated. One worker summarising the distinction explained:

> Well, you make the decisions, you're not going…and talking to your senior or anybody and saying 'what do you think?', because at the end of the day it's your decision, it's not his…at the end of the day I may listen to what he says…but…he's not going to railroad me into making a decision I think is wrong. But where if I was a social worker I couldn't do that.

For some workers this autonomy was felt to be liberating, for others it created anxieties about the possible implications should anything 'backfire'.

These anxieties may have practice implications. Even for the more experienced psychiatric hospital-based workers, concerns around the support available to them if 'something goes wrong' may influence the confidence with which workers feel able to question or challenge a medical recommendation to detain someone. Comments by workers in the study suggest that part of the decision-making process includes an assessment not only of the impact on society if someone is harmed, but also the impact on themselves as professionals entrusted with that responsibility. As one remarked: 'Risk is about whether or not you can go home at the end of the shift and sleep.'

This sense of personal responsibility, coupled with concerns about the support available from within their own departments, may have the unintended consequence of encouraging not autonomous decision making but a 'safety first' approach.

Wearing two hats: implications

A number of practice implications appear to stem from what one practitioner described as the 'dilemma of the two hats'.

First, as noted above, MHOs could be distinguished between those who saw the role as a limited legal function and those who perceived their responsibilities as encompassing both legal and welfare elements. As discussed by Ulas, these differences appear to have been partly influenced by the social work context within which the workers operated. For example, a number of workers based in generic teams suggested that although they would like to extend their role to include responding to social care issues, they felt constrained from doing so because of other social work responsibilities.

Second, workers' accounts highlight the potential conflict of interests between the MHO role of exploring alternatives in the community and the social worker's perception of the resource constraints faced by social work departments. Some MHOs within the study felt at a disadvantage, unable to fulfil their MHO role adequately because of limited alternative options. This was forcefully illustrated in one case where the worker felt caught between recommending an alternative which he felt was in the best interests of the client, and what the local authority was prepared to pay:

> Basically I knew what was in his interest was for the local authority to pay out an enormous sum of money to get him the proper treatment...[and I could see] the local authority turning around and saying 'no, we're not going to pay that much'.

The third practice implication arising from wearing two hats stems from the worker–client relationship and the appropriateness of combining both statutory and therapeutic roles. Although not an unfamiliar tension to social workers, practitioners nonetheless felt that, on occasions, adopting the MHO hat in the context of a pre-existing therapeutic relationship could prove counterproductive. As one worker commented: 'Quite often you're making decisions which the client isn't going to like, and sometimes you can work through that...and sometimes they'll tell you not to darken their doorstep again.'

As other commentators have suggested (Prior 1992; Tibbitt 1978) there is, at the heart of the MHO role, a conflict between the practitioner as an advocate for the individual and as a guardian of public safety. In instances where this duality of roles was potentially detrimental to a longer-term social work relationship, workers might look to other colleagues to 'come in and do the nasty bit'.

Where children were involved in cases it was not just a conflict of roles for the worker, but a potential conflict of interests. This was one issue which appeared to be more salient for the community-based MHOs than for those based in psychiatric hospitals. In part the conflict stemmed from an awareness of the possible impact of detention on both the parent and the child, and the need to weigh up the relative risks. But there was also an underlying question about the primacy of needs: who, in effect, was the client? Several area-based workers described situations where they had asked another worker to undertake a piece of statutory work in relation to a parent because of prior involvement with a family in relation to child care issues. The difficulty of acting in the interests of both parties, and being *seen* to act in their respective interests, was expressed by one worker who felt that for her to agree to a Section 26 could have been interpreted as a way for her to be able to admit the children into care. As the worker commented: 'I felt with my interest with the children it wouldn't be in the best interests of the client to be the MHO…it could have been seen for me to agree to the Section 26 because it would have suited for the kids to go into care.'

A fourth practice issue is the metaphorical nature of the 'hat': it is only visible to those who know. For the uninitiated, whether as client/patient, health or legal professional, or even social work manager, the 'hat' may have something of the invisibility of the emperor's new clothes.

A number of workers alluded to the confusions for clients and relatives of being both an MHO and a social worker. On the one hand this could mean that a pre-existing antagonism towards social workers on the part of the person being assessed could spill over into the assessment. On the other hand, several workers described how relatives may continue to contact the worker for advice on matters unrelated to the detention. In one case a practitioner involved both in detaining a client and arranging for her children to be taken into care found that her attempts to keep the two actions distinct were confounded by the client's husband:

> I did try to separate it, if I was going to see him…about the children…I had a
> specific agenda for that, and then other visits I made were specifically about

his wife. Although…the areas get fudged because he'd ask about the kids or ask about his wife.

Interviews with people who had been detained included several for whom the MHO was already their social worker. For these individuals any statutory element tended to be peripheral. One, for example, described the worker's role as 'well, he was bringing me clothes…and kept in touch with friends'. From the comments of a number of the people assessed, it appears that it was after detention, when what was sought was 'practical aid', that people would look to the MHO, *as a social worker,* for assistance.

But it is not just clients or relatives who may be bemused. Medical and nursing staff may be unsure of the worker's purpose at any one time; one MHO, for example remarked: 'I wonder if this one is confused because of the child care aspects and the nurses often thought…is she here as a mental health officer, or is she here as a so-cial worker?'

Conclusions

Presented very schematically, wearing the social work 'hat' carries with it implica-tions of shared responsibility by a team worker adopting an ostensibly welfare ori-entation geared towards future planning. When wearing the MHO 'hat' the worker functions as an independent practitioner whose focus is the application of legal criteria to the immediate situation. In reality, as suggested above, the two are not discrete: the worker brings the same skills and knowledge base to both situa-tions. Further, the worker is locked into an organisational infrastructure which is influential on both the opportunities the worker has to practise and the extensive-ness of the role beyond assessment. This interdependence implies that changes in the structure and function of the social work role will have repercussions for the practitioner in the MHO role and (potentially) vice versa.

As discussed by Ulas, the implementation of community care in 1994 threw into sharp relief questions relating to the organisation and deployment of MHOs. Additionally, it has perpetuated the potential tension between functions. Practice guidance accompanying community care legislation stresses the need to distin-guish between using an assessment as an instrument of social support and as an in-strument of social control: 'The former offers choice to the user, while the latter imposes solutions. The one should not be allowed to shade into the other without

all parties appreciating the full implications of that change'. (Social Services In-
spectorate/Social Work Services Group 1991, p.53)

While the focus may be distinct, the information collected in the course of the
MHO assessment has the potential to form the core of a comprehensive assessment. What needs further exploration is not only the relationship between the new
millinery of care management and the MHO role, but also the means for ensuring
that, where appropriate, information collected in one context feeds into the
care-planning process.

The issue, however, is not just one of information flow. The question remains as
to the scope available to MHOs to contribute to preventive and follow-through
work for people at risk of detention. The ever lengthening list of reports and inquiries exploring the role of mental health services in cases where people appear to
have slipped through the network of supports, with tragic outcomes (see, for example, Blom-Cooper, Hally and Murphy 1995; Boyd 1996; Ritchie, Dick and
Lingham 1994); the introduction of community supervision registers in England
from April 1994 and the introduction of community care orders in Scotland and
community treatment orders in England and Wales, all point to a very public, and
highly publicised, concern with ensuring continuing care (Atkinson 1996). Further research is required to explore the potential contribution MHOs and ASWs
can make to the longer-term care of people with enduring and severe mental health
problems. This needs to address issues of inter-disciplinary working, as well as the
intra-disciplinary contexts within which MHOs and ASWs *as social workers* operate.

Fundamentally, what is also required is an assessment of the resources available
both to provide alternatives to detention in hospital and to support people beyond
detention. Research in England is beginning to show the impact of services such as
Crisis Teams in terms of reducing hospital admissions (Muijen *et al.* 1992). At the
time of the study in Scotland in the early 1990s, workers felt constrained by the absence of alternatives other than to encourage someone to stay in hospital voluntarily. It may be that in the intervening period services such as those established
with the assistance of the Mental Illness Specific Grant will stimulate appropriate
alternative options.

Beyond the role of the MHO and ASW, and the issue of resources, is the experience of assessment and detention for the individual service user. What emerges
from the interviews with a small number of people assessed under the Act is the

sense of powerlessness; as Fisher argues, for this group of people 'concepts of choice and participation are nearly meaningless' (1990, p.225). What is required is research which gives a voice to those who have been through this experience: in this way services and providers, irrespective of which 'hat' they are wearing, can be even more responsive to the people they are intended to support.

References

Atkinson, J. (1996) The community of strangers: supervision and the New Right. *Health and Social Care in the Community 4*, 2, 122–125.

Barnes, M., Bowl, R. and Fisher, M. (1990) *Sectioned: Social Services and the 1983 Mental Health Act*. London: Routledge.

Bean, P. (1980) *Compulsory Admissions to Hospital*. London: John Wiley and Sons.

Bean, P. (1986) *Mental Disorder and Legal Control*. Cambridge: Cambridge University Press.

Blom-Cooper, L., Hally, H. and Murphy, E. (1995) *The Falling Shadow: One Patient's Mental Health Care 1978–1993*. London: Duckworth.

Boyd, W. (1996) *Report of the Confidential Inquiry into Homicides and Suicides by Mentally Ill People*. London: Department of Health.

Chodoff, P. (1984) Involuntary hospitalization of the mentally ill as a moral issue. *American Journal of Psychiatry 141*, 3, 384–389.

Emerson, R. and Pollner, M. (1976) Dirty work designations: their features and consequences in a psychiatric setting. *Social Problems 23*, 243–254.

Fisher, M. (1991) Defining the practice content of care management. *Social Work and Social Science Review 2*, 204–230.

Fisher, M., Newton, C. and Sainsbury, E. (1984) *Mental Health Social Work Observed*. London: George Allen and Unwin.

McGregor, C. (1983) *Mental Health Officers: A Study of Professional Practice Relating to Section 24 Admission*. Unpublished MSc Thesis, University of Stirling, Stirling.

Muijen, M., Marks, I., Conolly, J. and Audini, B. (1992) Home based and standard hospital care for patients with severe mental illness: a randomised control trial. *British Medical Journal 304*, 749–754.

Prior, P. (1992) The Approved Social Workers – reflections on origins. *British Journal of Social Work 22*, 105–119.

Ritchie, J., Dick, D. and Lingham, R. (1994) *The Report of the Inquiry into the Care and Treatment of Christopher Clunis*. London: HMSO.

Sheppard, M. (1990) *Mental Health: The Role of the Approved Social Worker*. Sheffield: Joint Unit for Social Services Research.

Smith, R. (1991) *A Study of Mental Health Officer Work in Scotland*. Stirling: Social Work Research Centre.

Social Services Inspectorate/Social Work Services Group (1991) *Care Management and Assessment: Practitioners' Guide.*

Tibbitt, J. (1978) *Social Workers as Mental Health Officers.* Edinburgh: HMSO.

Ulas, M., Myers, F. and Whyte, B. (1994) *The Role of the Mental Health Officer.* Edinburgh: Scottish Office Central Research Unit.

Unsworth, C. (1987) *The Politics of Mental Health Legislation.* Oxford: Clarendon Press.

CHAPTER 7

Ethnicity and Mental Health

Suman Fernando

Introduction

The importance of race and culture as issues in social work achieves a particular gravity, sometimes with considerable confusion, when it relates to mental health. However, the extent to which these issues are faced, and *how* they are faced, both in practical work and at the level of research, must determine the quality of social work with people with mental health problems – not just in case work (where personal prejudice and ignorance may be significant factors limiting the effectiveness of social work) but more generally in the organisation of services and training of social workers (where institutional racism and cultural insensitivity may actually reinforce racist structures in society at large). Dominelli (1988), in her book *Anti-Racist Social Work*, has argued cogently for the need to incorporate specific strategies for addressing racism in social work practice. Wider issues of multidisciplinary work of relevance to social work practice in the mental health field are encompassed in a multi-author book, *Mental Health in a Multi-Ethnic Society* (Fernando 1995a,b).

A major impediment to understanding what needs to be done both in practical work and research in the mental health field arises from the confounding of ideas about race and culture together with a lack of clarity about the meaning of ethnicity and racism – especially the way the latter is manifested in its institutional form. Therefore, this chapter attempts to describe (rather than define) the terms referred to before going on to discuss the way ethnicity and mental health are related in practice. Then, after considering issues concerned with the concept of (mental) 'illness' and health, practical problems for minority ethnic communities (including refugees and asylum seekers) arising mainly from racism and cultural insensitivity in the majority ethnic communities are described. Some ideas for future research based on practical need, rather than theoretical interest, are presented, and conclusions applicable to social work practice outlined.

Culture, race, ethnicity and racism

In a broad sense, the term 'culture' is applied to all features of an individual's environment, but specifically it refers to the non-material aspects of everything that a person holds in common with other individuals forming a social group. For example, it refers to child-rearing habits, family systems and ethical values or attitudes common to a group – what Leighton and Hughes (1961) call 'shared patterns of belief, feeling and adaptation which people carry in their minds' (p.447). So we could refer to a culture of a society, a community, a family or the culture or cultures of a system that involves a group of professionals – say psychiatrists, counsellors or mental health workers.

But no culture is ever static. There are always complex and varied changes over time and in successive generations, as new ideas, beliefs and patterns of behaviour permeate the group concerned. Further, external pressures play a significant part in determining certain aspects of culture; in fact, the culture of a community, family or group may be determined as much by social circumstances (e.g. poverty, racial harassment) as by custom. In other words, culture is as much fashioned by social pressures as determined by tradition.

The classifications of races, devised in Europe in the eighteenth and nineteenth centuries and largely based on skin colour, were constructed by biologists, physicians and anthropologists, who were later influenced by Darwinian ideas of evolution. They occurred in a context where the words 'black' and 'white' had been associated in the English language with heavily charged notions of good and bad and went hand in glove with prejudice from the very beginning. Then came slavery and colonialism, feeding into racial prejudice, and vice versa, consolidating the dogma of racism.

The concept of 'race', meaning some biologically determined entity recognisable by external appearance (or, rarely, by nominal religious affiliation or language), has been dismissed in scientific circles as a basis for dividing up the human race (Jones 1981). 'Human "racial" differentiation is indeed only skin deep. Any use of racial categories must take its justification from some other source than biology' (Rose, Lewontin and Kamin 1984, p.127). However, the tendency to think of people in terms of their 'race', referred to by Barzun (1965) as 'race thinking', persists; it is prevalent in most societies and all too often people are perceived, classified, discriminated against or favoured, and even destroyed, on the basis of what is seen as their 'race'. In other words, race, as we generally conceptualise it, is a biological myth but a social reality and, as such, a very powerful determinant of individual and group behaviour and of socio-cultural systems such as psychiatry, clinical psychology and counselling.

The term 'ethnic' may be used in some places as identical with 'race', but in Britain it is taken to mean a mixture of cultural background and racial designation, the significance of each being variable. It is essentially about self-perception – how people see themselves. A government paper about collecting ethnic health statistics states: 'Ethnic group describes how you see yourself, and is a mixture of culture, religion, skin colour, language, the origins of yourself or your family. It is not the same as nationality' (NHS Management Executive 1993, p.2).

So if racism is felt as a powerful force in society, people from various backgrounds and cultures may see themselves largely in racial terms (e.g. as 'black people') but also wish to identify in 'cultural' terms of religion or parental origin (e.g. as 'Muslims' or 'Asian'). The main broad ethnic groups referred to in British health surveys and research are African-Caribbeans, Africans, Asians and Whites, the two largest minority ethnic groups being South Asians and African-Caribbeans. In Britain, the term 'black people' is applied quite often to mean all ethnic minorities or, more specifically, Africans and African-Caribbeans, but in the USA and Canada the term 'people of colour' is preferred to 'black people'; however, in many countries on the mainland of Europe the term 'migrant' is still used (Fernando 1991c).

Race prejudice is basically a psychological state, a feeling or attitude of mind, felt and/or expressed as 'an antipathy based upon a faulty and inflexible generalisation' (Allport 1954, p.9); at a deeper level it may be likened to a belief that springs from 'ignorance, fear and the need to find a plausible explanation for perplexing physical and cultural differences' (Fryer 1984, p.133). Racism, however, is a doctrine or ideology – or dogma. As Wellman (1977) argues, once racial prejudice is embedded within the structures of society, individual prejudice is no longer the problem – 'prejudiced people are not the only racists' (p.1). Racism is not explicable by any one factor or event, either historically or in the present; it may be seen as having both social and psychological components — the former to do with power and economic domination, and the latter with a mixture of ideas, feelings and beliefs feeding on notions of 'race' fuelled by prejudice. Thus today, racism is fashioned by racial prejudice and underpinned by the power of economic and social forces. When implemented and practised through the institutions of society, it is called 'institutional racism'.

The manifestation of racism changes according to context and over time. Paul Gilroy (1993) argues that British racism now 'frequently operates without any overt reference to "race" itself or the biological notions of difference which still give the term its common-sense meaning' (p.23). 'Culture', seen as an immutable, fixed property of social groups, has become confounded with 'race', and racism is articulated in cultural terms. For example, in the field of cross-cultural psychiatric research, people from (industrially) underdeveloped countries are 'found' to be unable to discriminate between different types of emotion (Leff 1973) and 'West Indians' to deal with distress by 'cheery denial' rather than depression (Bebbington, Hurry and Tennant 1981). Naturally research findings like these (critically surveyed by Fernando 1988) result in statements such as the following, which appeared in a chapter by Lloyd and Bebbington (1986) in a recent British textbook of psychiatry:

> ...people from traditional cultures tend to express distress in somatic terms and fail to distinguish between the emotions of anxiety, irritability and depression [while] we in the industrial West have learned to make these distinctions and have developed a language to accommodate a subtle diversity of emotional experience expressed in psychological rather than somatic terms.

Racism enters into the diagnostic process at several levels. In the very personal interactions between psychiatrist and 'patient' involved in history taking and 'mental state' examination, images of black and brown people inevitably play a large part in judgements made (by the psychiatrist) about (the patient's) behaviour, beliefs and emotions — judgements that determine the diagnosis given (to the patient). And particular diagnoses carry particular images too, and images about 'illness' get confounded with images about people. For example, alienness is linked to images about 'madness' and also felt as an attribute about people who are 'foreign' for whatever reason. Further, when there is a view of schizophrenia as being caused by a 'bad' gene (a view that seems to be gaining ground), the idea of genetic inferiority gets linked to schizophrenia, while the ideology that sees black people as genetically tarnished is not an uncommon concept that informs thinking in western society. A carefully constructed study in the USA (Loring and Powell 1988) found that the perceived 'race' of a person is an important ingredient in diagnosis and that someone designated as 'black' (rather than 'white') is more likely to be diagnosed as 'schizophrenic' by both black and white psychiatrists. Unfortunately, an attempt to carry out a similar (but much smaller) study in England (Lewis, Croft and Jeffreys 1990) was seriously flawed through a lack of understanding of the nature of institutionalised racism (Fernando 1991a) for any conclusions to be drawn from it.

In the provision of mental health services, assumptions about 'cultural difference' in the personal attributes of black and brown people (e.g. suspicious nature of Asians, inherent aggressiveness of African-Caribbeans) may lead to professionals avoiding asking relevant questions (such as those about family interactions) or taking unnecessary precautions (such as calling the police when summoned to see black people in the community). The result is an essentially racist service arising from apparent sensitivity to 'cultural difference' and the alienating of brown and black people. At another level, over-zealous emphasis on 'cultural difference' may blind the professional to 'real' problems – again leading to injustice. As an experienced social worker, Shama Ahmed (1985, p.11), states:

> In social work there tends to be an uncritical reliance on cultural theories and culture-based explanations of behaviour, which frequently stop short of a more fundamental analysis which might be crucial in explaining the actions of minorities. It is significant that family disruption and breakdown are seen simply in terms of the innate deficiency of a culture, and the next critical step towards structural explanation is not taken.

Mental health and cultural difference

The concept of mental health is generally related to the concept of illness (or disease) and vice versa – the boundary between mental health and mental disorder hinging on the question of normality. Sabshin (1967) has described four approaches to normality as used by psychiatrists in the United States: normality meaning health as the absence of illness; normality as an ideal state of mind; normality as the average level of functioning of individuals within the context of a total group; and normality as a process that is judged by the functioning of individuals over a period of time. Yet mental health is generally conceptualised as something wider than, or perhaps somewhat different to, the absence of 'illness' or 'disorder'. Sudhir Kakar (1984), a psychoanalyst, states that the term 'mental health' is 'a rubric, a label which covers different perspectives and concerns, such as the absence of incapacitating symptoms, integration of psychological functioning, effective conduct of personal and social life, feelings of ethical and spiritual well-being and so on' (p.1).

The traditional medical approach is to see 'illness' as independent of culture, but there is a large anthropological literature that argues the cultural nature of what illness itself means. In other words, the relationship between 'illness' and 'culture' may be seen in two ways: cultural invariance or cultural relativity (of illness) (Box 7.1).

Box 7.1 Illness and culture

Culture determines the manifestation of illness

(pathoplastic effect of culture)

Each culture constructs its own illnesses

(pathogenic effect of culture)

The former maintains that concepts of health and illness are universal, although culture may determine the way illness is presented – the so-called 'pathoplastic' effect of culture – and misunderstandings derived from language differences may result in 'mis-diagnosis'. The latter states that each culture has its own 'health' and its own 'illness'; problems of diagnosis do not arise from misunderstandings alone but from the *cultural nature* of illness itself and, indeed, of the diagnostic system being applied. Unfortunately, it is not a simple matter of one or the other being correct. First, biological, social and psychological influences all determine the nature of what emerges as 'illness' in a particular cultural setting. Second, social construction is important but not the *only* consideration. And finally, cultures are not distinct and unchanging, and there is constant interchange between cultures, although powerful forces influence the nature of these changes – economic pressures, racism and even military might, to name just a few – all intertwined together.

Western psychiatry

Psychiatry arose in Western Europe to become allied to medicine through two avenues. First, with a separation of mind and body following Cartesian philosophy (Gold 1985) – Descartes' myth (Ryle 1949) – the study of the body was matched by a study of the mind. Second, in the late eighteenth century, cities grew and lunatics wandering about became a problem. The mind (as a sphere of study) and the control of lunatics (as a sphere of influence) were gradually taken over by medicine from religion. As European culture developed, the poetic and philosophical/religious models of madness present in its Greek roots were ignored and the medical approach (also present in Greek culture) came to predominate. Psychiatry then followed the directions taken by medicine. Essentially this meant the study of smaller and smaller fragments of the whole – the reductionist approach. The study of the body in this way (focusing on different organs and different functions) was imitated by similar study of the mind. The search for causes similar to the causes identified for medical conditions has continued. Neither Freud nor the behaviourists deviated much from this basic approach.

The medical model for collecting together matters to do with feelings, emotions, thinking, beliefs, willpower, behaviour, social interaction and even family life within the discipline of psychiatry is peculiar to Western European culture. This sort of process has not occurred in African, Asian (indigenous) American and other cultures, although something similar has been described in Tibetan culture, according to Clifford (1984). In those cultures, the matters brought together in psychiatry are seen in religious, spiritual, philosophical, psychological or medical terms – not in psychiatric terms. Therefore, the concept of mental illness itself being peculiar to western culture, the interface between (western) psychiatry and other cultures is seriously fraught when psychiatry is applied transculturally.

Ethnic minorities

The United Kingdom has seen a change in the ethnic composition of its population over the past 40 years, mainly as a result of migration from ex-British colonies in Asia and the Caribbean. However, more recently, there have been increasingly large numbers of people arriving in Britain as refugees and asylum seekers. So most communities within Britain are made up of various ethnic groups, that is, they are multi-ethnic.

In the 1991 census, an ethnic question was included for the first time, each person being asked to identify himself or herself in terms of ethnicity. And ethnic monitoring of service usage in the NHS is now commonplace in most parts of the United Kingdom – at least for local authority services and hospital-based mental health services – the basic categories used being those from the 1991 census (Box 7.2). Some figures for ethnic composition of parts of the UK are given in Table 7.1.

However, like the collection of statistics in general, ethnic monitoring is not an end in itself. In the field of mental health, the pressure to collect ethnic statistics arose because of concern about access to services, the quality of services *vis-à-vis* cultural and racial issues, and general dissatisfaction with the mental health services expressed by minority ethnic communities in Britain for many reasons, some of which are given later.

Box 7.2. Ethnic categories used for census (1991)

White

Black Caribbean

Black African

Black other

Indian

Pakistani

Bangladeshi

Chinese

Asian other

Other ethnic group

Table 7.1 Ethnic minority composition of population: 1991 census

Scotland	1.3%
Wales	1.4%
England	6.3%
Outer London	16.8%
Inner London	25.7%
Hackney, Tower Hamlets, Newham and Brent	33.7% – 44.9%
Leicester	28.5%
Slough	27.7%
Birmingham	21.5%
Luton	19.7%
Wolverhampton	18.5%
Bradford	15.6%

Since ordinary immigration by people other than those joining members of their family has been reduced drastically during recent years, most of the minority ethnic groups in Britain are composed of recent arrivals as refugees/asylum seekers and settled communities derived from earlier immigration. There have been very few British studies into the mental health needs of the former group but a considerable number of studies of settled communities. The next two sections will review some of the relevant studies, using mainly non-British studies that are of relevance to the British scene in the case of refugees, and British studies in the case of settled communities.

Refugees and asylum seekers

Studies after the last world war draw an association between diagnosed mental illness and degree of persecution and trauma (Krupinski, Stoller and Wallace 1973; Murphy 1955). However, while accepting the importance of specific traumatic events, some writers suggest that less tangible aspects of a refugee's experiences may well be as significant for mental health. Similarly, Muecke (1992, p.516) warns against the implications of using the now popular diagnosis of Post-Traumatic Stress Syndrome if by doing so one sanctions the 'continuing neglect of refugee suffering, suffering that is associated not only with the experience of persecution and trauma, but with…stigma, isolation and rejection'.

Many people arriving in the UK as refugees, seeking asylum on the grounds of persecution in other countries, are currently held in prisons and prison-like detention centres. A recent Australian article (Silove, McIntosh and Becker 1993) draws attention to the psychological harm done to asylum seekers by being kept in detention while their claims are being processed. In Britain, Bracken and Gorst-Unsworth (1991) document 'high levels of psychological disturbance' (p.657), with flashbacks to previous experiences and a multitude of symptoms among asylum seekers held in British prisons and comment:

> Detention on arrival leads to feelings of betrayal and despair. The psychological suffering of such people is intense and is often aggravated by their inability to speak or understand English. …Those who have endured torture and persecution because of their political and social ideals find it hard to comprehend why they should be included among those accused of criminal offences. (p.659)

The authors believe that detention on arrival in the country of refuge renders the later rehabilitation process, once a person is allowed to settle in the host country, almost impossible.

Questions of settlement are complex. It has been suggested (Berry 1991) that refugees, valuing their own cultural identity *and* good relations with the host population, aim to live in harmony in a pluralistic society (of many cultures existing side by side). But governments, concerned mainly with good relations being established, often pursue assimilation, which essentially involves a loss of specific identity as an ethnic group. There are many positions between 'pluralistic integration' and 'assimilation' and culture is never a static entity anyway. The best solution from the point of view of mental health must depend on many factors, including the extent of racism, economic opportunities in society and the presence of settled communities with whom refugees can identify. However, into this mixture we must add cultural variations in coping styles, difficulties of accessing mental health services and the inappropriateness of the services on offer – problems very similar to those encountered by settled minority ethnic communities.

Settled communities

There were hardly any studies of mental health among immigrants and ethnic minorities in the UK until a survey (Cochrane 1977) of admissions to mental hospitals found that, in comparison with the rate of admission for English born people, people born in Ireland, Scotland and Poland had higher rates, those born in the West Indies and the Americas had comparable rates, and people born in India, Pakistan, Germany and Italy had lower rates. Other similar studies followed, but hospital admission rates without taking into account the availability of services and admission policies were seen to be of limited value, particularly in a transcultural context where the use of services by different cultural groups may be very different and the way the services were structured and staffed tended to exclude some groups and favour others.

A community survey by Cochrane and Stopes-Roe (1981) found that Asian immigrants showed less evidence of emotional disturbance when compared with a matched English sample, but a study of general practice consultation rates in Oxford (Brewin 1980) showed that Asians and English people consulted GPs for emotional problems at very similar rates.

After several studies of inpatients in the 1960s and 1970s (e.g. Bagley 1971; Carpenter and Brockington 1980; Cochrane 1977; Dean *et al.* 1981; Hemsi 1967) had found that the diagnosis of schizophrenia was given to immigrants, especially those born in the West Indies, Africa and Pakistan, much more frequently than it was given to natives, the possibility of mis-diagnosis was raised by Littlewood and Lipsedge (1981). Then a prospective survey of African-Caribbean people referred to various psychiatric settings in Nottingham between September 1984 and August 1986 was published by Harrison *et al.* (1988). Here, 'ethnicity' was identified by physical appearance rather than birthplace and a standardised schedule was used for diagnosing schizophrenia. A calculated 'rate' of diagnosed schizophrenia compared with that already established in a previous community study gave striking results (Table 7.2). Among those born in Britain, the rate was 18 times in the 16–29 age group and among immigrants, 10 to 12 times (in both age groups). Although numbers were small, the rate for diagnosed 'mania' too was 12 times that in the general population. An earlier study (McGovern and Cope 1987a) in Birmingham had shown similar findings (Table 7.3).

Table 7.2. Diagnosis of 'schizophrenia' in Nottingham, 1984–86. Rates among African-Caribbeans compared with general rates (Harrison *et al.* 1988)

	Diagnosis of 'schizophrenia'	
	Aged 16–29	Aged 30–44
Immigrants	10 times	12 times
British-born	18 times	

Table 7.3 Diagnosis of 'schizophrenia' in Birmingham, 1980–83. First admissions aged 16–29. Rates among African-Caribbeans compared with rates among indigenous white people (McGovern and Cope 1987a)

	Diagnosis of 'schizophrenia'	
	Men	Women
Immigrants	5 times	4 times
British-born	7 times	14 times

Compulsory detention (forced admission)

The over-representation of both immigrant and British-born African-Caribbean and Asian men among those compulsorily detained in hospital under the Mental Health Act between 1975 and 1982 was first published in 1987 (McGovern and Cope 1987b) but is now accepted as established (Bowl and Barnes 1990; Depart-

Table 7.4 Compulsory Detention under Civil Orders, 1975–82. Rates of African-Caribbean and Asian men compared with those of white indigenous men (McGovern and Cope 1987b)

	Rates of compulsory detention	
	Aged 16–29	Aged 30–44
African-Caribbean immigrant	17 times	7 times
African-Caribbean second generation	9 times	–
Asian	1.5 times	3 times

Table 7.5 Compulsory Detention under Court Orders, 1975–82. Rates of African-Caribbean and Asian men compared with those of white indigenous men 1975–82 (McGovern and Cope 1987b)

	Rates of compulsory detention	
	Aged 16–29	Aged 30–44
African-Caribbean immigrant	25 times	7 times
African-Caribbean second generation	5 times	–
Asian	–	–

ment of Health and Home Office 1992; Fernando 1991b). In considering the civil sections (Table 7.4), in the 16–29 age group, the rate was 17 times that of indigenous white people among West Indian immigrants and nearly 9 times among the British born – both highly significant differences. In the case of the 30–44 age group, the rate for immigrants was nearly seven times higher. In the case of Asian people, in the 16–29 age group it was 1.5 times and in the 30–44 age group nearly three times higher. For 'offender patients' (Table 7.5), that is, people detained under those sections of the Mental Health Act applied by courts, the rate for West Indian immigrants between the ages of 16 and 29 was nearly 25 times that of the rate for indigenous white people and nearly 5 times in the case of British-born

African-Caribbeans. The corresponding rate in the 30–44 age group was 6.8 times (immigrants) and in the 45–65 age group 12 times higher.

Pathways to mental health care

A study of ten social services areas (Bowl and Barnes 1990) showed that African-Caribbeans were more likely to have been referred to psychiatric services by the police or social services in contrast to Asian people and indigenous whites, who were more often referred through GPs. An earlier study in Bristol (Harrison *et al.* 1984) found similar findings on ethnic differences in the pathway to hospital but, significantly, the extent of violent or threatening behaviour both before and after admission was remarkably similar in the two groups (West Indians and indigenous whites) studied.

Admissions to special (secure) hospitals

The hospital service in England and Wales for 'mentally disordered offenders' is based on three secure hospitals and several medium secure units. The former now carry out ethnic monitoring and unofficial figures suggest that 15 to 20 per cent of the inpatients in these hospitals are from ethnic minorities, predominantly African-Caribbeans. There was considerable concern recently about methods of control and treatment in these hospitals. An inquiry into Ashworth Hospital (Liverpool) found, among other serious concerns, evidence of extreme right-wing political activity with racial abuse being practised by the nursing staff (Blom-Cooper *et al.* 1992). Then, after the death of a young black man while in seclusion in 1991 – the third such death within seven years in the same hospital – an inquiry was set up. Its report (Prins *et al.* 1993) found extensive institutionalised racism and commented on the extent to which racist attitudes affect diagnosis and assessment of black patients.

Community mental health care

The use by ethnic minorities of community mental health services has not been studied systematically. A report on aftercare services in Leeds and Bradford, based on interviews with people from black and minority ethnic communities who had been discharged from psychiatric hospitals between September 1990 and August 1991, as well as carers of people with mental health problems (Baylies, Law and

Mercer 1994), found high levels of both inadequate preparation for discharge and low take-up and knowledge of community services. These problems arose from various factors, including language barriers, problems of physical access to centres, unmet need for counselling, inappropriateness of services and the lack of support for carers.

Treatment

Several observers have commented on the relatively low referral of ethnic minorities to psychotherapy services (e.g. Campling 1989), although there have been no direct studies of this phenomenon. The ethnocentric nature of most forms of counselling and psychotherapy may have something to do with this, but stereotypes of black people being unable to think in psychic terms may play a part (Fernando 1991b; Webb-Johnson 1991). Meanwhile, there has been growing concern among some psychiatrists and community organisations that ethnic minority patients are more likely than others to be treated by means of drugs (and high dosages of these) alone. In its *Third Biennial Report the Mental Health Act Commission* (1989), a statutory body appointed by the Secretary of State for Health (England and Wales), with a remit concerning the welfare of detained patients, reported an impression that high levels of medication were used for African-Caribbean patients in some hospitals. A study in Nottingham (Chen, Harrison and Standen 1991) found that high peak doses of neuroleptic drugs were used mainly for African-Caribbean patients and that patients from this ethnic group were more likely (compared with others) to be prescribed long-acting ('depot') preparations. A general resumé of current ethnic research is given in Box 7.3.

The reasons for these ethnic differences are far from clear. Many commentators (e.g. Browne 1995; Fernando 1991b), including the team that carried out the inquiry into the deaths at Broadmoor Hospital (Prins *et al.* 1993), have identified the perception of dangerousness as one of the crucial avenues through which racist misperceptions may influence psychiatric practice. Other stereotypes too may play a part in preventing a realistic appraisal of mental health needs of minority ethnic communities. For example, there is a powerful view that many Asian communities do not *want* statutory services for mental health needs because they 'look after their own', and that Asians 'somatise' emotional distress, seeking specifically medical remedies. Yet a recent study in London (Beliappa 1991) found a perceived need

---

Box 7.3 Racial and cultural issues: British findings

Black/Ethnic Minorities more often:

1. Diagnosed as schizophrenic

2. Compulsorily detained under the Mental Health Act

3. Admitted as 'offender patients'

4. Held by police under Section 136 of the Mental Health Act

5. Transferred to locked wards

6. Not referred for psychotherapy

7. Given high doses of medication

8. Sent to psychiatrists by courts

---

among Asian people for help from *outside* the family for what was clearly recognised in *their* terms as emotional distress. And this same study found that emotional problems (in the Asian sample) were seen 'in the context of personhood and social roles…within the parameters of normality, distinct from "illness" categories implicit within the medical model administered by the GP' (p.42).

The Mental Health Act Commission (1993) has expressed concern at the disadvantages that continue to be experienced by people from black and minority ethnic communities who come into contact with the mental health services. And dissatisfaction among minority ethnic communities with mental health services, and scepticism of the ways in which psychiatrists diagnose and treat what they call 'mental illness', is widespread (e.g. Webb-Johnson 1991).

Future research

Ethnic statistics

Basic information from ethnic monitoring of health and social services is likely to reveal either an under-use or over-use of one or other parts of a mental health service by a particular ethnic group. Clearly, the former may involve differential access resulting from differences in cultural sensitivity and/or appropriateness of services; the latter may reflect differential staff attitudes and/or institutionalised racism. Reliable ethnic statistics may help to elucidate these matters. However, statistical findings relating ethnic statistics to aspects of service provision should be viewed with caution for various reasons. For example, ethnic differences in relative rates of diagnoses (based on traditional western concepts of 'illness' and 'pathology'), such as 'schizophrenia' and 'depression', are unlikely to reflect morbidity in a meaningful sense for all ethnic groups for the simple reason that the validity of these diagnoses in transcultural settings has not been examined. (In this context, 'transcultural' means the use of a system derived in one culture in a very different cultural setting.) The under-use on a voluntary basis of a particular service setting by an ethnic group may reflect problems of access or appropriateness of setting; for example, if group x tends to under-use inpatient settings and over-use domiciliary settings for treatment, it may be correctly assumed that group x prefers the latter. But such a difference in the case of compulsory treatment may reflect staff preference or attitudes rather than user preference.

Research using the results of ethnic monitoring requires extremely perceptive and sensitive handling. Failure to do so may reinforce racist stereotypes and, worse still, impose ways of thinking that are culturally inappropriate, thereby aggravating the problems that minority ethnic groups already face in the mental health services.

Models of care and service development

The main thrust of research into ethnic issues in psychiatry is to search for medical–psychiatric explanations for diagnoses made on the basis of traditional (western) systems for categorising mental health problems; the perceptions of health and illness held among minority ethnic communities themselves are never used in gathering data – indeed these communities are seldom even consulted about the methodologies appropriate for research. It is clear that the traditional western models for analysing mental health problems (usually in terms of 'illness') require fundamental modification if 'medical' research in the field of mental health is to be relevant to the needs of a multi-ethnic society. Further, research into the way psychiatry functions as a social system aimed at developing models of care (for people with mental health problems) that are culturally sensitive is urgently needed.

Research into service development seldom involves users of services and black users get left out even more often than others in this respect. In a 'free market' approach, service development is closely tied up with issues of funding independent groups and organisations. A general policy on charitable funding, especially the funding of innovative services, is lacking and a recent report (Latimer 1992) finds that black groups face powerful institutional barriers when they apply for funding. It has been noted that 'many [innovative] projects started by black people have foundered on the question of finance' (Fernando 1995b, p.212). Research into ways of implementing 'equal opportunities' in the field of innovation and charitable funding is needed.

Migration

The social impact (on mental health) of migration, refugee trauma, the problems of acculturation in the face of xenophobia, and so on require study, especially in the case of recently arrived refugees. More importantly, there is an urgent need for objective research into the effects on, mental health of the ways in which host countries deal with refugees and asylum seekers. Both these areas of research have been seriously neglected in the UK.

Attitudes of majority community

In many parts of Europe most people referred to in Britain as 'ethnic minorities' are referred to as 'migrants' (Fernando 1991c). In Britain, too, many people from minority ethnic communities do not feel accepted – as Gilroy (1987) put it *There Ain't No Black in the Union Jack*. There is already much anecdotal information of hostility to ethnic minorities. So perhaps research is needed into institutionalised attitudes in health services that may reflect general social attitudes – and the effects of these on diagnostic methods and health care. In other words, in order to understand mental health issues of importance to ethnic minorities and the 'migrant' population of Europe, we need information about the ethnic *majorities*, the 'host' population, *vis-à-vis* the former groups, since the problems may well lie mostly (though not entirely) there. In doing so, we need to look at the problems encountered by ethnic minorities, including refugees and asylum seekers, in a holistic way – not just in terms of 'illness' but their total position in society, the ways in which they may be caught up in the interplay between judicial and psychiatric systems, their problems of identity, their needs in a cultural context, and so on.

Conclusions for social work practice

It will be evident from the earlier parts of this chapter that, apart from its ethnocentric nature, psychiatry is deeply imbued with racism. Thus the negative effects on black people of the diagnostic labels used by psychiatry are even more damaging than they might be in the case of others. A recent study in an inner-city area in England (Browne 1995) found that Approved Social Workers were aware that racist stereotyping (of black people) results in the over-use of compulsory powers ('sectioning') under the Mental Health Act – a fact that few psychiatrists seem to recognise. It is important therefore for social workers to guard against the influence of psychiatry on their thinking (i.e. the theoretical basis of their work) and their practice, especially in the use of compulsory detention.

There have been several recent publications that draw attention to the discriminatory nature of mental health services resulting in black people being seriously disadvantaged – for example, the *Fifth Biennial Report of the Mental Health Act Commission* (1993), the report published by the Confederation of Indian Organisations (Webb-Johnson 1991), and MIND's *Policy on Black and Minority Ethnic People* (MIND 1993). In publishing its findings after a consultative exercise with black service users, the Mental Health Task Force set up by the NHS Executive (Department of Health 1994) accepts that racism is a 'major contributing factor in the mental ill-health of black people' (p.23) and, even more importantly, that in failing to address issues of 'culture' in psychiatric treatment, there is a 'tendency to make assumptions about black people based on notions of their racial characteristics' (p.23).

Although changes affecting the vast bulk of the statutory services are at best marginal to the real problems, there have been several projects devised by non-statutory organisations throughout the UK that attempt to meet some of the concerns noted in this chapter. Information about these has been gathered together recently in a pack *Not Just Black and White* (Harding 1995). One of these projects that has stood the test of time (having been established in 1983) and achieved a well-deserved reputation is Nafsiyat, a centre in North London that claims to practise 'intercultural therapy'. The methods of working at Nafsiyat have been documented in articles by its founder, Jafar Kareem (1992) and its present clinical director, Lennox Thomas (1995).

The mental health user movement (also known as the 'psychiatric system survivor movement'), which has gathered pace in recent years, has now advanced to a stage where self-help and user-led alternatives to mental health services are being proposed and even acted upon (Lindow 1994). Although black people are over-represented at the 'hard end' of psychiatry, it is striking that few black people are involved in the user movement. According to two authors from the user movement, Mina Sassoon and Vivien Lindow (1995), one reason may be that 'the largely White survivor movement is presently influenced by an ideology governed by a western value system' that emphasises individual empowerment, while in other cultures 'control is sought in harmony and in consideration of the family and community' (p.99). These authors note that the campaigning for changes in services for black people 'has largely come from Black workers and others concerned with the plight of their particular community' (p.102) and that several mental health projects for black people, although not directly user-led, were developed 'alongside what Black users were saying about their experiences' (p.102). However, there *are* some black user-led projects – for example the Awaaz Mental Health Group in Manchester and the Black Carers and Clients Project in Brixton, both listed by Harding (1995) and referred to by Sassoon and Lindow (1995).

In summary, social workers in the field need to be aware of the limitations of the current 'illness' model used for analysing mental health problems, strive to minimise the effects of racism implemented through their educational systems and ways of working with people with mental health problems that are based on western psychiatry, and finally make efforts to empower and work in conjunction with black and minority ethnic people recognising the institutional impediments faced by them in all spheres of society.

References

Ahmed, S. (1985) Cultural racism in work with women and girls. In S. Fernando (ed) *Women: Cultural Perspectives. Report of Conference organised by the Transcultural Psychiatry Society* (UK), London.

Allport, G. (1954) *The Nature of Prejudice.* New York: Doubleday.

Bagley, C. (1971) Mental illness in immigrant minorities in London. *Journal of Biosocial Science 3*, 449–459.

Barzun, J. (1965) *Race: A Study of Superstition.* New York: Harper and Row (cited by Husband 1982).

Baylies, C., Law, I. and Mercer, G. (1993) *The Nature of Care in Multi-Racial Communities: Summary Report of an Investigation of the Support for Black and Ethnic Minority Persons after Discharge from Psychiatric Hospitals in Bradford and Leeds.* Leeds: School of Sociology and Social Policy, University of Leeds.

Bebbington, P.E., Hurry, J. and Tennant, C. (1981) Psychiatric disorders in selected immigrant groups in Camberwell. *Social Psychiatry 16,* 43–51.

Beliappa, J. (1991) *Illness or Distress? Alternative Models of Mental Health.* London: Confederation of Indian Organisations.

Berry, J.W. (1991) Refugee adaptation in settlement countries: an overview with an emphasis on primary prevention. In F.L. Ahearn and J.L. Athey (eds) *Refugee Children: Theory, Research, and Services.* Baltimore: Johns Hopkins University Press.

Blom-Cooper, L., Brown, M., Dolan, R. and Murphy, E. (1992) *Report of the Committee of Inquiry into Complaints about Ashworth Hospital.* London: HMSO.

Bowl, R. and Barnes, M. (1990) Race, racism and mental health social work: implications for Local Authority policy and training. *Research Policy and Planning 8,* 2, 12–18.

Bracken, P. and Gorst-Unsworth, C. (1991) The mental state of detained asylum seekers. *Psychiatric Bulletin 15,* 657–659.

Brewin, C. (1980) Explaining the lower rates of psychiatric treatment among Asian immigrants to the United Kingdom: a preliminary study. *Social Psychiatry 15,* 17–19.

Browne, D. (1995) Sectioning. The black experience. In S. Fernando (ed) *Mental Health in a Multi-ethnic Society. A Multi-Disciplinary Handbook.* London: Routledge.

Campling, P. (1989) Race, culture and psychotherapy. *Psychiatric Bulletin 13,* 550–551.

Carpenter, L. and Brockington, I.F. (1980) A study of mental illness in Asians, West Indians and Africans living in Manchester. *British Journal of Psychiatry 137,* 201–205.

Chen, E.Y.H., Harrison, G. and Standen, P.J. (1991) Management of first episode psychotic illness in Afro-Caribbean patients. *British Journal of Psychiatry 158,* 517–522.

Clifford, T. (1984) *Tibetan Buddhist Medicine and Psychiatry. The Diamond Healing.* York Beach, Maine: Samuel Weiser.

Cochrane, R. (1977) Mental illness in immigrants to England and Wales: an analysis of mental hospital admissions, 1971. *Social Psychiatry 12,* 23–35.

Cochrane, R. and Stopes-Roe, M. (1981) Psychological symptom levels in Indian immigrants to England – a comparison with native English. *Psychological Medicine 11,* 319–327.

Dean, G., Walsh, D., Downing, H. and Shelley, E. (1981) First admissions of native-born and immigrants to psychiatric hospitals in South-East England, 1970. *British Journal of Psychiatry 139,* 506–512.

Department of Health (1994) *Black Mental Health: A Dialogue for Change.* NHS Executive Mental Health Task Force. London: DOH.

Department of Health and Home Office (1992) *Services for People from Black and Ethnic Minority Groups. Issues of Race and Culture.* A Discussion Paper. London: Department of Health and Home Office.

Dominelli, L. (1988) *Anti-Racist Social Work. A Challenge for White Practitioners and Educators.* London: Macmillan.

Fernando, S. (1988) *Race and Culture in Psychiatry.* London: Croom Helm. Reprinted as paperback by Routledge 1989.

Fernando, S. (1991a) Racial stereotypes. *British Journal of Psychiatry 158,* 289–290.

Fernando, S. (1991b) *Mental Health, Race and Culture.* London: Macmillan.

Fernando, S. (1991c) Black Europeans. *Openmind 54,* 15.

Fernando, S. (1995a) *Mental Health in a Multi-Ethnic Society. A Multidisciplinary Handbook.* London: Routledge.

Fernando, S. (1995b) The way forward. In S. Fernando (ed) *Mental Health in a Multi-ethnic Society. A Multidisciplinary Handbook.* London: Routledge.

Fryer, P. (1984) *Staying Power. The History of Black People in Britain.* London: Pluto Press.

Gilroy, P. (1987) *There Ain't No Black in the Union Jack.* London: Routledge.

Gilroy, P. (1993) One nation under a groove. In P. Gilroy (ed) (1993) *Small Acts: Thoughts on the Politics of Black Cultures.* London: Serpent's Tail.

Gold, J. (1985) Cartesian dualism and the current crisis in medicine – a plan for a philosophical approach. Discussion paper. Journal of the Royal Society of Medicine 78, 663–666.

Harding, C. (1995) *Not Just Black and White.* An Information Pack about Mental Health Services for People from Black Communities. London: Good Practices in Mental Health.

Harrison, G., Ineichen, B., Smith, J. and Morgan, H.G. (1984) Psychiatric hospital admissions in Bristol: social and clinical aspects of compulsory admission. *British Journal of Psychiatry 145,* 605–611.

Harrison, G., Owens, D., Holton, A., Neilson, D. and Boot, D. (1988) A prospective study of severe mental disorder in Afro-Caribbean patients. *Psychological Medicine 18,* 643–657.

Hemsi, L.K. (1967) Psychiatric morbidity of West Indian immigrants. *Social Psychiatry 2,* 95–100.

Husband, C. (1982) 'Race, the continuity of a concept'. Introduction in C. Husband (ed) *Race in Britain: Community and Change.* London: Hutchinson.

Jones, J.S. (1981) How different are human races? *Nature 293,* 188–190.

Kakar, S. (1984) *Shamans, Mystics and Doctors. A Psychological Inquiry into India and its Healing Tradition.* London: Unwin Paperbacks.

Kareem, J. (1992) The Nafsiyat Intercultural Therapy Centre: ideas and experiences in intercultural therapy. In J. Kareem and R. Littlewood (eds) *Intercultural therapy. Themes, Interpretations and Practice.* Oxford: Blackwell.

Krupinski, J., Stoller, A. and Wallace, L. (1973) Psychiatric disorders in East European refugees now in Australia. *Social Science and Medicine 7,* 31–49.

Latimer, M. (1992) *Funding Black Groups. A Report into the Charitable Funding of Ethnic Minority Organisations.* London: Directory of Social Change.

Leff, J. (1973) Culture and the differentiation of emotional states. British Journal of *Psychiatry 123*, 299–306.

Leighton, A.H. and Hughes, J.M. (1961) Culture as causative of mental disorder. *Millbank Memorial Fund Quarterly 39, 3*, 446–470.

Lewis, G., Croft, C. and Jeffreys, A.D. (1990) Are British psychiatrists racist? *British Journal of Psychiatry 157*, 410–415.

Lindow, V. (1994) *Self-Help Alternatives to Mental Health Services.* London: MIND Publications.

Littlewood, R. and Lipsedge, M. (1981) Acute psychotic reaction in Caribbean-born patients. *Psychological Medicine 11*, 303–318.

Lloyd, G. and Bebbington, P. (1986) Social and transcultural psychiatry. In P. Hill, R. Murray and A. Thorley (eds) *Essentials of Postgraduate Psychiatry.* London: Grune and Stratton (second edition).

Loring, M. and Powell, B. (1988) Gender, race and DSM-III: a study of the objectivity of psychiatric diagnostic behavior. *Journal of Health and Social Behavior 29*, 1–22.

McGovern, D. and Cope, R. (1987a) First psychiatric admission rates of first and second generation Afro-Caribbeans. *Social Psychiatry 122*, 139–140.

McGovern, D. and Cope, R. (1987b) The compulsory detention of males of different ethnic groups, with special reference to offender patients. *British Journal of Psychiatry 150*, 505–512.

Mental Health Act Commission (1989) *Third Biennial Report 1987–1989.* London: HMSO.

Mental Health Act Commission (1993) *Fifth Biennial Report 1991–1993.* London: HMSO.

MIND (1993) *MIND's Policy on Black and Minority Ethnic People and Mental Health.* London: National Association for Mental Health.

Muecke, M.A. (1992) New paradigms for refugee health problems. *Social Science and Medicine 35*, 515–523.

Murphy, H.B.M. (1955) Refugee psychosis in Great Britain: admissions to mental hospitals. In H.B.M. Murphy (ed) *Flight and Resettlement.* Paris: UNESCO.

NHS Management Executive (1993) Letter to Professional Bodies 25 October 1993. Collecting Information about the Ethnic Group of Patients. Leeds: Department of Health.

Prins, H., Blacker-Holst, T., Francis, E. and Keitch, I. (1993) *Report of the Committee of Inquiry into the Death in Broadmoor Hospital of Orville Blackwood and a Review of the Deaths of Two Other Afro-Caribbean Patients. Big, Black and Dangerous?* London: Special Hospitals Service Authority.

Rose, S., Lewontin, R.C. and Kamin, L. (1984) *Not in our Genes. Biology, Ideology and Human Nature.* Harmondsworth: Penguin.

Ryle, G. (1949) *The Concept of Mind.* New York: Hutchinson.

Sabshin, M. (1967) Psychiatric perspectives on normality. *Archives of General Psychiatry (Chicago) 17*, 258–264.

Sassoon, M. and Lindow, V. (1995) Consulting and empowering Black mental health system users. In S. Fernando (ed) *Mental Health in Multi-ethnic Society. A Multidisciplinary Handbook.* London: Routledge.

Silove, D., McIntosh, P. and Becker, R. (1993) Risk of retraumatisation of asylum seekers in Australia. *Australian and New Zealand Journal of Psychiatry 27*, 606–612.

Thomas, L. (1995) Psychotherapy in the context of race and culture: an intercultural therapeutic approach. In S. Fernando (ed) *Mental Health in a Multi-Ethnic Society. A Multidisciplinary Handbook.* London: Routledge.

Webb-Johnson, A. (1991) *A Cry for Change. An Asian Perspective on Developing Quality Mental Health Care.* London: Confederation of Indian Organisations.

Wellman, D. (1977) *Portraits of White Racism.* Cambridge: Cambridge University Press.

Further reading

Beiser, M., Turner, R.J. and Ganesan, S. (1989) Catastrophic stress and factors affecting its consequences among Southeast Asian refugees. *Social Science and Medicine 28*, 183–195.

Foucault, M. (1988) *Politics, Philosophy, Culture. Interviews and Other Writings 1977–1984.* L.D. Kritzman (ed). London: Routledge.

May, R. (1992) Mental health care for immigrants in the Netherlands: a matter of quality, equality, policy or politics? Talk given at Autumn Quarterly Meeting of the Royal College of Psychiatrists.

Psychiatry in Europe: The Challenge of 1992, held in Birmingham, 14–15 October 1991.

Seligman, M.E.P. (1975) *Hopelessness: On Depression, Development and Death.* San Francisco: Freeman.

CHAPTER 8

Depression in Old Age

Maureen O'Neill

...Psychotherapy is not possible near or above the age of 50, the elasticity of the mental processes on which the treatment depends is as a rule lacking – old people are not educable. (Freud 1905)

...[the] assessor had focused on what they could not do, rather than building on what they could. Two-thirds had received no professional help and skilled counselling was lacking. This gives a clue for the future. If our society is to grow we must change the prophecies regarding old age. The current prophecy goes like this. Old age is a time of regret. Multiple losses and disability are associated with old age. So a priori, disabled older people will be depressed. This is untrue. Age and disability alone, or together, do not cause the depression. (Chester and Smith 1995)

Introduction

The above statements give a clue as to the approaches that are frequently adopted in relation to depression in old age. This chapter argues that mental health problems in older age tend to be treated as if they are an inevitable part of ageing and accepted by older people and professionals alike. It is therefore important that older people and those caring for them are encouraged to challenge this assumed inevitability so that the nature of each individual's problem is considered and the appropriate steps taken to improve the situation.

Society is too quick now to pronounce that the increasing population of older people is a burden and therefore their right to individual attention and recognition is reduced, rather than facing the fact that old age will come to all of us. Recognition must be given to the importance of people's individuality and their right to choose and take risks.

The Counsel and Care study entitled, *Older People's Sadness* (Chester and Smith 1995) describes what depressed older people feel about their lives. The study emphasised that the

> capacity to make simple choices about how we live our lives can be seriously threatened by lack of independence with ageing. Often this is due to physical disabilities of various sorts. The threat to independence, however, is compounded by the ability or willingness of those who care to keep open those choices rather than to take over because it is easier and quicker. Having choices is one of the most painful and humanising of the rights. Choosing one option involves letting go of another. Choices are always limited or limiting, but without them we lose a sense of individuality and freedom which is a crucial part of our being.

How common are mental health problems in older people?

The most common mental health problem among older people is depression, with 10 per cent of those over 65 being clinically diagnosed as suffering from depression (Mental Health Foundation 1993). It is also more common in women. To put the scale of depression in context in this age group, 1 per cent is known to be suffering from schizophrenia and 10 per cent of the total population over 65 will be diagnosed as having severe to moderate neuroses or personality disorders. These figures should be seen in relation to the total population in the UK being 58,191,000. The 1991 census showed that there were 10.6 million people of pensionable age (over 65 for men and over 60 for women) in the UK – 18.4 per cent of the population.

However, the diagnosis of depression in older people is complex. The effects of ageism in society are widely recognised. 'Ageism can reduce the status and expectations of old age for all generations, perpetuating negative views of inevitable and irreversible decline. Older people are expected to be miserable' (McEwan 1990) and are often reluctant to discuss their feelings.

Murphy (1984) reported that

> …70 per cent of depressed elderly people are unknown to their family doctors. Older subjects are less likely to go to the doctor with psychological symptoms. However, they frequently go with physical symptoms but the doctor either fails to spot the depression lurking behind them or, alternatively, while recognising that psychological factors are important, prescribes inappropriate sedative psychotropic medication and fails to tackle the true underlying depression.

Murphy (1988) also stresses that GPs could make a major contribution to preventing the disabling aspects of depression by being vigilant to the symptoms of depression in older people, which would include loss of appetite, changes in sleep patterns, and concentration and mood changes. Such symptoms need to be viewed in the context of the presence of physical illness and the psychosocial changes around the individual. It is therefore possible that the figure of 10 per cent of older people quoted previously is an underestimate of the extent of depression experienced by older people.

What are the factors that contribute to depression?

A number of studies point to 'loss' as a major contributor (e.g. Brown and Harris 1978). The loss could be a specific bereavement, loss of status, of financial or housing security and of physical well-being and especially the 'lack of an intimate confiding relationship with a spouse'.

Murphy (1982) in her study found that

> people over 65 were poorer financially; more likely to be living alone and in poor housing. In addition people over 65 years have more physical illnesses and are consequently often less mobile. They are more likely to have poor sight and hearing. Reduction in income and loss of status after retirement, bereavement of spouse, siblings and friends are commonplace events in old age.

The Counsel and Care study mentioned earlier also emphasises the link between depression and the lack of someone in whom to confide. Loneliness, which was linked to poor hearing and poor physical health, was particularly significant.

The study also stresses another important issue:

Our culture places great value on youthful energy and innovation as opposed to the experience and maturity of elders. This is bound to affect older people's self-image in a negative way. The demographic changes which are increasing the proportion of the population who are old and very old are often spoken of by politicians and others in almost cataclysmic terms; as a plague that will devour resources at an alarming and unsustainable rate. Against such a background it can be difficult for an older person, particularly someone in need of help with everyday living, to retain a positive image of themselves.

Wicks and Henwood (1988) also draw attention to the social features which affect the mental well-being of older people, which include poverty, poor housing, effect of caring for an older relative, cultural differences, isolation and loneliness. They particularly draw attention to:

- the poor quality of houses occupied by older people, being hard to heat and often lacking in amenities including inside toilets or exclusive use of a bathroom

- the problem of coping with owner-occupied housing requiring maintenance, adaptation and repairs

- the experience of people in old age reflects their financial and social status during their lives – work, marital status and earnings. Many retired people live on the basic state pension and are on the margins of poverty.

Norman (1988) stresses the particular isolation that older people from minority ethnic groups experience which arises from racism, language and cultural differences.

It is important to note that symptoms of depression are not only significant in the community. Surveys of older people in residential establishments found that residents suffered from a 'significantly depressed state' (Mann, Grapham and Asby 1984) and that in hospital populations symptoms of depression were common and frequently unrecognised (Bergman and Eastham 1974).

Diagnosis

As has previously been indicated, the detection of depression in old age is problematic, particularly among GPs who 'miss the overwhelming majority of the cases of potentially treatable depression which could be identified by psychiatric inter-view' (Bowers *et al.* 1990; Iliffe *et al.* 1991).

Katona (1994) points out that there is a clear need for appropriate, valid and re-liable techniques to detect depression in old age and to measure its severity. Such tests must be reliable in terms of stability for the testing and retesting of patients and also provide consistency of results when used by different practitioners. Iden-tifying suitable ways of detecting depression in old age must also be aimed at whether it is for formal diagnostic purposes on individual patients or for screening purposes to estimate the likely level of depression in a particular population.

It is essential that such diagnostic tools are sensitive enough to differentiate be-tween what might be ordinary symptoms of ageing, which could, for instance, in-clude sleep disturbance, loss of activity or greater susceptbility to fatigue, but which are also used as indicators of depression.

A number of diagnostic interview schedules have been developed especially for older people. Examples include the Geriatric Mental Status Schedule (GMS) (Copeland *et al.* 1976); and the Comprehensive Assessment and Referral Evaluation (CARE) developed by Gurland *et al.* (1977), who were also involved with develop-ing the GMS schedule. Gurland *et al.* (1984) have also devised a shorter version of CARE, SHORT-CARE, which has been found to be particularly acceptable in the primary care setting, with 100 per cent response rate and high criterion validity against clinical judgement (Katona *et al.* 1994). This schedule, which requires a trained interviewer, consists of 18 items and the complete interview takes approxi-mately 15 minutes to perform.

Other examples include self-completed rating scales such as the Geriatric De-pression Scale (GDS), which was devised by Yesavage *et al.* (1983) and was validated against the GMS interview in a British primary health care sample of elderly pa-tients by Evans and Katona (1993). The Crichton Royal Behavioural Scale enables a numerical value to be attached to a person's performance in various important ar-eas of behaviour, including communication, orientation, ability to perform tasks such as dressing and feeding, co-operation, restlessness and mobility.

What are the practice issues?

Murphy (1984) sets out the factors that could influence the prevention of depres-sion in older people:

- improvement of the financial and social status of the elderly

- improvement in the provision of easily accessible primary health care services with the hope of early detection and treatment of physical illness

- improvement of undergraduate medical education about disease in the elderly

- research into biological factors likely to be aetiologically important in severe depressive psychoses

- the provision of alternative social supports, for example day care facilities, clubs and voluntary visitors for elderly people who are living alone and have lost their major supportive relationship.

The government has a major role in enabling improvements to the financial and social status of older people and it is important to move away from the view that older people are a burden on society as they devour resources. There needs to be active encouragement to challenge ageist views and assumptions about the physical and mental changes experienced by older people.

A step towards greater recognition of depression in older people was taken by the Royal College of Psychiatrists and the Royal College of General Practitioners when they launched the 'Defeat Depression Campaign' in 1992. The campaign highlighted the extent of the problems experienced by older people and encouraged them as individuals to express how they 'feel' and not just their physical symptoms. It also drew the attention of GPs to the need to listen, to treat appropriately with anti-depressant drugs, to increase their knowledge of community-based resources and to use the screening tools already outlined.

The key values for a good life identified by the Department of Health (1989) in *Homes are for Living In* were adopted as a framework by the Counsel and Care study *Being Cared For* (1994), as follows:

- security

- privacy

- dignity

- independence

- rights

- choice
- fulfilment.

These basic rights create a platform on which all professional care workers can develop the range of services required as well as being inherent in the education and training for professionals and care workers alike. It is also important that through the assessment process, which is the responsibility of the social work or social services department under the community care legislation, that these values are reviewed for the individual and that as a result a multidisciplinary approach is adopted to ensure a properly integrated package of care.

The study undertaken by Counsel and Care (Chester and Smith 1995), *Older People's Sadness* illustrates that the loss of control and choice over everyday living has a large impact on the mental well-being of older people. This is particularly related to maintaining a house to the accustomed standard, choosing and buying food, choosing the time to go to bed and the ability to go out. Those interviewed demonstrated a reluctant acceptance of the levels of dependence. But the responses clearly show the requirement for a responsive homecare service, the need for conducive company and not to be confined within four walls. These provide clear indications to social work departments on the need to adapt current practice in determining the roles and provision of homecare services as well as the opportunities for day care.

Murphy (1988) points out that 'day care facilities, whether day hospitals run by health service professionals or day centres run by social services or voluntary agencies, provide diversion for the self-preoccupied and a convenient way for professionals to detect relapse and remission.' However, this points to the need to reassess regularly the needs of each individual so that changes are not missed and adaptations can be made to the care programme. A regular re-evaluation of an individual's requirements is as important in a residential or hospital setting as it is in the person's own home.

Most of the literature emphasises the importance of having someone to confide in and that it is very often the loss of such a person that precipitates depression. Blanchard, Waterreus and Mann (1995) claimed 'we are convinced that the improvement shown in people in our study relates to the personal counselling provided by the nurse rather than attendance at community facilities or anti-depressant medication'. However, Murphy (1988) raises the question as to whether those who are willing to be 'counselled' are the ones at risk of developing depressive illness. Subjects accepting such a service have already recognised their need to talk of their bereavement and believe in the value of support from others in a crisis. It is those who are ill at ease in interpersonal discussion who may be most at risk of breakdown and yet are the likeliest to refuse help.

Older People's Sadness confirms this observation and stresses the importance of having someone to talk to within the staff at a day centre, hospital or residential home in an informal way. Time should be allowed and importance attached to facilitating such discussion. The study strongly emphasises the need for agencies concerned with the welfare of older people to recognise and respond to this need for talking, particularly in the event of a loss in the person's life.

The opportunity to talk is invested with more potential than the administration of drugs about which most researchers advise caution. Wattis and Church (1986) stress the need to review the prescription of drugs to older people in terms of follow-up and side effects. Katona (1994) also stresses that anti-depressant drugs offer no guarantee of a response in elderly patients but that the new generation of anti-depressant drugs do represent a modest step forward in the treatment of depression in older patients.

GPs have a pivotal role in recognising depressive symptoms in older people and in referring them to psychiatric services and/or accessing community-based support. As Murphy (1984) emphasised, the improvement of undergraduate medical education is vital in this respect. But the vigilance required and the capacity for observation of changes should be enhanced through the initial training of all care workers and opportunities to refresh and retrain offered.

The fundamental values previously referred to and the spirit of community care provision requires active attention to the whole person rather than perceiving just their physical needs. Counsel and Care contends that if assessments were more focused on the rights of older people and action taken to provide the services which were appropriate, it would be likely that depression in older people could be substantially alleviated.

Conclusion

The prophecies relating to old age and depression need to be tackled through the education of primary health care teams, and clinical and care staff. Older people themselves must not be led to believe that depression is an inevitable part of age-ing. Imagination and enthusiasm must be brought to the management and treat-ment of what is a very disabling condition. However, the social problems which have been highlighted also need to be confronted and changes made if real strides in the treatment of depression in older people are to be made.

References

Bergman, K. and Eastham, E.J. (1974) Psychogeriatric ascertainment and assessment for treatment in an acute medical ward setting. *Age and Ageing 3,* 174–188.

Blanchard, M. Waterreus, A. and Mann, A.H. (1995) The effect of primary care nurse intervention on older people screened as depressed. *International Journal of Geriatric Psychiatry 10,* 289–298.

Bowers, J., Jorm, A.F., Henderson, S. and Harris, P. (1990) General Practitioners' detection of depression and dementia in elderly patients. *Medical Journal of Australia 153,* 192–196.

Brown, G.W. and Harris, T.O. (1978) *Social Origins of Depression.* London: Tavistock.

Chester, R. and Smith, J. (1995) *Older People's Sadness – A Study of Older People with Depression.* London: Counsel and Care.

Copeland, J.R.M., Kelleher, M.J., Kellett, J.M. and Gourlay, A.J. (1976) A semi-structured clinical interview for the assessment of diagnosis and mental state in the elderly: the Geriatric Mental State Schedule. *Psychological Medicine 6,* 439–449.

Counsel and Care (1994) *Being Cared For – A Discussion Document About Older People with Depression Living at Home.* London: Counsel and Care.

Department of Health – Social Services Inspectorate (1989) Homes are for Living In: *A Model for Evaluating Quality of Care Provided and Quality of Life Experienced, in Residential Care Homes for Elderly People.* London: HMSO.

Evans, S. and Katona, C.L.E. (1993) Epidemiology of depressive symptoms in elderly primary care attenders. *Dementia 4,* 6, 327–333.

Freud, S. (1905) *On Psychotherapy.* London: Hogarth Press.

Gurland, B.J., Kuriansky, J., Sharpe, L. *et al.* (1977) The Comprehensive Assessment and Referral Evaluation (CARE) – rationale, development and reliability. *International Journal of Ageing and Human Development 8,* 9–42.

Gurland, B.J., Golden, R.R., Teresi, J.A. and Challop, J. (1984) The SHORT-CARE: an efficient instrument for the assessment of depression, dementia and disability. *Journal of Gerontology 39,* 166–169.

Iliffe, S., Haines, A., Gallivan, S., Booroff, A., Goldenberge, E. and Morgan, F. (1991) Assess-ment of elderly people in general practice. *British Journal of General Practice 41,* 9–12.

Katona, C.L.E. (1994) *Depression in Old Age.* Chichester: John Wiley.

Katona, C.L.E., Evans, S., D'Ath, P. *et al.* (1994) The development of short screening ins-
    truments for detecting depression in elderly primary care patients. Submitted for pub.

Mann, A.H., Grapham, N. and Ashby, D. (1984) Psychiatric illness in residential homes for
    the elderly: a survey in one London borough. *Age and Ageing 13,* 257–265.

McEwan, E. (ed) (1990) *Age – The Unrecognised Discrimination.* London: Age Concern England.

Mental Health Foundation (1993) *The Fundamental Facts.* London: Mental Health Foundation.

Murphy, E. (1982) Social origins of depression in old age. *British Journal of Psychiatry 141,*
    135–142.

Murphy, E. (1984) Prevention is better: preventing mental illness. *Geriatric Medicine 14, 2,*
    75–79.

Murphy, E. (1988) Prevention of depression and suicide. In B. Gearing, M. Johnson and T.
    Heller (eds) *Mental Health Problems in Old Age: A Reader.* Chichester: John Wiley.

Norman, A. (1988) Mental disorder and elderly members of ethnic minority groups. In B.
    Gearing, M. Johnson and T. Heller (eds) *Mental Health Problems in Old Age: A Reader.*
    Chichester: John Wiley.

Wattis, J. and Church, M. (1986) *Practical Psychiatry of Old Age.* London: Croom Helm.

Wicks, M. and Henwood, M. (1988) The demographic and social circumstances of elderly
    people. In B. Gearing, M. Johnson and T. Heller (eds) *Mental Health Problems in Old Age: A
    Reader.* Chichester: John Wiley.

Yesavage, J.A., Brink, T.L., Rose, T.L. and Lum, O. (1983) Development and validation of a
    geriatric depression screening scale: a preliminary report. *Journal of Psychiatric Research 17,*
    37–49.

Further reading

Applegate, W.B. (1987) Use of assessment instruments in clinical settings. *Journal of the
    American Geriatric Society 35,* 45–50.

Gearing, B., Johnson, M. and Heller, T. (19) *Mental Health Problems in Old Age: A Reader.*
    Chichester: Wiley.

Murphy, E. (1985) Prevention of disease in the elderly. In J.A. Muir Gray (ed), London:
    Churchill Livingstone.

Scrutton, S. (1992) *Ageing, Healthy and in Control. An Alternative Approach to Maintaining the
    Health of Older People.* London: Chapman & Hall.

CHAPTER 9

Maternal Depression in Child and Family Care

The Design, Development and Use of an
Instrument for Research and Practice

Michael Sheppard

In a series of recent articles, Sheppard (1993a, 1993b, 1994a, 1994b) has provided considerable evidence suggesting a close relationship between maternal depression and child care problems in child and family care social work. The burden of the case derives from a number of observations about the link between child care problems and depression in women: that depression is found in women at about twice the rate of men, that mothers are particularly susceptible to depression, that working-class women are far more likely to suffer depression than other women, that depression in mothers is associated with low levels of social support, and that depression is associated with an increased incidence of child care problems. There is considerable evidence that these are exactly the groups which predominate in this area of practice (Gibbons, Thorpe and Wilkinson 1990; Packman, Randall and Jacques 1986). It is commonplace to observe that social workers often work with the most deprived groups in society, frequently with low levels of social support, with disrupted (and reconstituted) families.

The evidence on child care problems and maternal depression is particularly important because child and parenting problems provide the *raison d'être* for child care social work. The emotional and cognitive impact of maternal depression on children includes temperamental difficulties, delays in expressive language development, poor concentration span, and more somatic complaints and more negative self schemas than are characteristic of children of non-depressed women. Research on child behaviour and conduct shows considerably greater behavioural problems among children of depressed mothers, including more conflict and fighting, poorer parent–child relationships, poorer educational performance and possibly greater physical abuse by the parent (Zuvarin 1989). The social composition of child care social work clients, together with the association of parenting, and child emotional and behavioural problems with depression provide – because of social work involvement with these problems – a strong *prima facie* case for high rates of depression in mothers.

This evidence is significant in the light of the Children Act, 1989. The Children Act is founded on a philosophy that the best place for a child to be brought up is usually his/her family, and emphasises the importance of parental responsibility in the care of the children. There is considerable emphasis on parental strength and skills in discharging these responsibilities, and the deleterious effect of, for example, disability or illness in doing so adequately. Maternal depression, particularly where the mother continues to bear the major responsibility for child care, undoubtedly falls into this category. Packages of support are, in these circumstances, advocated as a means for retaining the child within the family (Department of Health 1991a, p.5). A further central concern of the Act is with child need, defined in terms of disability, (impaired) health and (impaired) development (Section 17 of the Children Act 1989). Since these specifically include physical, intellectual, emotional, social and behavioural development, the link between maternal depression and these issues is of obvious significance.

While, therefore, there is a great need for research in this area, there is as yet no systematic protocol developed specifically for social work, to identify ways in which social workers respond (if at all) to the presence of maternal depression. An instrument developed for this purpose could, in principle, be useful for both research and practice. Such an instrument would, however, need to possess a number of characteristics. It would need to be meaningful to social workers – that is, to reflect the ways they make sense of practice situations and the purposes of their work. It would need also to reflect 'theoretically relevant' dimensions of practice: that is, what we know about social and psychological factors associated with maternal depression. It would (for social workers) need to be easy to understand and efficient in the use of time. It should be able to reflect the severity of the client's problems and the nature of the social worker's intervention (direct and indirect). It should be capable, as a review or research instrument, of indicating change. Such an instrument would seek to provide a meaningful method for presenting both the way social workers saw the situation and the way they responded.

Goldberg and Wharburton (1979) some considerable time ago pointed out also the need for a case review format which would both aid accountability and help social workers in their conduct and planning of practice. This kind of instrument is, if anything, even more obviously important with the advent of care management and the emphasis on review and evaluation of intervention. It can help practitioners be precise about the problems, intervention, aims and central areas of concern; it can, as a result, enable them to make better informed decisions and take a more comprehensive view of planning; it can help create consistency in the collection of information so that all cases contain comparable information; and finally it can provide some indication of the complexity of the case and demands on the worker, thus assisting a workload management approach (see Parker *et al.* 1991). However, with the advent of care management, it is clear from government documents (Department of Health 1991b) that the place of social work in care management, which contains a number of 'levels' of practice, is at the 'professional' level (Sheppard 1995). Instruments developed for use in practice need, therefore, to reflect the specialist professional skills implied in this positioning of social work.

This chapter seeks to present the design, development and use of the Depression Social Assessment Schedule (DESAS), for use in three ways: research, agency monitoring of practice, and individual case examination and review. It does not, of itself, identify the presence of depression. This might be most effectively achieved by instruments such as the Beck Depression Inventory, the Zung Inventory or the General Health Questionnaire. It is designed, rather, to be used alongside such instruments. The discussion reflects the four key 'levels' in design and development: the principles for design, theoretical relevance, operationalisation and use in practice.

Principles for the design of DESAS

The DESAS is a questionnaire designed to glean information about the subject's social circumstances and the responses of the professionals involved (see Appendix). The focus of the questionnaire is the mother. This is important since, for example, the 'client' as defined by social services, may well be one of the children. DESAS was designed with two key factors in mind: to develop an instrument which would be meaningful to the social worker involved (Huntington 1981; Pavalko 1988), and to allow them to express their judgement of what they thought the client's circumstances were and the intervention they saw themselves to be undertaking.

A central characteristic, therefore, of the instrument, was that the classifications which comprised the structured questionnaire both incorporated occupationally relevant meaning and could be used with large samples (Marsh 1982). In this, there were two initial key elements. First, the definition of the concerns of the practitioners was presented in terms of 'problems' (hence problem categories), widely used in social work to define concern with clients (Hoghughi 1980; Perlman 1957; Reid 1978). The second involved the essentially psychosocial orientation of the social work practitioners, reflecting their domains of interest. Social work definitions of problems possess implicit standards influenced greatly by their position in social work or social services departments (Howe 1979), but also the occupational 'space' inhabited by social workers (Sheppard 1991). This essentially involves the combination of the 'internal' concerns of the psychological issues for the client and the 'external' ones of their environment and social situation. Although different approaches have different emphases (psychosocial, systems and ecological perspectives vary in this way), the focus is generally on the client, their family, their informal support systems, and formal supports in terms of agencies and professionals.

Depression-related variables in instrument construction

Social and relational problems of child care

Issues relevant for maternal depression were 'superimposed' on the concept of 'problems' and the concern with the domain of the . Three key initial dimensions – each related to social and relational domains – are relevant to the construction of an instrument with a psychosocial orientation for social workers. The first – the relationship between depression and social disadvantage – is widely known. Such information goes back as far as Hollingshead and Redlich (1958), Srole *et al.* (1962) and Myers and Bean (1968). More recent research shows that rates of depression are particularly high in women in inner-city areas (Moss and Plewis 1977; Richman 1977a; Richman, Stevenson and Graham 1982) and in working-class women (Brown and Harris 1978; Brown, Ni Brochlain and Harris 1975). These factors influenced the social and familial data section of the DESAS. In particular, findings that the prevalence of depression is greater among those with a child aged six or under, or three children aged 14 or under (Brown and Harris 1978; Brown *et al.* 1986) were reflected in this section.

Social and relational problems are widely associated with depression. This is obvious in one sense from the association of life events and difficulties with the onset of depression: they have causal power (Brown and Harris 1978; Brown *et al.* 1986) and can be easily formulated in terms of 'problems'. Studies have generally found a higher degree of social impairment in depressed subjects, as against comparison groups of non-depressed people (Corney 1984a; Weissman and Paykel 1974; Weissman, Paykel and Klerman 1972). Weissman and Paykel (1974) found that depressed women were particularly impaired in terms of their work role, and marital relationships and those with children were problematic. These indicate a range of areas which are significant for client problems. Those relating to disadvantage, such as financial and housing; to relationships (the relevance of social support is significant here, see below); and health (which is itself related to disadvantage) are all focused on in the instrument.

The additional dimension of child care is particularly important in this context. This is obviously the case, since the instrument is designed for use in work with children and families. However, there is extensive evidence of the relationship between depression and child care problems (Sheppard 1993a, 1994a). A general impairment in role performance, including communication problems, lack of involvement, guilt, resentment and mother–child friction has been found in depressed mothers (Pannacione and Wahler 1986; Weissman *et al.* 1972; Zuvarin 1989). Child problems have also been associated with depression: these include more somatic complaints, more negative cognitions about self, more extensive behavioural problems and impaired task performance compared with children of non-depressed mothers (Cox *et al.* 1987; Forehand *et al.* 1988; Welner and Rice 1988; Welner *et al.* 1977). These point to two further dimensions in the assessment of problems: parenting and child problems, both of which are included as domains of the problem section of the instrument.

Social support and depression

This leads to the second key theoretical dimension of depression in the development of the social assessment schedule. This is the concern with social support as a theoretical construct of interest in the study of depression. Social support has been widely related to depression in mothers (Sheppard 1994a), with potentially major implications for social work practice in child care. For example, it is possible to glean from the research that the following groups of mothers are among those at highest risk for depression: mothers without a confidant (in the sense used by Brown and Harris 1978); mothers with a hostile, condemnatory partner; single unemployed mothers; single mothers with low expressive support; and employed (dual role) mothers with low instrumental support (Sheppard 1994a). Such information may be useful in 'targeting' those at greatest risk for depression.

The concepts of social network and social support are central to the ways in which social workers work (Pincus and Minahan 1975; Whittaker and Garbino 1983). Social support is a complex concept which may at times be too easily simplified. It is important to understand, first, what it is. Weiss (1974) usefully defines it as 'provisions of social relationships', an approach which has been widely adopted. Social support, furthermore, is a multi-dimensional concept rather than one which is unitary (Sheppard 1993a; Thoits 1982; Vieil 1985): it can be divided up in terms of who provides it, what is provided and the effect of its provision.

There is a correlation between maternal depression and poor levels of support. Whether depression is caused directly by poor levels of support *per se*, or because of its absence in the face of life events, the mobilisation and provision of support would appear to be efficacious. The same goes for its provision for individuals who are depressed. Beck (1974) has distinguished such individuals who place great importance on their relationships and, therefore, through *personality factors*, are particularly vulnerable to social support deficits.

However, we should not limit social support to a relatively passive or instrumentally based notion. Social support is not simply about the provision of material help – money, help managing the house, and so on. It is also about the emotional side of an individual's problems – affective support. Hence it is possible to identify examples within DESAS of both these types of support. For instance, the domain of 'practical/facilitative work' is distinguished from 'emotional/supportive' work by the social worker, and encouraging the provision of 'material help' is distinguished from 'reducing interpersonal conflict' in the section on work with the in-formal network. Furthermore, it is not simply about 'being there' and listening to a client when they are distressed. It can be more actively therapeutic, even to the point of using specialist techniques such as cognitive behavioural therapy to help them resolve their problems. This is evident in the distinction between emotional support and ventilation and esteem-building activities undertaken by the social worker. Finally, it is not simply about groups (although groups can supply support). Individuals as well as networks can supply social support. These considerations were reflected in the classification of intervention in DESAS.

The conduct of intervention was usefully distinguished in terms of its type of support (affective or instrumental) and relational context (formal or informal) (see Vieil 1985). Where the intent, as is the case in DESAS, is to indicate the nature of the support provided, then these distinctions are important. The distinctions of re-lational context are clear in the section on intervention. Thus there are three broad dimensions: direct work by the social worker, informal support from relatives and friends, and formal support from outside agencies and professionals. Hence, one area of informal support and two areas of formal support are included in the sched-ule. This not only corresponds with a social support approach to social work inter-vention, but is consistent with long-standing distinctions within the social work literature. Direct and indirect work are terms distinguishing the locus of interven-tion which have been widely used in social work, and which are consistent with the overall psychosocial approach characterising social work (Whittaker 1974). It is, of course, also consistent with the resource-mobilising nature of care management: that much of the intervention is likely to be given by providers other than the care manager himself or herself. In child care it has been recognised that a hard and fast division between purchaser and provider may not always be sustainable (Depart-ment of Health 1991b; Sheppard 1995) – hence the need to take into account the direct work undertaken by the social worker himself or herself.

Psychological factors

Beyond these considerations, there is an extensive psychological literature. There is, of course, a variety of theories about depression: the most well known are the cognitive theories of Beck (1967), the link with the formation of attachments and early loss (Bowlby 1969, 1980) and the 'learned helplessness' ideas of Seligman

(1975). These cannot be properly explored here, but they possess key characteristics that can be identified which helped in the construction of the instrument.

The first is an attempt to understand depression, or at the very least the predisposition to depression, in terms of past events impacting on the individual. In the case of attachment theory, it is the disturbance and disruption of the maintenance of attachment bonds, or their outright termination, which are seen to underlie the development of a variety of pathological disturbances. This is most clearly evident in the loss of a parent at an early age – consistently found in studies of depression to be significant when such loss occurs before the age of 17 (Bifulco, Brown and Harris 1987; Harris, Brown and Bifulco 1986; Roy 1980, 1981), and in its most famous formulation, for women the loss of a mother before the age of 11 (Brown and Harris 1978). With learned helplessness, it is the result of powerlessness to affect negative situations (or the perception of powerlessness) that is significant. The individual learns from experience that they are unable to exercise any significant influence over external events that are impinging on them (Overmeir and Seligman 1967; Seligman 1975). Depression is the result of the realisation by an individual that they are unable to control these external events and a consequent belief that they will not be able to do so in the future. With cognitive theories, depression reflects some sort of developing schema about the world (Beck 1967). These past events are seen to affect the way in which depressed individuals view their world, with the outcome that they develop negative cognitions associated with depression. For the depressed person, their appraisal of themselves and their experiences is pervaded by a sense of loss. They perceive themselves as having lost objects or attributes of significant value to them. The appraisal of loss pervades the evaluations concerning the self, the world and the future (the so-called 'negative cognitive triad'). This negative triad is latent in those vulnerable to depression, and its development occurs in the early learning history of an individual which predisposes the individual to depression (Beck 1974). The research on parental loss is as relevant to cognitive theorists as those interested in attachment theory.

The second key element is the distinction between depression as something arising from the way individuals construct their world, and depression as a response to actual events. In the first formulation, depression is associated with negative cognitions which do not necessarily bear any relationship to what is actually happening to the individuals concerned. This is most apparent in the work of Beck.

For Beck, the congruence between the external event and its cognitive appraisal by the individual is low, and affective disturbance is the consequence of this poor congruence. The individual liable to get depressed will be constantly interpreting events in a negative way (not justified by the events themselves): that the actions of their friends indicate they do not 'really' like them; that their partner is not 'really' interested in them; that they will not really succeed in the accomplishment of a task (Beck 1967).

An alternative way of viewing depression is that it is an understandable response to adverse life situations. In this case it is the actual uncontrollability of the event which leads to a perception of the self as helpless. This underlies the more sociological formulation of Brown and his colleagues (Brown and Harris 1978; Brown *et al.* 1975). They emphasise, in particular, provoking agents – severe life events and major long-term difficulties – and vulnerability factors, such as loss of mother before age 11, low intimacy and three or more children at home aged under 14. Their conception of 'contextual threat' seeks to understand how seriously an individual might view an event in terms of their own life and expectations. It contains both an objective dimension (such as the event itself) and an interpretive dimension (the way an individual might be expected to respond to this event). Brown and Harris, however, do not wholly abandon psychological formulations, strongly associating these experiences with the development of low self-esteem.

From these formulations emerged certain key factors for DESAS. Depressed individuals are liable to possess negative cognitions and a sense of hopelessness, hence some recognition of the need to alter cognitions was significant. They might also be expected to have low control, or a low sense of control, over their environment – hence the issue of developing ways of increasing control was significant. Finally, all theories indicated that depression is pervaded by low self-esteem: negative conceptions of the self (cognitive theories), a sense of being unable to control significant areas of one's life (learned helplessness) and the development of negative schemas about the self (attachment theory) would all be associated with low self-esteem. These, together with the recognition of the need emotionally to support vulnerable individuals, underlie the personal problem-solving and emotional supportive domains of direct work. There are also relevant issues in the sections on work with informal networks (e.g. reassurance of worth) and work with formal organisations (e.g. therapeutic work on parents) which reflect these elements. The

link between disadvantage, helplessness, hopelessness and low self-esteem is reflected in the social and demographic variables examined (such as familial loss/dis-
ruption and indices of deprivation).

Operationalising DESAS

In order to develop an appropriate instrument, it was important not simply to rely
on the ways that the occupation as a whole made sense of practice situations, but to
test out its appropriateness with practitioners themselves. This would (a) make sure
that the main constructs used (such as problems) were relevant and meaningful to
the practitioner, and (b) allow the development of specific categories which would
accurately reflect the ways in which social workers saw the particular circumstances of the clients.

In constructing DESAS, existing instruments were drawn upon, although none
of these adequately dealt with this specific area. The end product, it should be
emphasised, while making use of existing schedules, was quite different from each
of these schedules, with a specific focus on the particular concern of the DESAS
itself. Two instruments were initially drawn upon: one focusing on social problems
(Fitzgerald 1978) and the other on child care (Parker *et al.* 1991). Although useful,
each alone was not adequate to the specific task of this research. The General Practice Research Unit Problem Classification (GPRUPC) (Fitzgerald 1978) did not
fully indicate the type and range of social problems to be examined. However,
when developed in concert with the practitioners, it was possible to create an
instrument which was relevant to their child care practice. Hence, for example, the
GPRUPC contained useful categories, such as housing, financial and home management problems, but did not include the categories of sexual abuse/violence or
specific reference to clinical depression or psychotic disturbance, and the distinction in both ill-health and deviant behaviour, between the subject herself and significant others.

The GPRUPC did not, furthermore, provide a specific focus on parenting and
child problems – hence the need for a further instrument. The child care instrument
was too detailed and time consuming, involving different sections for different age
groups (Parker *et al.* 1991). Two approaches were made: first to conflate the categories through which child problems could be defined (reducing the total number
down to nine) – for example, emotional difficulties, behavioural difficulties, poor

social involvement - without making the problems age specific. In this way these categories could be used where appropriate.

The other instrument, the Arizona Social Support Interview Schedule (Barrera 1981) was developed primarily for use with the women themselves (rather than the social workers). However, its classification of social support made it useful in providing the detail of the nature of the support provided by informal carers. This involved a distinction between support *providers* and support *provided*. The latter involved identifying who was providing support. The former related to the classification of 'support elicited', which included, for example, material help, advice or guidance and reassurance of worth.

Pilot stage

Beyond the developmental framework emphasising occupational meaning and theory-relevant factors, and some consideration of instruments already in use, a 'moderating' function was carried out by the social work teams and their team managers. Fourteen social workers and their team managers were involved. This was undertaken with two child care teams, one in a rural and the other in a severely deprived urban area. This combination was particularly helpful, in view of the possible differences which might occur between two such differing geographical areas. The result, it was expected, would be that it was relevant to all types of social work team, whether urban or rural or a combination of both.

This work involved a constant refining of the instrument at the development stage, which took place over a period of six months. This was undertaken through a number of meetings with practitioners and also through additional meetings with the team managers. Practitioners were able to amend the instrument as appeared appropriate. A further element involved both of the team managers working with some of the social workers, using the forms in relation to their cases before the study began. This, in effect, constituted a 'pilot' of the instrument with the kinds of case for which it was intended to be appropriate. The effect of these measures was to alter the instrument in certain respects from its original form. This was the case, for example, with the inclusion of 'sexual abuse/violence' to the woman herself in the adult relationship part of the problem section of DESAS, and with the inclusion of the category 'acute psychological distress', designed to indicate a level of distress which, while being severe, was below the level which could be considered to be clinical depression. As a result, we were able to ascertain both whether the instrument was adequate to the task and how much time it took to complete.

The final element of the instrument was its need to be practical to use and to reflect the agency base from which social workers carry out their tasks. The agency base was reflected in the section on case status. This involved three central elements: the nature and extent of child protection concerns, the legal status of the case (particularly whether or not a child from the family was accommodated and any offending behaviour), and the status of the case in the preventive pathway (referred, allocated, existing caseload, in accommodation). These very much reflect the institutional concerns of social workers and social services agencies with child care in general, and prevention and child protection in particular. As a result it was possible to obtain information on the agency-defined classification of the case being one involving child abuse (reflected in the 'category' of the case and whether a child had been on the child protection register) separate from the more detailed parenting and child care problems involved as identified by the workers. It also reflects the processing of cases – whether a client was referred, and if so whether or not allocated for longer-term care management, and so on. This provided definitions of what might be defined as the 'agency/legal' status of the case.

On a practical level DESAS was designed to be easy and, given its comprehensive nature, quick to use. Within the broad areas of problems and intervention undertaken, there were divisions and subdivisions which were designed to help 'direct' the social worker to areas containing problems or forms of intervention relevant to the case. Hence the instrument was divided into four broad areas: social and demographic, agency/case status, client problems and intervention undertaken. From this, further divisions and subdivisions were developed which would help direct the social worker to use the instrument quickly and efficiently. For example, within the client problem section, five divisions were made: social factors, relationship problems, ill-health, parenting problems and child problems. This meant, for example, that if the client had no health problems, the social worker could 'skip' that section entirely, rather than laboriously going through each health category one at a time. If, however, there was a health problem, the social worker could quickly focus on that section and identify from it the relevant health problem.

Reliability and validity of DESAS

DESAS was assessed in terms of its reliability and validity. The issue of validity relates to the extent to which it can be considered to be measuring what we think it is measuring, that is, is it really measuring the social problems and intervention process it is intended to measure? The issue of reliability is about the extent to which the instrument reliably reflects the perceptions of the practitioners themselves, rather than reflecting some arbitrary factors which influence its completion. The data for this part of the development of DESAS are based on forms completed by eight social workers (not involved in its development) evenly divided between two districts. One group (District B) completed the forms on their own, while the other group (District A) completed DESAS with a researcher, who filled in the form during an interview with the practitioner. Altogether forms were completed for 41 families in District A and for 50 families in District B.

Validity

The assessment of validity has in part been discussed. DESAS possesses clear theoretical validity, since its main dimensions were derived from existing literature. It possesses also face validity in that it was developed in detail with social work practitioners. Clearly, the categories developed made sense to the social workers and were considered capable of meaningfully representing their practice. This was subsequently confirmed by the capacity of practitioners, with or without the researcher, to complete the instrument. Beyond this, DESAS may also be considered to possess 'content validity'. An instrument possessing content validity should contain sufficient items to cover the full range of relevant concerns, and to cover them in a balanced way. Both social workers and team managers took part in determining the adequacy of the instrument in this respect.

We can also assess its validity in the extent to which its use is consistent with expectations derived from extensive research findings, which have been summarised earlier. This relates to 'construct validity', which is based on the way a measure relates to other variables within a system of theoretical relationships. By focusing on the broad problem domains, all of which may be expected to be associated with the presence of depression, it is possible to discover the extent to which they were, in fact, associated with depression (Table 9.1).

**Table 9.1 Correlation between maternal depression and
the five problem domains of DESAS**

	Problem				
	Relationship	Health	Parent	Child	Social
Correlation	0.27	0.23	0.25	0.09	0.002
Significance: p =	0.01	0.03	0.02	0.40	0.980

The data shown in Table 9.1 may at first not seem entirely to confirm the validity of DESAS. Although there are clear and significant correlations between relationship, health and parenting problems and maternal depression, this was not the case with child and social problems. However, these data may not, after all, be surprising. This was not a study of the general population: the social composition of this client group meant that it was highly deprived. It would, perhaps, be surprising if there were great differences in the social problems suffered by depressed and non-depressed women given the high state of disadvantage suffered by *all* these families. Likewise, this client group is actually defined by the presence of child problems – emotional, behavioural, cognitive and so on. We should, therefore, hardly be surprised if child problems are a feature of families *without* depressed mothers as well as those *with* depressed mothers. On reflection, therefore, the relationships between depression and associated problems are rather what would be reasonable to expect, suggesting the validity of the dimensions of problems 'tapped' by DESAS.

A further way of examining the validity of DESAS is to identify the extent to which there are relationships between broad problem domains in the ways that might be expected, in view of existing research. Are parenting problems associated with child problems, or relationship problems (in adults) associated with child problems? The data shown in Table 9.2 broadly indicate that such associations do exist. Of particular and central interest for both maternal depression and the concerns of child care social work is the relationship between child and parenting problems. These data show the relationship to be significant. The same may be stated about the association between relationship and parenting problems. Other

Table 9.2 Correlation between problem domains in DESAS

		Child	Parenting	Health	Relationships
Social	Correlation	-0.08	0.38	0.12	0.29
	Significance: p	0.40	<0.001	0.25	<0.01
Relationship	Correlation	0.30	0.22	0.15	
	Significance: p	<0.01	0.04	0.16	
Health	Correlation	0.03	0.14		
	Significance: p	0.80	0.20		
Parenting	Correlation	0.27			
	Significance: p	0.01			

significant correlations exist between social problems and parenting and relationship, but not child or health, problems. Health problems were also not associated with child or parenting problems.

We cannot be surprised to find relationships between parenting problems and, respectively, child and relationship problems. Furthermore, the pressures of social problems are such – and their association with disadvantage – that it is also not surprising to find them associated with parenting and relationship problems. The absence of an association between child problems and health and social problems may be because of the centrality of child problems to all cases, regardless of the other problems which were present. Child care social work, after all, focuses on the child.

Overall, therefore, there are good reasons to consider that DESAS is validly constructed in relation to problem areas. This involves face validity, content validity and construct validity.

Reliability

The reliability of DESAS involves the issue of the extent to which the problems and intervention identified by the social workers 'really' represented their perceptions of problems and intervention. This is based on a test–retest process, through which the stability of the domains and categories constituting the instrument can

Table 9.3 Test–retest correlations of broad problem domains in DESAS

	District A		District B	
	Present	Severe	Present	Severe
Social problems	0.90	0.86	0.77	0.96
Relationship problems	0.86	0.88	0.75	1.00
Health problems	0.95	1.00	0.91	0.94
Parenting problems	0.94	1.00	0.96	0.96
Child problems	1.00	1.00	0.76	0.96
Mean correlation	0.93	0.95	0.83	0.96

Note: All data have a significance of $p < 0.0001$.

be ascertained. This was achieved by asking the social workers to complete the form in relation to the same family twice, the two completions separated by one week. There were, however, no tests of inter-rater reliability. It was not the concern of the research to discover if all practitioners were consistent in their perceptions of client circumstances. Rather, the concern was to be sure that DESAS accurately reflected the way in which each social worker defined the situation, and their intervention.

We may first concentrate on broad problem domains. A test–retest correlation in a broad problem domain is defined as a situation where the individual problem identified in the initial completion of the instrument fell into the same domain as that identified in the second completion of the instrument.

Table 9.3 shows high levels of test–retest correlations across all problem domains. This means that social workers were very consistent in identifying, in general, social, relationship, child, parenting and health problems in relation to particular families. Interestingly, while there is very little difference between Districts A and B in the mean correlation of severe problems, District A showed noticeably higher mean correlation for non-severe problems than District B.

Table 9.4 Test–retest correlations for problems and severe problems. Data indicate number of problems with test–retest correlations*

Correlation	Problems		Severe problems	
	District A	District B	District A	District B
Over 0.9	26	12	25	21
0.8–0.9	8	10	2	7
0.7–0.8	1	10	2	2
0.6–0.7	1	10	2	1
Total problem areas assessed	35	36	31	31

*Where no clients were considered to have problems in a particular problem area, they were excluded from correlations.

The same task may be performed in relation to the individual problem areas constituent of the broad problem domains. The correlations for severe and non-severe problems are shown in Table 9.4.

The data show the test–retest correlations for individual problem areas in the two districts. These data clearly show high levels of correlation in all individual problem areas. This is the case with both districts and also in relation to rating of severity of problems. It is also the case in relation to primary problem. The test–retest correlation for District A was 0.9 and for District B 0.88. On this evidence, DESAS is capable of reliably reporting social workers' perceptions of client problems and also the severity of these problems. This means that DESAS is, by extension, capable of reliably indicating practitioners' perceptions of change in client circumstances if it is used in a longitudinal research design. As with broad problem domains, however, the correlations were greater in District A than District B. Hence nearly three-quarters of problems identified in District A had a test–retest correlation of 0.9 or greater, compared with only 33 per cent of problems in District B. Although less marked, correlations of severe problems were also greater for District A: 81 per cent had a test–retest correlation of 0.9 or more compared with only 68 per cent in District B.

Intervention

Direct work by social worker

The same process of testing reliability was carried out in relation to intervention. The main focus and forum for intervention for District A showed, respectively, correlations of 0.91 and 0.86. For District B the correlations were, respectively, 0.84 and 0.87. Table 9.5 shows the five broad areas of direct intervention by social workers.

Table 9.5 Test–retest correlations: broad areas of direct work

	District A	District B
Assessment	0.94	0.68
Practical help	0.85	0.74
Emotional support	1.00	0.72
Personal problem solving	1.00	1.00
Direct work with children	1.00	1.00
Mean correlation	0.96	0.83

Note: All correlations are highly significant at $p<0.0001$.

Table 9.5 shows, again, high levels of correlation between initial and second completions of DESAS by the social workers. This was particularly high for both groups in relation to personal problem solving and direct work with children. Although correlations are still impressive, they were rather lower for District B in relation to assessment, practical help and emotional support. As with previous data, the mean correlation was higher for District A than District B.

These data may be examined in relation to specific areas of direct intervention by the social worker, and results are shown in Table 9.6.

Table 9.6 Direct work by social worker, services provided/shadow purchased and resources purchased

Correlation	Direct work		Services provided		Resources purchased	
	District A	District B	District A	District B	District A	District B
Over 0.9	9	4	6	2	7	6
0.8–0.9	1	1	1	5	4	2
0.7–0.8	3	5	2	1		2
0.6–0.7		2				1
0.5–0.6		1		1		
Total examined	13	13	9	9	11	11

Note: Direct work refers to number of activities with the corresponding correlations; services provided and resources purchased, to the number falling into the corresponding correlation.

These data show highly acceptable correlations across individual intervention areas of direct intervention for both districts. However, as with previous data, District A performed rather better than District B. Thus while correlations of 0.9 or better were evident in 69 per cent of District A families, this was the case with only 31 per cent of District B families. The same applies to services provided and resources purchased by social workers in their capacity as care managers.

Indirect intervention

Indirect intervention was divided into two: support from the informal network sought for the mother by the social worker and services purchased (or shadow purchased) by the social worker from formal sources of support. Table 9.7 shows the type and source of support sought by social workers from the woman's informal network.

The data in Table 9.7 again show highly acceptable test–retest reliability across all areas, although some, such as material help and reassurance of worth in District

Table 9.7 Informal support sought for client by social worker:
test–retest correlation

	Type of support			Source of support	
	District A	District B		District A	District B
Material	1.00	0.82	Partner	0.85	0.94
Advice/ guidance	0.69	0.96	Mother	1.00	0.75
Reassurance of worth	1.00	0.96	Father	1.00	0.86
Child care	0.89	0.71	Other relatives	0.75	0.65
Practical	0.93	0.84	Friends	0.85	0.81
Social participation	1.00	0.68			
Conflict reduction	0.88	0.75			
Mean	0.91	0.80	Mean	0.89	0.80

Note: All correlations are highly significant at $p<0.0001$.

A, had rather better correlations than others, such as advice and guidance from the same district. As with previous data, correlations of both type and source of support were rather higher in District A than District B.

Conclusion

DESAS provides a framework whereby factors associated with depression can be identified and researched in a way which pays appropriate attention to the occupational meanings characteristic of social work, of theoretical and empirical areas established to be significant in the understanding of depression, and where the psychosocial focus is consistent with the focus of social work itself. It has been operationalised in such a way that it may be used in practice, and it is capable of identifying clearly some of the key elements of practice in this area. As a result, it may be used both as an instrument for research and an instrument which can monitor, on an individual level, the processes of practice.

Although both groups showed highly acceptable levels of validity and reliability, it is particularly noticeable that test–retest correlations were consistently higher for District A than District B. There may have been various reasons for this, but the one clearly identifiable constant which directly bore on this issue was the presence of a research assistant in all completions of DESAS by District A, whereas DESAS was completed by the worker alone in District B. Although the researcher only acted as a 'recorder' for the social worker by filling in the form to the social worker's verbal instructions, and made no attempt to influence the social worker, it seems likely that the presence of the researcher somehow contributed to a higher level of reliability.

However, even District B showed highly acceptable levels of test–retest correlations, indicating a high degree of reliability. DESAS is clearly a form which can be used in practice even where completed by the social worker/care manager themselves. This is of particular significance where the advent of care management has thrown the traditional expectations of the social work role into such turmoil. DESAS, bringing together the range of relevant psychosocial factors in relation to depression both provides a form demonstrating the enormous complexity of situations with which social workers work and the high levels of skill required of practice, but does so in a way which is consistent with the traditional role of social work. It fits with the occupational 'space' in which social work resides. Furthermore, DESAS provides a way of more openly indicating the practice of the social worker, and hence encouraging accountability. When used by all social workers in relation to all cases in a district, DESAS can show, collectively, the nature of problems and practice in that district. It can, so to speak, be used as an 'in practice' research tool.

DESAS is, then, able to provide a fairly clear picture of the psychosocial aspects of the clients' situation and the social workers' intervention in a way which would easily be allied to an assessment of depression. DESAS, it may be anticipated, is an instrument which could be used alongside depression instruments as a means for investigating the relationship between the woman's depression and a range of psychosocial problems and intervention measures appropriate for social work.

References

Barrera, M. (1981) Social support in the adjustment of pregnant adolescents: assessment issues. In B.H. Gottlieb (ed) *Social Networks and Social Supports.* Beverley Hills: Sage.

Beck, A. (1967) *Depression: Clinical, Experimental and Theoretical Aspects.* New York: Harper and Row.

Beck, A. (1974) The development of depression. In R.J. Friedman and M.M. Katz (eds) *The Psychology of Depression: Contemporary Theory and Research.* New York: Wiston Wiley.

Bifulco, A., Brown, G.W. and Harris, T.O. (1987) Loss of parent, lack of parental care and adult psychiatric disorder: the Islington study. *Journal of Affective Disorder 12,* 115–128.

Bowlby, J. (1969) *Attachment and Loss, Vol. 1.* London: Hogarth Press.

Bowlby, J. (1980) *Loss: Sadness and Depression. Attachment and Loss Vol. 3.* London: Hogarth Press.

Brown, G. and Harris, T. (1978) *Social Origins of Depression.* London: Tavistock.

Brown, G., Ni Brochlain, M. and Harris, T. (1975) Social class and psychiatric disturbance amongst women in an urban population. *Sociology 9,* 225–254.

Brown, G.W., Andrews, B., Harris, T.O., Adler, Z. and Bridge, L. (1986) Social support, self esteem and depression. *Psychological Medicine 16,* 813–831.

Corney, R. (1984a) The mental and physical health of clients referred to social workers in local authority and general practice attachment schemes. *Psychological Medicine 14,* 137–144.

Cox, A.D., Puckering, C., Pound, A. and Mills, M. (1987) The impact of maternal depression on young children. *Journal of Child Psychology and Psychiatry and Allied Disciplines 28,* 6, 917–928.

Department of Health (1991a) The Children Act 1989 *Guidance and Regulations Vol II. Family Support, Day Care and Education Provision for Young Children.* London: HMSO.

Department of Health (1991b) *Care Management: Practitioners' Guide.* London: HMSO.

Fitzgerald, R. (1978) The classification and recording of 'social problems'. *Social Science and Medicine 12,* 255–263.

Forehand, R. and Combs, A. (1988) Unravelling antecedant–consequent conditions in maternal depression and adolescent functioning. *Behaviour Research and Therapy 26,* 5, 399–405.

Gibbons, J., with Thorpe, S. and Wilkinson, P. (1990) *Family Support and Prevention: Studies in Local Areas.* London: National Institute for Social Work/HMSO.

Goldberg, E.M. and Wharburton, W. (1979) *Ends and Means in Social Work.* London: George Allen and Unwin.

Harris, T.O., Brown, G.W. and Bifulco, A. (1986) Loss of parent in childhood and adult psychiatric disorder: the role of adequate parental care. *Psychological Medicine 16*, 641–659.

Hoghughi, M. (1980) Social work in a bind. *Community Care*, 3 November, 17–23.

Hollingshead, A.B. and Redlich, F.C. (1958) *Social Class and Mental Illness.* New York: John Wiley.

Howe, D. (1979) Agency function and social work principles. *British Journal of Social Work 9*, 29–48.

Huntington, J. (1981) *Social Work and General Medical Practice: Collaboration or Conflict?* London: George Allen and Unwin.

Marsh, C. (1982) *The Survey Method: The Contribution of Survey to Sociological Method.* London: Allen and Unwin.

Moss, P. and Plewis, I. (1977) Mental distress in mothers of pre- school children in Inner London. *Psychological Medicine 7*, 641–652.

Myers, J. and Bean, L. (1968) *A Decade Later: A Follow-up of Social Class and Mental Illness.* New York: John Wiley.

Overmeir, J.B. and Seligman, M. (1967) Effects of inescapable shock upon subsequent escape and avoidance learning. *Journal of Comparative and Physiological Psychology 63*, 28–33.

Packman, J., with Randall, J. and Jacques, N. (1986) *Who Needs Care?* Oxford: Blackwell.

Pannacione, V.F. and Wahler, R.G. (1986) Child behaviour, maternal depression and social coercion as factors in the quality of child care. *Journal of Abnormal Child Psychology 14*, 2, 263–278.

Parker, R., Ward, H., Jackson, S., Aldgate, J. and Wedge, P. (1991) *Assessing Outcomes in Child Care.* London: HMSO.

Pavalko, R. (1988) *The Sociology of Occupations. Second edition.* Itasca, IL: Peacock.

Perlman, H.H. (1957) *Social Casework: A Problem Solving Process.* Chicago: University of Chicago Press.

Pincus, A. and Minahan, A. (1975) *Social Work Practice: Model and Method.* Itasca, IL: Peacock.

Reid, W. (1978) *The Task Centred System.* New York: Columbia University Press.

Richman, N. (1977a) Behaviour problems in pre-school children: family and social factors. *British Journal of Psychiatry 131*, 523–527.

Richman, N., Stevenson, J. and Graham, P.J. (1982) *Pre School to School: A Behavioural Study.* London: Academic Press.

Roy, A. (1980) Early parental loss in depressive neurosis compared with other neuroses. *Canadian Journal of Psychiatry 25*, 503–505.

Roy, A. (1981) Vulnerability factors and depression in men. *British Journal of Psychiatry 138*, 75–77.

Seligman, M. (1975) *Helplessness: On Depression, Development and Death.* San Francisco: Freeman and Co.

Sheppard, M. (1991) *Mental Health Work in the Community: Theory and Practice in Social Work and Community Psychiatric Nursing.* London: Falmer.

Sheppard, M. (1993a) The external context for social support: towards a theoretical formulation of social support, child care and maternal depression. *Social Work and Social Sciences Review 4,* 1, 27–59.

Sheppard, M. (1993b) Maternal depression, child care and social work: the significance for research and practice. *Adoption and Fostering 17,* 2, 10–17.

Sheppard, M. (1994a) Maternal depression, child care and the social work role. *British Journal of Social Work 24,* 33–51.

Sheppard, M. (1994b) Child care, social support and maternal depression: review and application of findings. *British Journal of Social Work 24,* 287–310.

Sheppard, M. (1995) *Care Management and the New Social Work: A Critical Analysis.* London: Whiting and Birch.

Srole, L., Langer, T.S., Michael, S.T. and Opler, M.K. (1962) *Mental Health in the Metropolis.* New York: McGraw Hill.

Thoits, P. (1982) Conceptual, methodological and theoretical problems in studying social support as a buffer against life stress. *Journal of Health and Social Behaviour 23,* 145–159.

Vieil, H. (1985) Dimensions of social support: a conceptual framework for research. *Social Psychiatry 20,* 156–162.

Weiss, R. (1974) The provisions of social relationships. In Z. Rubin (ed) *Doing Unto Others.* Englewood Cliffs, New Jersey: Prentice Hall.

Weissman, M. and Paykel, E. (1974) *The Depressed Woman.* Chicago: University of Chicago Press.

Weissman, M., Paykel, E. and Klerman, G. (1972) The depressed woman as mother. *Social Psychiatry 7,* 98–108.

Welner, Z. and Rice, J. (1988) School aged children of depressed parents: a blind and controlled study. *Journal of Affective Disorder 15,* 3, 291–302.

Welner, Z., Welner, A., Mcrary, M. and Leonard, M. (1977) Psychopathology of children of inpatients with depression: a controlled study. *Journal of Nervous and Mental Disease 164,* 6, 408–413.

Whittaker, J.K. (1974) *Social Treatment.* Chicago: Aldine.

Whittaker, J.K. and Garbarino, J. (1983) *Social Support Networks.* New York: Aldine.

Zuvarin, S.J. (1989) Severity of maternal depression and three types of mother–child aggression. *American Journal of Orthopsychiatry 59,* 3, 377–389.

Further reading

Black, J., Bowl, R. and Burns, D. (1983) *Social Work in Context.* London: Tavistock.

Brown, G. and Harris, T. (1986) Stress, vulnerability and depression. *Psychological Medicine 16,* 739–744.

Brown, G., Bifulco, A. and Harris, T. (1987) Life events, vulnerability and onset of depression: some refinements. *British Journal of Psychiatry 150,* 30–42.

Campbell, E., Cope, S. and Teesdale, J. (1983) Social factors and affective disorders: an investigation of Brown and Harris's model. *British Journal of Psychiatry 143,* 548–553.

Cohen, J. and Fisher, M. (1987) Recognition of mental health problems by doctors and social workers. *Practice 3,* 225–240.

Corney, R. (1984b) *The Effectiveness of Attached Social Workers in the Management of Depressed Female Patients in General Practice.* Cambridge: Cambridge University Press.

Department of Health (1989) *An Introduction to the Children Act, 1989.* London: HMSO.

Fisher, M., Newton, C. and Sainsbury, E. (1984) *Mental Health Social Work Observed.* London: George Allen and Unwin.

Howe, D. (1986) *Social Workers and their Practice in Welfare Bureaucracies.* Aldershot: Gower.

Huxley, P. and Fitzpatrick, R. (1984) The probable extent of minor mental illness in adult clients of social workers: a research note. *British Journal of Social Work 14,* 67–73.

Huxley, P., Korer, J. and Tolley, S. (1987) The psychiatric 'caseness' of clients referred to an urban social services department. *British Journal of Social Work 17,* 507–520.

Isaac, B., Minty, E. and Morrison, R. (1986) Children in care: the association with mental disorder in parents. *British Journal of Social Work 16,* 325–339.

Richman, N. (1977b) Depression in mothers of pre-school children. *Journal of Child Psychology and Psychiatry 17,* 75–78.

Seligman, M., Abramson, L., Semmel, A. and Baeger, C. (1979) Depressive attributional style. *Journal of Abnormal Psychology 88,* 242–247.

Sheppard, M. (1994c) Postnatal depression, child care and social support: a review of findings and their implications for social work. *Social Work and Social Sciences Review 5,* 1, 24–47.

Weissman, M. and Klerman, G. (1977) Sex differences in the epidemiology of depression. *Archives of General Psychiatry 34,* 98–111.

Appendix

Depression Social Assessment Schedule

Social / Demographic Data

1.   Is the mother

A single parent?   ☐

Married?   ☐

Living with a common law partner?   ☐

2.   If married/with common law partner, is the husband/partner the natural father of any of her children?

Yes ☐   No ☐

3.   To your knowledge:

Was the woman/mother previously married?   Yes ☐   No ☐

Did she previously have a common law partner?   ☐   ☐

If so

Was her former partner/husband the father

of any of her children?   ☐   ☐

4.   Age of parents:

	Under 18	18–30	31–44	Over 44
Age of mother/woman	☐	☐	☐	☐
Age of partner/husband (if she has one)	☐	☐	☐	☐

5.   Number of children in family

Age	Under 1	1–6	6–14	14–18
Male	☐	☐	☐	☐
Female	☐	☐	☐	☐

6.   Housing status:

Owner occupied	☐	Bed/breakfast	☐
Private rented	☐	Hostel/lodger	☐
Council	☐	No fixed abode	☐
Other (state)	☐		

7. Number of rooms in house/accommodation available to family ☐☐

8. Is the mother in paid employment?   Yes ☐ No ☐
   Occupation?
   Is the partner (if any) in paid employment?   Yes ☐ No ☐
   Occupation?

9. Source of income:
   Wages   ☐
   Benefits   ☐
   Wages plus benefits   ☐

10. Does the family own (to your knowledge):
    a refrigerator   Yes ☐ No ☐
    washing machine   Yes ☐ No ☐
    car   Yes ☐ No ☐

11. To your knowledge, does she receive regular child care help, such as looking after the children or providing practical help (more than once a week), from any of the following?
    Mother   ☐
    Father   ☐
    Sister/brother   ☐
    Friends   ☐

12. Does she live within half a mile of the nearest dwelling (as an estimate)?
    Yes   ☐
    No   ☐

13. To your knowledge, has the woman/mother ever been the recipient of
    Higher education (university/polytechnic)?   ☐
    Further education/sixth form college/'A' level   ☐
    education?

Case Status

1.   Departmental classification of case:
        Category One: physical emotional harm   ☐
        Category Two: loss of independence   ☐
        Category Three: quality of life   ☐

2.   Are the children on the 'at risk' register or *known* to have been abused?
                                                   Yes ☐ No ☐

        Indicate if this is for any of the following reasons:
            Physical abuse   ☐   Neglect/failure to thrive ☐
            Sexual abuse   ☐   Other (state)   ☐
            Emotional abuse   ☐

3.   Legal status of the case: are any children currently
        accommodated (voluntarily)   ☐
        in care   ☐

4.   Type of case (referral, allocation, caseload, accommodation, in care)
      Is this case one that has
          (a) just been referred and not allocated   ☐
          (b) just been referred and allocated   ☐
          (c) a case on existing caseload with no children
               in accommodation care   ☐
          (d) a case with children accommodated in care   ☐

5.   Offending behaviour: are social services involved because of offences by a
      child in the family?
                                     Yes ☐   No ☐

Case Review Questionnaire

PROBLEMS IN THE CASE

Please indicate, in the following, which problems have been, in your view, experienced by the client/family since your last review. *Please indicate the severity of each problem by ticking the appropriate box* (marked mild, moderate and severe). *If any problems were not present, simply do not tick the relevant box.* For example, if there were no housing problems, ignore that category.

Adult Problems and Needs

SOCIAL FACTORS

		Present 1	Severe 2
1. *Housing*	e.g. tenancy problems, homeless, overcrowding, physically unsuitable for needs	☐	☐
2. *Financial*	e.g. indebtedness, poor financial management	☐	☐
3. *Occupation*	e.g. difficulties with employers, problems with workmates/colleagues, threat of unemployment	☐	☐
4. *Problems with formal institutions*	e.g. difficulties with agencies (e.g. DSS, legal system, police, health) lack of knowledge of welfare rights or available resources	☐	☐
5. *Problems of race and culture*	e.g. subject to racism causing them distress; difficulties arising from language, limited opportunities for religious pursuits	☐	☐
6. *Home management*	e.g. cooking, cleaning, shopping, personal care of self maintenance/repair of house	☐	☐
7. *Deviant behaviour*	(a) Problems associated with subject's criminal behaviour (b) Problems associated with close adult family/friend's criminal behaviour (c) Drug/alcohol abuse	☐	☐

Relationship Problems

		Present 1	Severe 2
1. *Marital/partner*	e.g. persistent arguments with partner, poor communication, violent behaviour, extended absence, sexual problems	☐	☐
2. *Extended family*	e.g. persistent arguments, poor communication, distressing extended absence	☐	☐
3. *Friends*	e.g. arguments, disputes or poor communication with friends, neighbours and work colleagues	☐	☐
4. *Lack of relationships*	Persistent isolation, limited social network	☐	☐
5. *Sexual abuse/ violence*	e.g. subject to racism causing them distress; difficulties arising from language, limited opportunities for religious pursuits	☐	☐
6. *Bereavement/loss*	of close family/friends/partner, causing distress	☐	☐

Ill-Health

		Present 1	Severe 2
1. *Physical health*	(a) Long-term disability/illness in woman (b) long-term illness/disability in close adult family	☐	☐
2. *Reproduction*	e.g. problems with contraception, unwanted pregnancy, infertility	☐	☐
3. *Mental health*	(a) Psychotic disturbance in woman (subject) e.g. schizophrenia, mania (b) Clinical depression in woman (subject) (c) Acute psychological distress in woman (d) Psychiatric disturbance in close adult family	☐	☐

Parenting Problems

		Present 1	Severe 2
1. *Physical care of child(ren)*	e.g. concern about inadequate hygiene, adequacy of clothing, care when ill etc.	☐	☐
2. *Provision of guidance*	e.g. little/no guidance about right or wrong behaviour; unclear behavioural boundaries, lack of action when child misbehaves, etc.	☐	☐
3. *Provision of positive affect towards child(ren)*	(a) Lack of concern about them; limited attachment/bonding (b) Hostility towards/excessive criticism of children	☐	☐
4. *Involvement with child(ren)*	e.g. shows no interest in their interests, limiting communication or even contact with the child	☐	☐
5. *Unrealistic expectations*	expectations of child inappropriate to age, e.g. in tasks or understanding	☐	☐

Child Problems

		Present 1	Severe 2
1. *Emotional difficulties*	e.g. persistent distress, depression, anxiety, irritability	☐	☐
2. *Behavioural difficulties*	e.g. habitual defiance, aggressive behaviour, tantrums	☐	☐
3. *Cognitive difficulties*	e.g. poor concentration, poor language development	☐	☐
4. *Poor social involvement*	e.g. social withdrawal, disinclination to play, few/no friends, lack of involvement with peers or family	☐	☐
5. *Uncertainty/ confused identity*	unclear sense of 'self', e.g. relating to family of origin, sexuality, race/culture (arising e.g. from adoption, fostering, step-parent status, confused sexuality)	☐	☐
6. *Physical health*	illness/disability	☐	☐
7. *Somatic problems*	e.g. soiling, bed wetting (age inappropriate) disrupted sleeping, poor appetite/not eating enough	☐	☐
8. *Educational*	(a) Educational underachievement (b) Behavioural problems: e.g. truancy, disruptive behaviour at school	☐	☐
9. *Deviant behaviour*	e.g. drug/alcohol abuse, delinquency/criminal behaviour	☐	☐

PRIMARY PROBLEM

Which of the problems that you have already indicated are present in this case do you consider to be the main or primary problem? Please ring one number only from the alternatives below.

Adult social

1   Housing

2   Financial

3   Occupation

4   Problems with institutions

5   Race/culture

6   Home management

7   Criminal behaviour (woman's)

8   Criminal behaviour (adult close family)

9   Drug abuse

Adult health

10   Illness in woman

11   Illness in adult family

12   Reproduction

13   Psychosis in woman

14   Clinical depression in woman

15   Acute psychological distress in woman

16   Mental illness in close adult family

Adult relationship

17   Marital/partner

18   Extended family

19   Friends

20   Lack of relationships

21   Sexual abuse/violence

22   Loss/bereavement

Parenting

23   Physical care of children

24   Guidance

25   Poor attachment/bonding to child

26   Hostility to child

27   Poor involvement with child

28   Unrealistic expectations of child

Child problems

29   Emotional

30   Behavioural

31   Cognitive

32   Poor social involvement

33   Identity

34   Physical health

35   Somatic

36   Educational underachievement

37   Social behaviour/truancy

38   Deviant behaviour

Case Review Questionnaire
INTERVENTION

1. Please estimate the total number of interviews undertaken in relation to this case in the last six months (put number in relevant box) □□□

2. How long has social services been involved in this case? (If less than one month indicate number of days; if less than one year indicate number of months, if more than one year indicate number of years.)

    years □□ months □□ days □□

DIRECT WORK BY SOCIAL WORKER/CARE MANAGER WITH CLIENT/MOTHER

Please indicate by ticking the appropriate box which of the following activities you have carried out since the last review or since allocation or, if the case was not allocated, those activities undertaken on duty.

A.

1. *Assessment/information gathering*

B. *Practical/facilitative*

2. Information/advice: child care
                         other

3. Encouraging social skills

4. Direct financial support (e.g. section 17 money)

C. *Emotional–supportive*

5. Emotional support/ventilation

6. Esteem support/encouragement (e.g. praising achievements, encouraging life plans)

7. Encouraging/facilitating contact with friends/ membership of social/sports clubs/interest

D. *Personal problem solving*

8. Promotion of self-understanding (helping mothers understand themselves and their actions better)

9. Decision-facilitating activities (discussing future options/helping with life plans/ambitions)

10. Esteem building activities (changing cognitions about self, task achievement activities, e.g. cognitive behavioural therapy)

E. *Direct work with children*

11. Therapeutic work (e.g. life story book, helping them express their feelings)

12. Child assessment (including disclosure work)

13. Befriending/relationship building or sustaining

WORK WITH INFORMAL NETWORK

1. *Encouraging the provision of support*

This refers to encouragement of the individual(s) interviewed, such as friends, relatives or neighbours, to provide the following support for the client. Please indicate by ticking the appropriate boxes who, if anyone, you directly encouraged to provide support, and what support you encouraged them to provide. Note that this is about you encouraging them to provide the support *whether or not* they subsequently provided it.

(a) Support provider(s)

Partner	Other relatives
Mother	Friends
Father	

(b) Support elicited

Material help	Other practical help
Advice/guidance	Encouraging increased social
Reassurance of worth/praise	participation
Help with children	Help reduce interpersonal conflict
Other [specify]	

WORK WITH FORMAL ORGANISATIONS AND NETWORKS

1. Advocacy on behalf of clients or contact with outside agencies: please indi-
    cate which of the following agencies/professionals you have contacted
    since the last review:

Health visitor	Drug/alcohol service	Legal services
GP	Housing	Police
Paediatrician	Probation	School
Psychiatrist	Education welfare	Other [specify]
Psychologist	Family conciliation	

SERVICES PURCHASED

1. Services purchased (or shadow purchased) by care manager:

Specialist assessment	Befriending support/support group
Parenting skills development	Budgeting help
Relief care of children	Direct work with children
Therpaeutic work on parents	Family therapy
Practical support	Other [specify]

2. Resources from which these services were purchased:

Family centre	Family Aid
Children's home/resource unit	Home help
Fostering	Other social worker
Adolescent support worker	NSPCC
Child psychiatry/psychology	Family conciliation
Drug/alcohol unit	Childminder

CONDUCT OF INTERVENTION

1. *Main forum for work.* Please indicate the most significant activity carried out in case management. Please circle the appropriate number. Please circle *only* one.

(a) *Direct work by care manager:*

Assessment	1
Practical facilitative	2
Emotional supportive	3
Personal problem solving	4
Direct work with children	5

(b) *Informal network*

Assessment through informal network	6
Encouraging network support	7

(c) *Work by purchased service*

Specialist assessment	8
Parenting skills development	9
Relief care for children	10
Therapeutic work on parent(s)	11
Befriending support group	12
Practical support	13
Budgeting help	14
Direct work with children	15
Other [specify] _____	16

2. *Main focus for work.* Please indicate who was the prime focus for your intervention (i.e. who you concentrated on to improve/resolve the situation).

Subject (mother)	Partner	Subject and partner
Child(ren)	Other family	Other social network
Formal agencies/professionals		

CHAPTER 10

Evaluation of Social Work Services for People with Mental Health Problems

Allyson McCollam and Julia White

Introduction

This chapter reviews some of the issues connected with the evaluation of mental health services. In doing so the authors concentrate for several reasons mostly on those services which fall within the ambit of the social work and voluntary sectors. First, much of the detailed evaluative work which has been carried out in mental health to date has been in these sectors, whereas health care settings tend to have generated surveys and larger-scale investigations. Second, as the fulcrum of mental health provision moves away from psychiatric institutions to community-based services, the role and scope of the social work and voluntary sectors are set to expand.

Evaluation is one of a number of tools which can be employed to review performance, along with routine monitoring, clinical audit, quality assurance systems, inspection, cost–benefit analysis, surveys, and so on. The selection of a particular method to measure performance reflects the nature of the task under scrutiny and the rationale for carrying out a review. There are a variety of sources which interested readers may wish to consult for an overview of these different options and their application (Connor and Black 1994; Cheetham *et al.* 1992; Sykes *et al.* 1992).

Evaluation is assuming ever greater significance in the planning and provision of services for people with mental health problems. Pressure on finite resources means funders increasingly expect evidence of the impact of a service to justify its continuation. The development of an array of innovative services and innovative approaches to the delivery of services calls for efforts to assess effectiveness and to adjudge applicability in other contexts. The move towards community-based mental health care also implies a reordering of professional roles and responsibilities, and in such an environment, evaluation provides an opportunity to review and refine practice.

It is understandable therefore that there is a growing awareness among service users, carers and professionals in the statutory and voluntary sectors that they need to be conversant with the terminology and methods of evaluation. This chapter considers the process of evaluation and some of the issues which arise when conducting an evaluation in a mental health setting. It also looks at how a completed evaluation can be used to best effect. Before doing so, however, it is important to clarify what is meant by evaluation.

Monitoring and evaluation

Monitoring and evaluation are often harnessed together and are sometimes mistakenly used interchangeably. *Monitoring* refers to the process of recording in a systematic way what is taking place. It is undertaken to elicit facts to describe a piece of work or an event, to review what is happening relative to what should be happening. Most mental health services are engaged in some form of monitoring, whether it be recording attendances at a day centre or occupancy rates in a supported accommodation project.

The methods used to collect information will reflect ideally the purposes for which that information is sought. Where monitoring is viewed as burdensome and as a distraction from 'real' work, it can be very helpful to review why that information is needed and what will be done with it.

Evaluation is about constructing explanations of what takes place and making judgements about the merit of an activity by measuring it against specific criteria (Goldberg and Connelly 1982). It is concerned with effectiveness and outcomes, in relation to the aims and objectives of the service. Monitoring gathers information on broad trends and features, whereas evaluation is more concerned with the detail, with the connections between different features and with explanation.

The different models of evaluation have been described in depth elsewhere. It is common to distinguish the classical version of evaluation from the pluralistic approach (Smith and Cantley 1984). As evaluation has gradually become insinuated into the field of social care and social work, there is a growing recognition of the necessity of finding methodologies which do justice to the complexity of these activities and the social world in which they take place (Cheetham *et al.* 1992). This has led to a loosening up of the definitions of evaluation to allow the creative development of approaches which fit more comfortably with the ethos and the purposes of the activity under scrutiny (Feuerstein 1987).

Coupled with that is the recognition that evaluation need not be the exclusive domain of the professional researcher or academic. For some years, social workers have been exhorted to review their own work with rigour (Sheldon 1986). There is growing evidence that workers on the ground are conscious of the need to equip themselves with the skills needed to carry out evaluations, or at least to understand evaluations of their own work conducted by others (Scottish Evaluation Forum/Nuffield Centre for Community Care Studies 1995).

Why evaluate mental health services?

There are a number of factors which work together to strengthen the case for giving greater priority to evaluation in the planning and delivery of services for people with mental health problems:

- the swell of new projects with the advent of specific grant
- increased competition for funding which means that providers must produce information on what they do and demonstrate the effectiveness of their work
- purchasers must be able to make informed decisions about resource allocation
- individual workers need to be able to take stock of their own work and judge whether their time and energies are being used most fruitfully
- the recognition that service users should have a greater say in provision requires that mechanisms be established to glean users' views

- the goals of many mental health services are often to support and maintain people in the community, and there is a need therefore for careful evaluation to do justice to the particular complexities of mental health work

- the changing patterns of provision as hospitals are replaced by community-based services and the shifting boundaries between professional roles support the case for evaluation of the impact of such changes on service users' lives

- service users and staff often feel they are working in isolation and lack information on, or contact with, similar services. Evaluation affords a means of providing information and of highlighting aspects of good practice.

Stages of evaluation

The various stages involved in an evaluation are set out in Figure 10.1. As illustrated, these stages do not necessarily follow in fixed linear sequence – it may

Define project aims

Define purposes of evaluation

Determine focus and audience:

what is being evaluated, and for whom?

Specify the timescale for the evaluation

Describe work of project

Choose evaluator

Select methods

Collect information

Analyse and write up results

Use results internally

Disseminate results externally

Figure 10.1 Stages of evaluation

prove necessary to review the progress of the evaluation and make adjustments. Experience does suggest that careful planning and preparation are crucial to ensure the evaluation is viable and acceptable.

Planning and preparation
Defining the focus

Evaluation can be used in a wide variety of contexts and at many different levels. The focus of a study can vary across a number of dimensions. It may concentrate on:

- a particular service, such as supported accommodation, involving either a single provider (McCollam 1988) or a range of providers (Buglass and Dick 1992; Petch 1992)

- a system of services working with a specific group of people, for example, those with long-term mental health problems (Knapp *et al.* 1992; Smith 1991)

- a group of service users whose engagement with particular services is tracked over time (Leff 1993; Pickard *et al.* 1992)

- a one-off piece of work, such as a consultation event or training day

- issues of process and quality in addition to outcomes.

When consideration is being given to carrying out an evaluation, it is important that the focus of the proposed work is clearly defined to avoid confusion and ambiguity later. Probably the most familiar usage of evaluation is when a service is assessed over a time-limited period. While it remains important that a body of knowledge is accumulated about the effectiveness of different services in different contexts, there is a definite absence of information about how the individual elements of service provision knit together and about how changes in one element impact on the others. This might entail adopting a wider perspective across the mental health care system as a whole to review the balance and range of provision. Alternatively, an evaluation might take as its starting point the experience of individual service users to track the impact of the overall service system on the lives of those who use it.

Defining the purpose of the evaluation

There is a difference between deciding that an evaluation should be carried out and homing in on what should in fact be investigated. The authors' experience of working in a consultative capacity on evaluation with projects and groups suggests that there is a tendency to approach this part of the work back to front. It can be very misleading to start to collect data for an evaluation when the questions to be addressed have not been clearly formulated in advance. The danger is that the form the evaluation takes will then be determined by the information generated, rather than the purpose of the investigation dictating the types of method to be used.

The purposes of the evaluation should not be confused with the objectives of the service or work being assessed. Where the aims and objectives of a service are well defined, it is often necessary to translate these into concrete achievable tasks, which can then be measured. Where a service has no formal definition of its aims and objectives, or these are now out-dated, the evaluation exercise would need to begin by rectifying this situation. Indeed, the effect on a project of having to reach agreement on its aims and objectives can be one of the beneficial results of taking on an evaluation!

Perhaps one of the reasons that evaluation can seem so daunting to those unfamiliar with it is the prospect of doing justice to the complexity of the work undertaken. While this is undoubtedly a challenge, in reality most studies select specific aspects of the work to investigate. It may be, for example, that the principal concern is with reviewing the take-up of a service and the evaluation will therefore survey referring agents. It is generally better in the first place to tackle a discrete aspect of the service's operation – one which is manageable and not unduly disruptive. Once that is concluded it is always possible to look at other areas.

There is also often apprehension among service users and workers that the service or project may be judged on the basis of criteria which do not necessarily reflect its 'true' nature. This is often an issue when an evaluation has been instigated by funders and is being carried out by an external evaluator. It underlines the importance of discussion and negotiation among all concerned from the outset to allay concerns as far as possible and to ensure that all parties stand to derive some gain from the exercise.

Box 10.1 Purposes Of Evaluation

Value for money

- efficient use of resources
- rational basis for resource allocation
- enables better targeting

Quality

- refines practice
- uses feedback to match services to users' requirements
- highlights good practice
- ensures standards are adhered to
- helps validate new approaches

Effectiveness

- reviews impact on service users
- uncovers possible unexpected consequences
- identifies gaps in provision
- promotes critical reflection
- encourages change and development
- aids decision making

Audience

Evaluation is a means of achieving an end, rather than an end in itself, and it is helpful to consider in advance for whom the final product is intended. This is likely to have an effect on the nature of the investigation and on how the results are presented and disseminated. A recent survey by the Scottish Association of Mental Health (SAMH 1994) of the views of service users on training, employment and day activities resulted in the production of two reports, one for Local Enterprise Companies and training providers, and another for social work departments and health boards. The broad content was similar, but each version had a different emphasis.

Evaluation in the contracting process

Including plans for evaluation from the earliest stages when purchasers and providers are discussing project objectives, allows all those involved to negotiate a strategy for evaluation which fits in with the project's operation and timescales.

It is important at this stage that expectations of the service are clarified and agreed, and focusing on the proposed evaluation can encourage that.

Evaluation, even on a small scale, has resource implications, and while additional costs are sometimes built into project proposals, unless the nature of the evaluation has been considered in some detail, the amount set aside for this purpose is often very small and is vulnerable to being cut if budgets have to be pared.

If service providers know in advance what funders expect in the way of evaluation, they are then able to determine whether there are additional areas of their work which they wish to evaluate, or whether they want to examine some aspects in greater depth.

All too often projects find themselves required to produce an end-of-funding cycle review of their work with insufficient warning or discussion of what is entailed. This can be very difficult to accommodate if the project has not been collecting the necessary monitoring information as the foundation for evaluation.

An area of increasing concern is where projects have several sources of funding and therefore are expected to report back in different ways, possibly using different criteria to assess achievements. The effects of 'patchwork' funding can be very stressful for projects. Joint commissioning offers a solution in that it brings together the different parties to reach a joint agreement on a service's aims and objectives, timescales and so on.

Evaluating innovation

Innovation may mean that the work itself or the particular approach adopted is new. It may involve applying a tried and tested approach in a new context or with a different group of service users. When innovative services are set up, there is an important opportunity to build in from the beginning information systems which allow the work to be evaluated.

Evaluating innovative projects presents certain challenges, however. It requires adaptability and flexibility, both in terms of the methods used and on the part of the evaluator. Innovative services often evolve organically, and to begin with goals may not be firmly defined. The work of the service can alter substantially and it may be realistic to start with small-scale monitoring activities, gradually extending into evaluation as the service assumes a more coherent form.

One of the interests in evaluating innovative work is to define what is different about that approach, how it compares with more 'traditional' approaches and to assess how it might be replicated in other contexts. This can have particular implications for how the evaluation is carried out, and calls for resourcefulness and imagination in designing the evaluation.

Evaluation can be useful to innovative projects in the longer term, as it can review how the original idea develops. Projects which are deemed to be successful or ground breaking can sometimes find it very difficult to change in response to evolving needs, as a result of their status as show-pieces. They may attract a great deal of attention, which only detracts from their core purposes and prevents them from developing further their innovative methods and services.

Carrying out an evaluation

Some mental health issues

We do not intend to give an account here of the various methods which can be used to evaluate. This is amply covered elsewhere (Connor 1993; McCollam and White 1993; McIver 1991; NHS/SCC 1994). We will however explore a number of specific considerations related to the evaluation of mental health services.

It is increasingly recognised as important that the evaluation process should itself promote mental health and empower service users (SEF/NCCCS 1994). On a purely pragmatic basis, if service users agree to participate in the evaluation by completing questionnaires or being interviewed, but receive no information subsequently about the results and how they are to be used, they are likely to become disillusioned and less inclined to take part in further research initiatives.

In addition, many people experiencing long-term mental ill-health already have low self-esteem and a sense of powerlessness (Shepherd, Murray and Muijen 1994). Evaluation can provide an opportunity to promote a more positive image of, and a more proactive role for, service users (Rapp, Shera and Kisthardt 1993).

Involving service users will affect the way the evaluation is organised:

- users will require accessible information about the evaluation
- all participants should be made aware of the time allowed for the evaluation
- training should be provided for specific tasks as necessary, for example interviewing or analysing information
- opportunities to 'learn by doing' should be included. Experienced evaluators working alongside users and workers with no previous evaluation experience can enable greater experience at a more meaningful level.

The intention to involve service users in an evaluation has to be taken into account from the planning stages, in relation to general issues such as the pace and the methods of evaluation. There are, however, several more specific issues which require closer attention.

Boundaries

During the course of an evaluation, the roles of staff and users can alter, which may at first be disconcerting for participants. Service users, who until now may have been used to receiving services without comment, are now asked to give their opinion on those services; staff used to coordinating and providing services are asked to describe what they do; members of management committees used to making decisions may now have to justify those decisions. These temporary changes can have an unsettling effect on the service which must be taken into account when carrying out an evaluation.

Consent

While those wishing to be involved in an evaluation should be given every opportunity to participate, it should also be possible to decline. Informed consent is perhaps easier to obtain when carrying out a survey or interviews, but should also be sought in less clear-cut situations, for example in a comparative study looking at the involvement of residents in different types of supported accommodation provision.

Role conflict

This can arise when it has been decided to carry out a self-evaluation. A member of staff who assumes the role of evaluator should be careful to explain the change of role to all participants. There may be difficulties because the evaluator already knows a great deal about potential interviewees; because the evaluator has access to confidential information which would not otherwise have been available; or because service users prefer the member of staff to occupy their former role.

The role of the evaluator

The evaluator's role is crucial to the success of an evaluation in any setting, and there are certain qualities and skills which are worth seeking out. Previous experience of carrying out an evaluation is important, as is familiarity with the type of work being evaluated. It helps to have someone who is flexible and adaptable and can adopt innovative approaches to their work, someone who is a good communicator with an interest in individuals and their responses to different situations.

In working with mental health service users, providers and managers, it is important that the evaluator can negotiate, smooth out misunderstandings and ensure that everyone is involved in the process. Box 10.2 presents a number of practice points relating to the role of the evaluator.

Interviewing service users

Interviewing in a mental health context requires sensitivity on the part of the researcher, especially if questions touch on matters of mental health and hospitalisation. The individual's rights to privacy and to withhold information have to be respected. Our experience suggests that many people who have had treatment for mental health problems become accustomed to disclosing personal details in their role as patient, and the interviewer needs to take time and care to explain the boundaries, to and the purpose of, the interview. In other instances the person being interviewed may need repeated reassurances about confidentiality and about how the information will be used.

An important part of the interviewer's task is to ensure that the purpose of the interview is clearly understood. Providing written information in advance to each person who will be interviewed or who will take part in a group discussion can be useful, as people may be apprehensive and not able to absorb what they are told

Box 10.2 The evaluator's role

The evaluator's role	Practice points
Keep regular contact	Staff and users should know when visits are to take place and what their purpose is. They should be able to contact the evaluator between planned visits.
Build up a relationship of trust	Not being critical is most important here. The evaluator has to show how a project works and what it is doing. She should aim to be detached from the successes and failures of the work, as these are simply a part of the process of the project's development.
Negotiate ways of carrying the evaluation	The evaluator needs the cooperation of out the people she is working with. If they become enthusiastic about the evaluation, so much the better!
Adapt methods of assessment to the needs of different projects	Try to avoid a 'blueprint' approach. What has worked with one group of users may be seen as intrusive and unnecessary by another.
Work in a supportive way	The evaluation process may impose extra workloads on people who are already overworked. Try to fit into existing routines.
Offer a flexible input as far as possible	Assistance and advice outside of regular meetings may be welcomed, especially if the project is new or innovative.
Adopt a sensitive approach	Be alert to aspects of the evaluation which may seem threatening to users and staff. Seek to reassure people of the confidentiality of the evaluation.

face to face. It also affords an opportunity for people to give thought in advance to what they want to say to the interviewer, rather than being put on the spot, which can be a stressful experience.

The pacing of the interview or discussion needs to allow for the fact that some people with mental health problems may find it difficult to concentrate for lengthy periods and may welcome a break. In addition, there may be particular times of the day when someone feels more able to focus on a discussion because of the effects of their medication.

The setting in which the interview or meeting takes place can influence the outcome. If someone is being interviewed in a setting where they feel ill at ease, or where there are likely to be repeated interruptions, the interviewer may well find it hard to keep someone's interest. Making people feel comfortable and as far as possible in control of the situation will help the encounter run smoothly.

The language and terminology used in an interview or discussion can influence the degree to which participants become engaged in the process. It can be helpful to spend a brief time addressing this at the outset to agree on acceptable terms and to avoid alienating people subsequently. People with mental health problems tend to be stigmatised and marginalised as much by the attitudes and reactions of others as by the effects of their particular difficulties. It is important to ensure that the experience of being evaluated does not reinforce negative images, in the way the evaluation is both conducted and presented.

Self-evaluation

Self-evaluation is often considered when:

- the service to be evaluated is innovative and the provider wishes to retain control over the evaluation process
- there is agreement that service users should be involved in the planning and management of the evaluation
- resource constraints preclude the employment of an outside evaluator
- there are strong feelings that a member of staff should take on the role of evaluator because of their understanding of the project's purpose and ethos
- there is concern about how the outcome of the evaluation will reflect on the service.

Self-evaluation can in time lead on to the employment of an outside evaluator. It can enable a service to participate in the evaluation process without exposure to the pressures often associated with a more comprehensive evaluation exercise. Reviewing the use of staff time or examining the effectiveness of communication systems within a project can stand alone as small-scale evaluations or can be used as the basis for a more in-depth analysis of a project's operation.

For many small voluntary organisations, self-evaluation will remain the only option available. As it can be incorporated into the everyday work of the service, disruption can be minimised and the evaluation adapted as the service evolves (SEF/NCCCS 1994). Appropriate methods which can be used by smaller organisations are now being refined, and a better understanding of the resources needed by such groups is being developed (Moore and Whitting 1993). However, the amount of extra work involved in carrying out a self-evaluation should not be underestimated, either by services which elect to embark on an evaluation or by purchasers who may require providers to carry one out.

Outcomes

Different perspectives on success

In the field of mental health the issue of outcomes continues to generate much discussion – in terms of both definition and measurement. As the funding arrangements for service provision tie providers to the attainment of specific outcomes over a defined period, debate on what constitutes an acceptable outcome assumes a new urgency. Definitions of outcomes, moreover, need to be sufficiently broad to encapsulate both health and social care services for the full range of individuals with mental health problems, not just the traditional users of psychiatric care.

Choosing outcomes

The *choice* of outcome measures for any service should be tied closely to the service's objectives, to ensure that its achievements can be assessed. However, it is important that mental health services set out with realistic expectations of what they might achieve. Many services play a relatively small, though significant, part in a person's life, and it needs to be acknowledged that their impact is likely to be limited in terms of effecting change. Added to that, many of the services people receive are unable to tackle the major difficulties users face – such as unemployment, poverty and poor housing – so that their potential influence is diminished.

Broadly speaking, outcomes can be divided into:

- those which are service based, and consider performance or activity

- those which review the service's impact on its users.

Service-based outcomes tend to be more straightforward and easier to collect. They include:

- the extent to which the objectives are being met
- details on the content of the service
- frequency of contact with service users
- quality of provision
- costs.

The importance of accumulating even quite basic data on the type and quantity of services provided should not be underestimated. Without this sort of information as a foundation, it is difficult on the one hand to know whether, in discussions of outcomes, we are comparing like with like. On the other hand, it remains impossible to begin to explore how particular types of service produce particular effects. As the range of services available to people with mental health problems looks set to develop in new ways in Scotland with the demise of the old-style large psychiatric hospitals, the accumulation of a body of descriptive information on what types of service are being developed would be enormously valuable.

Box 10.3 Service user outcomes

Maintenance	of current state or level of skills or well-being
Stabilisation	in crisis
Change and growth	in skills and capacities, including progression to follow-on services
Prevention	of deterioration

The different orders of *outcomes focused on the service user* are shown in Box 10.3. These could be applied across different domains, such as psychiatric symptoms, employment status, social networks and skills, self-esteem and quality of life.

Difficulties have sometimes arisen in the past when an unrealistic or inappropriate expectation of change exists as an index of success. This may have been imposed by funding bodies or been generated by the service because of a lack of experience in the field or because of over-ambition to win approval and secure funding. Recognition that other orders of outcome are equally valid and important would relieve many projects from the pressure of performing to standards which are simply unobtainable in many instances, but also inappropriate for that type of work.

A further confounding factor is the short-term nature of many of the funding options available to services for people with mental health problems. This means that the time within which projects are expected to produce evidence that objectives have been achieved is often remarkably brief. This would suggest that methods need to be devised to ensure that a service's overarching objectives are broken down into goals which are attainable within the time-frame under scrutiny.

In supporting in the community people with a range of mental health problems which vary in severity and in duration, mental health provision serves a number of different functions, which can render comparisons of the outcomes of different services difficult. The extent to which the results of evaluation are used as a tool in decision making and in the process of resource allocation is in any case a moot point (Bulmer 1986). But it is important that the relative value to be attached to different sets of outcomes is fully and openly debated.

Measuring outcomes

As services strive more and more to offer an individualised service to their users, this can complicate attempts to aggregate outcomes, and produce misleading results for the project as a whole. Often people who use a service start out from different baselines in terms of skills, levels of symptoms and so on. Additionally, they may use the same service for a variety of reasons and have quite different aspirations (McCollam 1993).

Evaluation methodologies need to find ways of taking cognisance of these sorts of variation among users and of devising appropriate methodologies. Kopp (in CEDEFOP (European Centre for the Development of Vocational Training) 1990) offers an interesting example of how this might be effected in a vocational training project for people with mental health problems. Thus, for example, follow-up information on the employment status of graduates from the training programme states the proportion in work or unemployed and the proportion who did not have employment as a goal. The achievements of individual trainees are assessed relative to their starting point on joining the programme.

The types of softer outcome which are so fundamental to much of mental health practice pose particular challenges when it comes to measurement. We look briefly at three such outcomes commonly used in the mental health field.

QUALITY OF LIFE

Quality of life is mentioned frequently in policy statements as one of the corner-stones of community care. The key issues in measuring quality of life appear to centre around the balance to be struck between objective and subjective measures and around the criteria to be used in arriving at some summary statement. Evidence indicates that the experience of mental health problems does not significantly colour how an individual assesses her quality of life, except for areas directly relating to health (Lehmann 1983).

The method chosen to explore quality of life will depend very much on why that information is sought. In some instances, there may be an interest in assessing the impact on quality of life of service usage, elsewhere the concern may be to identify areas where quality of life could be improved by specific interventions. The first exercise would require precise and specific measurement; the second would entail a more exploratory, discursive approach (Kerruish in Leiper and Field 1993).

SATISFACTION WITH SERVICES

The case for including in an evaluation mechanisms to gather the views of service users is now well established in social services research. The inclusion of users' perspectives in the evaluation of mental health services is increasingly seen as a way of giving a marginalised group more of a voice. There are, however, a number of conceptual and practical problems. In the first place, there is a general and well-documented tendency for service users to report high levels of overall satisfaction with services received (Cheetham *et al.* 1992). Yet what is of interest to those who fund, manage or provide services is 'honest' feedback – both positive and negative – from users on the strengths and weaknesses of a given service.

Overall ratings of satisfaction are therefore not particularly helpful, as they tell us little about specific aspects of services nor about variations between different service users in levels of satisfaction. The same service may fulfil different purposes for different users, thus it is important to consider the basis on which an individual formulates their opinion. In a study of shared living (Cooper *et al.* 1993), it was found that some residents set great store by the availability of close companionship, whereas others were content to know that other people were to hand if needed. Residents had differing priorities, which were reflected in their perceptions about the benefits of group living.

In order to consider how users perceive services, qualitative methods are called

---

Box 10.4 Measuring user satisfaction: an example

A 'bottom-up' approach to consider satisfaction with services was employed in a training project run by the Scottish Association for Mental Health. The project staff started out by discussing with groups of trainees not only what they found helpful about the project but also how to phrase and present a questionnaire for wider distribution to current and past trainees. This resulted in changes to the substance and the wording of the draft questionnaire, and in the development of a useful and flexible instrument (SAMH 1994).

---

for to enable the interviewer and the service user to engage in a loosely structured exploratory discussion. This allows issues raised by the individual to be considered in some depth, and provides the researcher with an opportunity to seek to understand the service user's views. It seems that more effective approaches use several different methods to access service users' views, employing, for example, focus groups and individual interviews, written exercises and discussions (NHS/SCC 1994).

There are also indications that more accurate, detailed information is provided when the researcher has spent time getting to know people and has regular contact with participants during the research (Cornwell 1984). This may encourage those taking part in the evaluation to express their private accounts rather than more socially acceptable public accounts (Kerruish 1995).

It has been suggested (Petch 1992) that users' views may change over time as they become more confident and have raised expectations of the services provided.

Added to this individual effect, the growing user movement (see Chapter 11) is enabling service users to adopt a more critical approach collectively and to express dissatisfactions with provision (Scottish Users' Conference 1993).

The actual methods used to explore service users' views may not be the only obstacle to obtaining 'honest' feedback from service users. The following factors may also be pertinent:

- where people have not previously received any services, they may feel grateful for what now exists and reluctant to criticise

- the distinction needs to be made between users' views on the impact of a service and their views on the process by which that service is provided

- users may not have sufficient information on, or knowledge of, alternative service models to allow them to arrive at an informed opinion

- there may be concerns about being 'disloyal' to workers who provide the service, and who may be perceived to have considerable power

- there may be doubts about the independence of the evaluation and worries that the views expressed will be held against people

- it may be that service users have become sceptical about providing feedback – perhaps they were not informed of what was done with the information provided in the past or feel that the views they expressed were not heeded (McIver 1991)

- users are less likely to contribute to an evaluation if it is perceived to be focused on issues which are not a priority for them, to the neglect of their own agenda for change.

It may not be possible to eliminate these factors when carrying out an evaluation, but it is important to be alert to them.

The credibility of the evaluation among service users may be considerably enhanced if users themselves are involved throughout the process, from planning to implementation and dissemination. A recent study of case management undertaken by the Sainsbury Centre for Mental Health is an example of a user-led piece of research (Beeforth *et al.* 1994). The authors contend that the opportunity to speak to fellow users rather than professional researchers encouraged respondents to be more forthcoming and more critical.

SELF-ESTEEM

Many mental health services set out – explicitly or implicitly – to enhance the self-esteem of service users, both in the type of support provided and the way in which that support is delivered. Where a service is targeted at people with long-term mental health problems, whose self-esteem and confidence may have been eroded gradually, this can be an important strand to any work undertaken. In attempting to assess changes in the self-esteem of service users, it may not be considered appropriate to deploy psychological rating scales. Such instruments undoubtedly have their place, but may not be considered suitable in settings where the ethos is non-clinical.

The alternatives are to use self-report or reports from 'interested others'. In asking service users directly about possible changes to self-esteem, some ingenuity is called for to translate the abstract concept into meaningful images and language. One possibility is to find out what types of activity or situation the person finds it difficult to cope with, and then to monitor whether there are any changes in this over time. People can be encouraged to keep diaries or log-books to ease recall.

Where personal and social development is in itself a focus of intervention, then the programme of work undertaken can build in a regular review exercise to record progress. This provides a useful record for service users and workers and can also be aggregated to give an overview of the impact of the project as a whole (Scottish Further Education Unit 1989).

Interpreting outcomes

The question of what constitutes a positive outcome often remains open to interpretation in the field of mental health. The classic example is that of hospital admission and readmission. If the goals of an accommodation unit include the prevention of hospital admission, then the fact that a resident from a supported accommodation project goes back into hospital for a brief stay to have her medication reassessed under close supervision is ostensibly a disappointing outcome. Yet that same person may have managed to retain a base in the community for over 11 months of the year, and will be enabled to return to it on discharge. The assumption that hospital admission represented a failure of the community support service for that individual might need to be recast, if reviewed in the context of that same person's previous history and own perceptions of her situation.

To date, evaluation of mental health services has tended to focus on client outcomes and to neglect detailed elucidations of the types of interaction which take place in various service settings. Yet without some understanding of the process of, for example, outreach support, the value of information about the impact of that service is necessarily limited. Where an evaluation has explored in some depth the nature of the service individuals receive as well as the impact of that service on those recipients, the task of establishing the relationships between these two sets of data is challenging but nonetheless of considerable importance to the future development of policy and provision.

Relationships between costs and other outcomes

With the advent of the purchaser–provider relationship, costs have assumed a more overt importance in planning and delivering services than previously. However, it is still the case that relatively little is known about the *efficiency* of different patterns of mental health services (O'Donnell 1991). The growing body of research into the reprovision of services to replace psychiatric hospitals in the south east of England is helping to fill this void, not only in terms of data on costs but more fundamentally in terms of methodologies to gather cost information (Knapp *et al.* 1992).

There is unlikely to be a simple formula to enable decision makers to weigh up the costs and effectiveness of different approaches. Such decisions are ultimately value judgements about whether the benefits of one approach are worth the costs, relative to other opportunities which may have to be foregone as a consequence. The way ahead seems to lie in acknowledging that we cannot choose to ignore the financial part of the equation in evaluating services. On the contrary, greater transparency in terms of costs can only lead to more effective deployment of the limited resources available.

Using evaluation

Evaluation is not an end in itself, yet it is not uncommon for most time and energy to be devoted to the collection of data and the collation of results. The subsequent stages in the cycle – disseminating and implementing the results – are often neglected.

Implementation of findings

The results of a piece of evaluative research can have repercussions at various levels:

- there may be immediate implications for the day-to-day operation of a service, and for relationships between service users and staff within it
- the organisation providing the service may be prompted to review how it functions
- there may be wider implications for policy and practice at a more global level.

The aspect of evaluation which seems to be overlooked very often is that any changes precipitated need to be carefully managed and supported. Organisations and institutions have an in-built resistance to change, and determined strategies are required to alter fixed practices. Individuals tend to regard change as threaten-

---

Box 10.5 Factors which influence the extent to which findings are implemented

- Acceptance of evaluation as a legitimate activity by all concerned
- Acknowledgement of the interests of different stakeholders
- Recognising and working with the power differentials between groups
- Discussing fully and openly the effects of changes proposed
- Provision of training to enable people to absorb changes required
- Resources made available to implement changes
- Support to follow through the change process

---

ing, and therefore preparation, information and support are called for to sustain the effort needed to absorb change.

A cautionary note is needed here lest the impression is created that evaluation research necessarily has a direct impact on decision making at practice and policy level. The evidence points to a creative tension rather than a direct relationship, in that evaluation can help to structure discussion and frame issues in a coherent way (Cheetham *et al.* 1992). However, the plurality of interests at stake and the range of considerations other than the results of an evaluation which have a bearing on decision making complicate the relationship immeasurably (Weis 1986).

Dissemination

Dissemination is about communicating the results of the evaluation. It is not simply about producing a final report for the funders of the evaluation. Time and effort are needed to tailor the methods of dissemination to the various audiences, including service users (McCollam and White 1993).

Even where an evaluation is carried out as an internal exercise there is still a task to be done to ensure that those implicated are informed of the results. This is in part a question of good practice as well as of accountability – that those who have participated in or supported the exercise are entitled to learn of its outcome. It is also an opportunity to share information and review working practices constructively.

Where respondents are given feedback on the results of an evaluation and informed of how these are to be put into effect, they are more likely to wish to repeat the experience in the future (Thornton and Tozer 1994).

Feeding back the findings of the evaluation can be a delicate task, demanding sensitivity and tact of the evaluator. Service staff and managers may be wary of any implicit criticism within the evaluation, and easily become defensive. Service users may feel their perspectives have not been given sufficient regard in comparison with other considerations. For these reasons it is often advisable to have several interim sessions to review the evaluation, especially if it is a large study and one which arouses concerns. This has the added advantage of enabling the evaluator to check some of the preliminary findings of the research for accuracy, and to elucidate areas of uncertainty.

In practice, feedback sessions can often be more of a dialogue than a formal presentation of findings, as the results tend to elicit debate and discussion.

Conclusions

Mental health service evaluation is slowly evolving to keep pace with the increasing diversity of provision. The future contains risks, but also many opportunities.

Perhaps the greatest danger in the current climate is that evaluation will become corrupted and used solely as a rationing device, when in fact it has much to contribute to the development of quality mental health services.

Set against that is the growing recognition both that evaluation should reflect the values and principles of good mental health practice, and that it is in fact an intrinsic part of such practice. The growing interest of service providers and users in this topic illustrates that evaluation affects all those involved in mental health provision, not just managers and funders.

Evaluation represents a means of empowering service users and staff. It can provide information on how a service operates, it offers an opportunity for different groups to voice their opinions, and it throws into relief the effectiveness of the service in achieving its objectives.

The challenge is to ensure that the skills and knowledge required to take an active part in evaluating services are made more widely accessible.

References

Beeforth, M., Coulan, C. and Graley, R. (1994) *Have We Got Views for You. User Evaluation of Case Management.* London: Sainsbury Centre for Mental Health.

Buglass, D. and Dick, S. (1992) *Not Just Somewhere To Go.* Edinburgh: Scottish Association for Mental Health.

Bulmer, M. (1986) *Social Science and Social Policy.* London: Allen and Unwin.

CEDEFOP (1990) *Vocational Rehabilitation of the Mentally Ill in Office and Computer Services.* Berlin: European Centre for the Development of Vocational Training.

Cheetham, J., Fuller, R., McIvor, G. and Petch, A. (1992) *Evaluating Social Work Effectiveness.* Buckingham: Open University Press.

Connor, A. (1993) *Monitoring and Evaluation Made Easy. A Handbook for Voluntary Organisations.* Edinburgh: HMSO.

Connor, A. and Black, S. (eds) (1994) *Performance Review and Quality in Social Care. Research Highlights 20.* London: Jessica Kingsley Publishers.

Cooper, R. *et al.* (1993) *Shared Living in Supported Housing.* York: Joseph Rowntree Foundation.

Cornwell, J. (1984) *Hard-Earned Lives: Accounts of Health and Illness from East London.* London: Tavistock.

Feuerstein, M. (1987) *Partners in Evaluation: Evaluating Development and Community Programmes with Participants.* Hong Kong: Macmillan.

Goldberg, E.M. and Connelly, N. (1982) *The Effectiveness of Social Care for the Elderly.* London: Heinemann Educational.

Kerruish, A. (1995) Basic human values: the ethos for methodology. *Journal of Community and Applied Social Psychology 5*, 2, 121–143.

Knapp, M., Cambridge, P., Thomason, C., Beecham, J., Allen, C. and Dartun, R. (1992) *Care in the Community: Challenge and Demonstration.* Aldershot: Ashgate.

Leff, J. (ed) (1993) The TAPS project: evaluating community placement of long-stay psychiatric patients. *British Journal of Psychiatry 162,* Supplement 19.

Lehmann, A.F. (1983) The well-being of chronic mental patients: assessing their quality of life. *Archives of General Psychiatry 40*, 369–373.

Leiper, R. and Field, V. (eds) (1993) *Counting for Something in Mental Health Services.* Aldershot: Avebury.

McCollam, A. (1988) *Working at Sprout. The Evaluation of an Employment Project for People with Experience of Mental Illness.* Edinburgh: Scottish Association for Mental Health.

McCollam, A. (1993) 'Before, I was on my own.' *An Evaluation of an Employment Support Service.* Edinburgh: NSF (Scotland).

McCollam, A. and White, J. (1993) *Building on Experience.* Edinburgh: Scottish Association for Mental Health.

McIver, S. (1991) *Obtaining the Views of Users of Mental Health Services.* London: King's Fund Centre.

Moore, J. and Whitting, G. (1993) *Enhancing Practice Through Evaluation: Opportunities for the Voluntary Sector.* Birmingham: Thamesdown Evaluation Project.

NHS/SCC (1994) *Consulting Consumers. A Guide to Good Practice for the NHS in Scotland.* Edinburgh: HMSO.

O'Donnell, O. (1991) Cost-effectiveness of community care for the chronic mentally ill. In H. Freeman and J. Henderson (eds) *Evaluation of Comprehensive Care for the Mentally Ill.* London: Gaskell.

Petch, A. (1992) *At Home in the Community.* Aldershot: Avebury.

Pickard, L. *et al.* (1992) *Evaluating the Closure of Cane Hill Hospital.* London: Research and Development in Psychiatry.

Rapp, C. *et al.* (1993) Research strategies for consumer empowerment of people with severe mental illness. *Social Work 38*, 6, 727–735.

Scottish Association for mental Health (1994) *The Best Place to Be, Even When Things are Bad. How Trainees View their Training Projects.* Edinburgh: SAMH.

Scottish Further Education Unit (1989) *Personal and Social Development Handbook.* Edinburgh: SFEU.

Scottish Users' Conference (1993) *Care in the Community 'Our Needs'.* Edinburgh: Scottish Users Conference.

SEF/NCCS (1995) *Evaluation: Making It Work for Us. Self-Evaluation and Community Care.* Glasgow: Scottish Evaluation Forum and Nuffield Centre for Community Care Studies.

Sheldon, B. (1986) Social work effectiveness experiments: review and implications. *British Journal of Social Work 16*, 223–242.

Shepherd, G. *et al.* (1994) *Relative Values. The Differing Views of Users, Family Carers and Professionals on Services for People with Schizophrenia in the Community.* London: Sainsbury Centre for Mental Health.

Smith, G. and Cantley, C. (1984) Pluralistic evaluation. In J. Lishman (ed) *Research Highlights 8: Evaluation.* London: Jessica Kingsley Publishers.

Smith, R. (1991) *Consumers' Views. A Study of Opinion of Mental Health Service Users in Grampian Region.* Grampian: Joint Mental Health Group.

Sykes, W. *et al.* (1992) *Listening to Local Voices. A Guide to Research Methods.* Leeds: Nuffield Centre for Public Health Services Studies.

Thornton, P. and Tozer, R. (1994) *Involving Older People in Planning and Evaluating Community Care: A Review of Initiatives.* York: University of York, Social Policy Research Unit.

Weis, C. (1986) Towards the future of stakeholder approaches in evaluation. In R. House (ed) *New Directions in Educational Evaluation.* Brighton: Falmer Press.

CHAPTER 11

Service Users' Perspectives on Social Work Activities for People Experiencing Mental Health Problems

Julia White and Allyson McCollam

Introduction

Purchasers and providers of social work services are becoming increasingly interested in the effectiveness of those services – what impact do they have on people's lives; are they accessible to those who want to use them; what changes will be needed in future to ensure appropriate service provision?

With the development of the users' movement (Barnes and Wistow 1994; Dean 1994), there is a new opportunity for the future development of services to be guided by the views of service users. Individual choice and the rights of the consumer now have a renewed political significance, as well as being the 'flavour of the month' (Citizens' Charter 1991; Department of Health 1991; NHS Executive Mental Health Task Force User Group 1994).

Mental health service users have been at the forefront of the users' movement, often working across traditional service boundaries as they seek to bring about change within the broad spectrum of mental health services. Social work staff, councillors and those working in related statutory and voluntary agencies now have access not only to the views of service users but also to the experience of those service users who have worked alongside providers and purchasers (Evans and Hughes 1993; Scottish Association for Mental Health unpublished).

In this chapter, we shall begin by discussing definitions of some terms in current use and review the reasons for promoting user involvement in mental health social work services. We shall then look in more detail at the different types of involvement at the strategic level, in terms of planning and evaluating services, in direct service provision and in assessment and care management.

More than feedback

Descriptions of mental health service users' views on the social work services provided for them have so far tended to rely heavily on information gleaned from consumer feedback. Recipients of social work mental health services have been asked for their views via surveys, questionnaires, and individual and group interviews, and have often expressed pleasure in having been asked to contribute. While these reports may give us useful information on the topics under scrutiny, they rarely allow service users the opportunity to comment freely from their own perspective.

In order to elicit a wider range of views on a greater variety of topics, we would argue that it is vital to allow service users opportunities to participate in social work activities on a more meaningful basis than is generally available to them through simply giving feedback on the services they receive (Connor and Black 1994).

In this chapter we shall focus on ways of discovering users' views other than through feedback mechanisms. However, direct comment by service users on social work provision will form part of the discussion in this chapter (see also Chapter 10).

Some definitions

Before exploring the perspectives of service users, comment is needed on the term 'service user' itself. Social work has traditionally dealt with 'clients' and health care agencies with 'patients'. Both these terms imply a particular type of relationship between staff and those receiving a service which the latter now often regard as disempowering and constraining. The preferred terminology – service user – is a more neutral term and it can apply across different types of organisation and different disciplines.

The term 'user' is not acceptable to all, however. It carries strong connotations of illegal drug use which mental health service users may wish to avoid. For some, more appropriate terms include 'member' – of a club or group – and 'survivor' –

having survived the experience of receiving mental health services. It is important that the use of these – and other – terms is discussed with individuals and their own particular preferences taken into account.

The term 'mental health service user' is generally used to denote someone who is or has been a recipient of care or treatment from the formal psychiatric services, but that definition is unduly narrow. In considering the perspectives of service users it may be helpful to examine in more detail the different bases on which individuals engage with services. This will have a bearing on how they regard provision and on how their opinions might be elicited and their involvement promoted.

It is possible to distinguish between:

- those who receive formal psychiatric services on either a voluntary or an involuntary basis. Provision for this group will increasingly become a responsibility of social work departments, as the role of psychiatric hospitals becomes more narrowly defined

- those with experience of mental health problems who receive care and support from other sources outside hospital, for example primary health care services, social work/care agencies based in the community

- those engaged with social work/care services, but whose mental health problems either remain hidden or do not become the focus of any help offered

- potential service users: current levels of take-up cannot be equated with need as there is likely to be a number of individuals who, for various reasons, do not avail themselves of services from which they might benefit.

People use services on a short-term or a long-term basis, or intermittently. Many people now belong to a user group and some service users have subsequently been employed as mental health workers. It is evident therefore that it is a simplification to view service users as a homogeneous body with a common set of interests and views. Any attempts to consult users, or to gain feedback, need to acknowledge the range of experiences and diversity of perspectives, and approach with caution the issue of representativeness (Lindow 1991; White 1995a).

For our purposes here, we shall be taking a broad definition of 'service users' to consider how those with experience of mental health problems (past or current) stand in relation to the provision available to them.

Why promote participation?

A number of forces have come together in recent years to promote a more active interest in the perspectives of service users and in how they might become more involved in planning, developing and delivering provision. There has been a growing political emphasis on choice and on consumer involvement across all sectors of public services (Croft and Beresford 1990) and on the rights of consumers, as evidenced by the proliferation of charters. Coupled with that, the legal affirmation of an individual's rights to access personal information held on file by social work departments, health and housing authorities (Villeneau 1992) has provided additional impetus to more open ways of working and has emphasised further that public services are accountable to those who use them.

In the fields of social care and social work, successive policy statements have reproduced the themes of choice and involvement. The Wagner Report (1988) into residential care stressed the concepts of individual choice and of control over one's own life. This was echoed in Griffiths' report (HMSO 1988) on community care in the same year, whose recommendations included the provision of individually tailored packages of care, the promotion of competition among providers to promote wider choice for service users, and the strengthening of the lines of accountability between providers of services and their users.

The White Paper *Caring for People* (1989) and the NHS and Community Care Act (1990) brought significant changes in the provision of all community care services, the effects of which are now being felt. In different ways these changes denote a redefinition of the role of service users, outlined in Box 11.1.

Box 11.1 Legislative changes

- Community care plans are to be developed in consultation with service users

- Individual needs assessments are to be carried out to devise appropriate packages of care, reflecting as far as possible individual preferences

- There is a requirement that local authorities devise complaints procedures

---

The promotion of service user participation is in keeping with the overall aims of care in the community. Indeed, services for people with mental health problems often have as a broad aim the maximisation of individual autonomy and potential. There is also a growing recognition that issues of process and of service quality – for instance how users experience and perceive services – are of crucial importance and can influence the effectiveness of provision (York and Itzhaky 1991). It is conceivable that the way in which support is offered may have a bearing on the outcome for those who use that support.

However, the recurring themes of choice and of accountability conceal the fact that very different motivations drive the same policy. On the one hand, these concepts are espoused by those who set out to rationalise service provision and enhance its efficiency and effectiveness, by more accurately targeting scarce resources. Choice in this context is about the opportunity to select among competing providers.

On the other hand, choice and accountability are regarded as fundamental in the process of ensuring that individual citizens are enabled to gain greater control over their own lives and over the services they use (Lupton and Hall 1993). Choice here relates to the ability to contribute to decisions about the type and range of provision.

These two divergent philosophies have very different implications for the rights of service users and for their roles. In the first 'consumerist' model, users are consulted or surveyed as a means of refining existing practices, but the initiative and the decision-making power remain vested in the organisation. The second 'citizenship' model allows service users a direct say in all parts of the process from planning and development to management. The co-existence of these two approaches to user involvement generates confusion and conflicting expectations of what is entailed.

An illustration of these differing interpretations of choice and involvement is given in Box 11.2 (White 1995b, used by kind permission of the Scottish Forum for Public Health Medicine).

Box 11.2 Aspects of user involvement

Receiving information	a key facet and one that is often skipped or done half-heartedly or too late in the consultation process
Being consulted	preferably carried out in the early stages of drafting a report or making a decisionand repeated at a later stage in the process
Participating	enabling people to attend meetings and planning groups means being clear about the time commitment involved, about the payment of expenses and fees, and about how any training needs may be met
Gaining control	users and carer groups require resources which are under their control if they are to participate on a regular basis in planning. This enables individuals to be trained and to gain information on particular topics while allowing the group to maintain its own functions and tointroduce new people to the planning process

---

Why is user participation important in mental health social work services?

It is increasingly apparent that many mental health service users want a more active part in provision which extends beyond that accorded to them in the narrowly circumscribed consumerist model of involvement (Audit Commission 1994; Scottish Users' Conference 1993). While individuals are generally pleased to comment on services and provide feedback on their experiences, they also want opportunities for greater involvement.

There is now a growing awareness by service users that they are able and entitled to exert some influence both over the development of services generally and over the particular services that they use (Barnes and Wistow 1994). Statements of good practice for use in the development of social work community care services also assert that users should be involved (Caring for People 1989; Wagner 1988).

It has become clear that activities in this area may result in improvements in individual care, better take-up of services and more effective services, as well as enabling individual service users to gain more control over their lives (NHS Executive Mental Health Task Force 1994).

By participating at some level in the planning and provision of mental health services, users can break down some of the preconceptions that those providing services may have and begin to tackle the stigma experienced by many people using those services. When those who provide services are felt to be on the side of the service user, the services in themselves become more valuable and more effective (Smith in Dean 1994).

A group of users will often be more effective than a single person trying to change or affect a service system. This is particularly true of people who have experienced mental ill-health. Seizing the chance to talk together, to share problems and concerns, has similarities with the process of the Women's Movement in the 1970s, where reducing the isolation experienced by individual women had powerful consequences for those following after (MIND 1986).

The exchange of information can be a powerful tool for change, as, for example, when the issues discussed include self-harm and eating problems (Campbell in Dean 1994). The support offered by, and found in, a users' group is often seen as life changing in the impact felt by the individual user, despite the stresses of becoming more involved: 'What people involved in rights and users' organisations are now showing is that we can do these two crucial things: make change and support each other' (Beresford in National Institute for Social Work (NISW) 1993).

How did it begin?

During the 1960s and 1970s, peoples' experience of psychiatric hospital and their treatment under the Mental Health Acts led many to question the role of professional workers and their use of resources for people experiencing mental ill-health. The Mental Health Act (1983) and the Mental Health (Scotland) Act (1984) were intended to set limits on the power of professionals to admit people to hospital and to treat them without their consent. However, service users felt that they experienced a loss of their civil liberties once they entered a psychiatric hospital and that there was very little that they could do about this: 'I was told that I would be sectioned if I did not take the anti-depressants' (Rogers, Pilgrim and Lacey 1993).

In the United Kingdom at this time there was much interest in what other countries were doing. In Holland, in the 1970s, the first patients' councils or committees were set up in psychiatric hospitals to answer patients' complaints about the services they received. Every Dutch psychiatric hospital is now required to have a patients' council and a worker responsible for developing its activities (Gell in Winn 1990).

In the United States, mental health service users were beginning to look at the need for crisis services, and it was argued persuasively (Chamberlin 1988) that the best people to run such services were users, who were the only people able to provide the intensive support and rapport that someone going through a crisis would need.

The first initiative along these lines to be started in Britain began in Nottingham in 1986, when the Nottingham Patient Council Support Group was established. The requirement for membership was past or present experience of using mental health services (Gell in Winn 1990). The group aimed to:

- create user-only meetings in wards, day units and community mental health centres and support such groups in taking up issues raised by them
- influence the planning and management of mental health services
- educate workers both locally and nationally about the need for user involvement.

The Insight Group in Brighton was also developing at this time (Beeforth in NISW 1993). It aimed to ensure that the local statutory services continued their commitment to involving service users in the planning of mental health services. This was achieved by a number of different methods:

- group members sat in on mental health planning and steering groups
- a users' charter was developed for the Brighton area
- support was given to help establish a local peer advocacy scheme.

Individual initiatives such as these have led to the development of a wide variety of user-led projects and services. Networking organisations such as Survivors Speak Out (Campbell in Winn 1990) and the Scottish Users' Network (Smith in Dean 1994) have created links between individual service users, self-help groups and service-providing organisations, enabling them to share information and expertise and to offer support and opportunities for further involvement to each other. Further examples of user participation are given later in this chapter.

Taking participation forward: the workers' role

A feature of some successful user participation initiatives in recent times has been the presence of workers who act as 'allies' to service users. These are people working in mental health services who have tried to facilitate user participation, most frequently in voluntary organisation settings and through those with community development and 'consumer' roles (Lupton and Taylor 1995).

Wilson (1991, 1994), in her work on self-help groups, talks of 'firm believers', that is, professionals who have influenced colleagues towards a more positive view of user participation. Of those workers with an interest in facilitating user participation, some will have had personal experience of the difficulties faced by mental health service users (Harding in NISW 1993).

There are workers, however, who are uncomfortable with the idea of service users getting together to campaign or lobby, and it is likely that they will prefer to negotiate change on an individual rather than on a group basis (Campbell in Dean 1994).

It is necessary to acknowledge the power that social work staff can exert over service users in their efforts to become more involved in the services they receive. Many people with experience of mental ill-health have experienced being seen as untrustworthy, so that their period of ill-health is seen as a cause of imbalance in other areas of their life (Lucas 1992). For this reason, workers may be uneasy about users being given responsibility for handling money, which will have implications for the funding of user-led groups and for the introduction of user-controlled budgets for individual care (Cresswell 1995). It has also been suggested that some workers have furthered their careers through pioneering user participation (Beeforth in NISW 1993).

Promoting participation at the strategic level

The involvement of service users in aspects of an organisation's functioning which have traditionally been seen as internal management concerns is radical and challenging for all parties. However, if the intention is to promote the model of involvement which affirms that service users have a right to increased control and choice over the services available to them, then it is a natural progression to consider how their role can be extended into all areas of an organisation's work. Before beginning a user participation initiative on an organisational level, it is worth bearing in mind the following points:

Users' roles

No service users should be made to participate. The service offered to users should be largely unaffected by their choosing to participate or to opt out. In the case of services offered to an individual, of course, participation by the user may mean that the service received is more finely tuned to that user's requirements.

Staff roles

All staff will need to be involved, regardless of the opportunities they have for contact with service users and of the type of job they have. All staff will have opportunities to influence both service users' opinions of themselves and the quality of service offered. Points of contact with service users should be reviewed for each job/project/section.

Expectations

It is important that expectations are clarified before the exercise begins. The constraints within which users, management and staff have to operate should be made explicit.

Previous experience

Use any previous experience of user consultation or involvement within the organisation to inform current initiatives. It is easy for staff to decide to ignore past unsuccessful efforts, but service users may choose not to.

Existing information

Review all existing organisational policy with regard to user participation. Amend/rewrite as necessary. Jargon should be avoided as far as possible (Hannaway and Kelly 1994; HMSO 1991) and abbreviations listed in an appendix. Presentation of information must take into account the effects of medication on eyesight and on reading ability: video and audio tapes are also effective ways of passing on information.

Guidelines

Provide guidelines as to acceptable or preferred ways of communicating with and working with service users. There will be many members of staff who will feel un-prepared to alter their current work practices without guidance.

New appointments

Appoint staff with previous relevant experience to carry forward this area of work. Experience in community development work will be useful, both in terms of direct contact with user groups and also in promoting an organisational understanding of how to work effectively with service users and user groups.

Resources

Providing sufficient and appropriate resources is one of the obvious and most effective ways of promoting user participation. Without adequate resources, participation will be dependent on those who can afford to become involved.

Resources required include:

- travel expenses, particularly in rural areas; expenses for child care and care of other dependent people; for subsistance; and for consultancy fees. Service users should have access to a standardised fee when asked to contribute to meetings and conferences
- training: access both to training courses to obtain practical skills and to conferences and seminars
- meeting rooms: users will need access to meeting places near to public transport routes and which are physically accessible
- support: practical support, such as help with transport or child care; emotional support.

Promoting participation within an organisation

Core activities within an organisation, such as recruitment and training, quality assurance and inspection, and monitoring and evaluation, all influence the type of provision offered and the way in which services are delivered.

Recruitment and training

There are a limited number of examples of user involvement in the recruitment of staff, and these tend to be in accommodation projects (Villeneau 1992). Wider opportunities to contribute to staff training are gradually opening up, although such developments are still piecemeal and narrowly defined. Many users regard as particularly important involvement in training concerned with their rights under the Mental Health Act (Harrison and Beresford 1994).

Feedback from social service trainers, educators and students suggests that much could be gained by all concerned if there were greater user involvement in community care training (Central Council for Education and Training in Social Work 1994). The benefits to service users who take part are considerable – they have a chance to learn new skills, their confidence and self-esteem are increased, and they have a sense of being able to put their experiences to good use (Evans and Hughes 1993; SAMH unpublished).

Key points in consolidating service users' contributions to training include:

- careful consideration of why such involvement is sought, to avoid tokenism
- financial support to groups set up for this purpose
- attention to the practicalities of the training, that is, suitable timing of sessions and locations for service users
- clarification of what is expected of service users
- training and back-up to enable users to develop skills and confidence
- recognition that users' inputs should extend beyond direct discussions of their experiences as service users to look at areas such as curriculum development
- attention to the professional attitudes and practices which might devalue or marginalise inputs from service users.

Quality and inspection

Involving people who use services in defining and monitoring quality standards can ensure that provision is both relevant and wanted. Many quality assurance systems contain opportunities for service users to feed in their views on provision. However, this tends to maintain the notion of service users as passive, reacting to requests for information or comment at the behest of professional workers and organisations.

Arguably a more influential role is conceivable if service users participate in discussions from the earliest stages about what constitutes a good quality service. Kerruish and Smith (in Leiper 1993) describe how the quality of residential services for people with long-term mental health problems was monitored using a quality component framework based on the outcomes of group discussions with residents.

Elsewhere, Villeneau (1992) examines in a series of case studies how the principles of good housing practice can be implemented by working closely with residents, staff and management. Areas prioritised for action included privacy, health and safety, crisis procedures and hospital admission, and the selection of new residents.

The Social Work Services Inspectorate inspection of day services included two lay inspectors, who were involved from the outset in deciding how inspections would be conducted, in visiting projects, in presentations of preliminary findings and in drafting the report. Their presence on the inspection was said to add new dimensions to the exercise and helped gain the confidence of the project users whose views were being canvassed (Kiddie and Leckie in SAMH 1993).

Research and evaluation

Traditionally the role of service users has been restricted to that of providing feedback on the services received. Latterly, however, there is evidence of an encouraging tendency to draw users more directly into the research process from the earliest stages, so that they have a part in formulating the questions the research will ask.

A recent investigation of service users' views on case management by the Sainsbury Centre for Mental Health was a user-led piece of research (Beeforth *et al.* 1994). This approach was adopted partly for pragmatic reasons, as it was felt that people who were to be approached for information would respond more readily and more freely to other service users than to professionals. This proved to be largely substantiated. There was also a 'missionary' aspect to the research in that it sought to prove to other organisations that this model of research is respectable, viable and useful.

Research on users' views of day activities by the Scottish Association for Mental Health involved service users from the early stages (Buglass and Dick 1992). Tasks undertaken by users included assessing questionnaire responses, planning and participating in one-to-one and group interviews, and speaking at the launch of the report. This was a deliberate attempt to move away from the often-repeated scenario in which the role of service users is to fill out a questionnaire and then to hear no more of the research or its results. All participants were invited to the launch and received a copy of the report.

To undertake a piece of research in collaboration with service users may well be more time consuming, but is likely to yield new ideas and perceptions which repay the effort. The work involved can be minimised by using existing user groups as the starting point for discussion. Focus groups can be utilised to highlight areas of concern which might be investigated and to refine the research questions.

If users are to collect the information, support and training may be necessary. The range of tasks entailed in research means there is often scope to use the particular skills of different individuals at different stages.

The experience of participating in research can be an empowering one for service users. It gives access to new information about how services operate, and an opportunity to acquire techniques and skills which have applications in other contexts.

Implications of increased user participation for service users, staff and organisations

Evidence (Barnes and Wistow 1994; Social Services Research and Information Unit 1992) suggests that the involvement of service users has both costs and benefits for them as well as for workers and organisations.

Although there is a growing acknowledgement that mental health service users have a right to be involved in provision, the fact remains that in practice this is as yet rarely implemented consistently, for some of the reasons highlighted in Box 11.3.

Box 11.3

	Risks	Benefits
Service users	• pressure and stress – expectation that users should participate • frustration – may not change very much • tokenism – extent of involvement still determined by staff/organisation	• confirmation of worth • chance to develop/brush up communication skills • opportunity to shape current and future provision
Staff	• coping with unrealistic expectations • demands change in attitudes and ways of working • challenges to professional identity • loss of control over resource allocation – fears about equity	• better quality and more responsible services • greater job satisfaction • greater transparency of work • encourages more open relationships between service users and staff
Organisations	• may require radical changes in working practices and relationships • vulnerability – greater openness may generate criticism and demands for change • tension between demands of service users and other, external demands, for example, from legislation	• better quality and more responsive and accountable services • opportunities to develop innovative work in line with users' preferences • direct and immediate access to service users views

---

User participation in practice

We shall now look in some detail at a range of practical examples of user involvement across the different areas of social work activity in order to review the extent to which user participation is in evidence and to suggest ways in which progress in this direction might be encouraged. It is suggested (Flynn and Hurley 1993) that those involved in local authority community care services must bring users into every element of the process of providing services. If not, it is the purchasers and providers who are seen as the key players and the service user perspective is neglected.

A wide range of service users should be consulted and given opportunities to participate. This will require purchasers to play an active role in the consultation process, particularly in making contact with black and ethnic minority community groups (Health Education Board for Scotland/CDF/SFPHM 1994). Different approaches will be required to consult effectively with users from urban and from rural areas, with particular attention being paid to the timescales involved in different settings (White 1995b).

Participation in service planning

The expectation that service users and carers should be involved in the process of devising community care plans for a locality affords an opportunity for both groups to influence crucial decisions on the development of provision. As authorities become more experienced in developing plans which are both useful and usable, and are increasingly required to focus on specifying targets and on identifying resources to attain these (Scottish Office 1994), community care planning is becoming more sophisticated and more powerful in shaping patterns of provision.

Local authority efforts to involve service users in this evolving process have, however, encountered a number of difficulties. Often authorities will have had relatively little previous experience of working in collaboration with service users at this level, and will themselves be coming to grips with the community care planning process. While there is a dearth of information on the particular experiences of mental health service users in this area, a number of issues relating to the role of service users in general have been identified and are worth noting here:

- it is important that service users have an opportunity to participate from the outset in the construction of plans, in addition to commenting on drafts

- direct consultation with user groups is vital, rather than relying solely on voluntary organisations as a proxy for users' views (Scottish Council for Voluntary Organisations 1992)

- the issue of representativeness of any users co-opted to planning groups must be carefully considered. Whom do they represent? How are they s/elected? How do they consult with their constituency of interest (Bewley and Glendinning 1994)? Do they have to be representative for this particular task or should they be asked to participate as individuals?

- participation and consultation demand a great deal of effort and energy from service users, which will only be sustained if the exercise is perceived as useful and fruitful. Too frequently plans produced fail to state how the consultation process contributed to the final version, or what the general feedback was from groups consulted on the draft proposals (Wistow *et al.* 1993). The example of Borders Regional Council is worth noting: in parallel to the published community care plan for the region, a report was produced detailing those organisations which had responded to the draft, along with their comments

- efforts to engage service users in planning will be undermined if it becomes apparent that it is mere window dressing and that the real decisions, for example about purchasing plans, are being made in another arena

- planning a consultation exercise requires considerable preparation, and attention to detail is important to ensure   success. There is a danger of consultation fatigue among staff and some groups of service users, and an impatience to see returns on efforts. For these reasons the objectives of the exercise need to be clear to all concerned to avoid raising false expectations (Barker 1995).

In order to facilitate user involvement in planning, there are several approaches an authority can take. It can opt to:

- support existing initiatives, such as self-help groups, and draw them into the consultation process (Craddock in Scottish Association of Health Councils (SACH) 1993)

- set up new initiatives for the explicit purpose of consultation, such as Lothian Regional Council's Consumer Involvement Officers. They have a focus on all community care service users and the purpose of their job includes:

  - 'enabling the social work district to consult effectively with consumers (users and potential users and their informal carers) in the planning, delivery and monitoring of community care services'

  - 'promoting and facilitating consumer involvement with social work services and other related services provided by other agencies within the district'
  (Extract from job description for Consumer Involvement Officers, used by kind permission of Lothian Regional Council Social Work Department.)

- stage one-off events such as conferences or focus groups. This method has been well used in the health service to canvass views on proposals for provision and to review good practice.

These approaches can be linked together: in Skye, a two day workshop marked the starting point for a joint initiative to develop locality community care planning. The workshop was a means of gauging support and of identifying issues to be addressed in subsequent work.

To date, attention has focused on the *process* of how users might participate more fully in planning. The *impact* of service user involvement in terms of determining priorities for service development still remains to be seen. While there is a relatively high degree of consistency in the types of service which users want to see developed (Audit Commission 1994; Scottish Users' Conference 1993), the early round of community care plans in Scotland did not reflect the emphases of service users (McCollam 1992). Ultimately, the effectiveness of user involvement policies will be gauged by the extent to which their views are listened to and acted upon.

Participation in purchasing services

There are relatively few examples of user participation in purchasing social work services for people experiencing mental ill-health. This is partly because of the limited role played by social work departments until recently in the provision of mental health services.

Mental health services have traditionally received a low allocation of resources from within social work departments. Legislative responsibilities for children and elderly people coupled with the prevailing poor public image of people who use mental health services have allowed the provision of mental health services to remain at a minimal level.

Many of the mental health services now provided by social work departments, which include both direct services and those purchased from voluntary organisations and other agencies, have been developed following the community care reforms and are still comparatively new.

Social work departments have relatively few resources with which to purchase mental health services, whereas health boards have areas in which they can make savings, for example from closing wards in psychiatric hospitals, freeing up resources for replacement mental health services.

The third reason is that the purchaser/provider split is less obvious at present within social work departments. The NHS reforms created new bodies which would provide services, leaving health boards with the responsibility for buying appropriate services from the new hospital trusts. In social work, however, the main change in terms of purchasing following the community care reforms was the direction that social work departments should reduce the number of resources provided directly by the department and instead buy services from private and voluntary agencies. This is a gradual process, requiring the separation of service provision from the departments' other functions. There have therefore been fewer obvious opportunities for user involvement in the social work purchasing process.

One possible area for increased user participation is in the prioritisation of projects under consideration for Mental Illness Specific Grant (MISG) funding. There are many well-established user groups and forums based within local authority areas which would be able to offer recommendations for purchasing based on their knowledge of the needs and requirements of local service users. The yearly cycle of MISG funding makes it a particularly appropriate area for user participation, it being known well in advance when bids are to be prepared and when the prioritisation process takes place. This allows for forward planning and for time to consult user groups. With sources of funding which have no clearly defined cycle, or where bids have to be prepared at short notice, consultation is often cut short or overlooked altogether.

Some more recently developed projects have been set up with the express purpose of encouraging and enabling users' voices to be heard. These include projects funded by MISG such as:

- the Consultation and Advocacy Promotion Service (CAPS) in Lothian. CAPS works with user groups and individuals to promote understanding of advocacy and to increase opportunities for service users' voices to be heard in the processes which affect them. The organisation offers training and support for user groups and information on local and national groups

and projects funded by the health service, such as:

- the Newcastle Mental Health Consumer Group. This group is funded to monitor the purchasing contract between the health authority and the mental health trust. Service users look at how health services are provided on wards and in day centres and feed information back to both purchaser and provider (Sherlock 1993)

and jointly funded projects, such as:

- the Glasgow Advocacy Network. This organisation is funded by Strathclyde Regional Council, Greater Glasgow Community and Mental Health Services Trust, and the Glasgow Association for Mental Health to coordinate the development of locally based groups of representatives of mental health service users. The network is user led, with service users involved in the planning, management and evaluation processes. A network of service users' councils is being established within each of the city's health sectors to provide a structure by which service users can make their views known.

Voluntary agencies are well placed to initiate projects which they see will fill a gap in current provision:

- the Edinburgh Association for Mental Health (EAMH) set up a consultation programme focused on enabling people from minority ethnic groups to participate in discussions about mental health services. An initial study commissioned by the Association found that minority communities were not using mental health services and that services were not seen as accessible or acceptable. Two consultation events took place, the first for members of minority communities and the second for those from service-providing agencies and members of minority communities.

These events were preceded by a period of development work, during which personal contacts were made within the different communities and the forthcoming events were publicised (EAMH 1992).

As well as ongoing models of participation, there are examples of one-off exercises, such as:

• two seminars initiated by the Scottish Needs Assessment Programme Working Group on Mental Health on involving service users in assessing the need for, commissioning and monitoring health service provision for people experiencing mental ill-health. The seminars brought together service users with experience of participation to review different models of participation and to make recommendations about the methods used to consult users about health services in the future (White 1995b).

If social work departments wish service users to become more involved in their purchasing decisions, one factor which it is important to acknowledge is that information about purchasing issues is often hard to obtain. Hogman (in NISW 1993) suggests that users will find information about levels of resources and an understanding of the planning cycle helpful in this context. To encourage better access to information, Moyes (in SAHC 1993) suggests that there is a need for a communications strategy involving different approaches to communication at different stages in the purchasing cycle.

One starting point for increased user participation is the contracting process. It has been suggested that 'three-way contracts', which include the viewpoints of the service user as well as the purchaser and the service provider, are particularly important in relation to social care (Association of Metropolitan Authorities 1990). Flynn and Hurley (1993) comment that contracts can be explicit about the role of service users and the level of involvement or control they expect to have. Local government reorganisation and the formation of unitary authorities may also provide opportunities for increased user participation within the agendas being set at this time.

Participation in service provision

User participation in providing services is in the process of being developed at present. While there are, as yet, few examples of totally user-led resources, many service users have had experience of being involved in service provision, often as a member of a project steering group or management committee:

- self-help and support groups run for the benefit of their members, with decisions being taken by member-run committees. Some groups are supported by a worker, at least in their early stages

- day and drop-in centres run by workers with service users as members of their management committees. Service users may be involved in recruiting and training staff or in the long-term development of the day resource

- service users employed as consultants on short-term pieces of work, such as setting up a new support group, delivering a training course or running a consultation exercise.

Examples of user participation in running services tend to exist within social work departments/SSD-funded services rather than social work departments/SSD direct service provision, as can be seen in the following descriptions:

- day resource: the Mental Health Services Consumer Group, Grampian has recently been funded to open a day resource at the Royal Cornhill Hospital in Aberdeen. The group has a campaigning and promotional role, aiming to monitor existing services and to be involved in the development and improvement of services within the community. It also encourages a free exchange of ideas between professionals, users and members of the public (promotional material)

- drop-in centre: the Brixton Community Sanctuary is a user-run resource and support centre set up with local authority funding two years ago. The principles on which the Sanctuary operates are decided by users and everyone takes responsibility for creating a safe environment where people are respected. Users can participate in art and poetry groups and a range of information is also provided (Knibbs 1994).

Participation in assessment and care management

In mental health, the fact that the relationship between care management and the care programme approach remains ill-defined (Stalker *et al.* 1994; Stone 1992) means there is considerable scope for confusion among professional workers let alone among service users about roles and responsibilities.

What is clear is that care management is perceived to have substantial benefits by mental health service users. These benefits include:

- the opportunity for users to develop a trusting relationship with their manager, which serves as the foundation for their care

- allowing service users more control over decisions about what happens to them and more choice

- opening up access to, and coordinating a range of, services

- providing accessible, practical help and advice

- improved relationships and better communication between service users and their families (Beeforth *et al.* 1994).

Social services staff generally consider that the system of individual needs assessment and of key workers should allow mental health service users a greater say in their own care and treatment (Schneider 1993). Whether this in fact happens is a moot point. For example, a review of the assessment proformas used by different social work departments revealed that more space was devoted specifically to record carers' views than service users' views (Stalker *et al.* 1994).

Users may be precluded from taking an active part in their care planning by a lack of information about the process and about the services which might be available to them (SSI 1995).

As Hudson (1993) observes, the concept of needs-led assessment requires a change in perspective for both service user and worker. In the context of care management with older people, she notes that to make full use of the opportunity which care management represents, users require a better knowledge of the range of options and support to speak out and voice preferences and dissatisfactions.

In an analysis of how the transfer of power from workers to users within the assessment process is constrained, based on discussions with social services staff, Macdonald and Myers (1995) identify four sets of factors:

- structural issues relating to the non/availability of services from which the user can choose

- procedural controls such as the workers' power in assessing and defining need, in influencing what information is passed on and how the whole process is recorded

- cultural issues reflecting the fact that service users often have little experience of participating proactively and lack confidence in how to handle that

- practical difficulties where service users may have problems articulating or communicating choice.

The authors conclude that there is a clear gap between the idea of transferring power and its realisation in practice.

The changes required in professional practice are developed further by Ellis (1994). In a study of participation in needs assessment of people with a disability (but not including those with mental health problems) she found a reluctance among practitioners to surrender professional authority or power to service users. Information was not shared openly with users and the assumptions on which professionals based their decisions were not overtly discussed. This made it very difficult for service users to challenge assessors' judgements or to discern the criteria used to ration scarce resources. Ellis suggests that rights to representation, information and a written statement of need would go some way to counter the discretionary powers of professionals.

Needs assessments generally concentrate on current needs. Yet many people with enduring mental health problems are concerned about what may happen should they become unwell again, and it is important that this should be covered in the assessment process (Beeforth *et al.* 1994; Bleach and Ryan 1995). Options such as crisis-cards, advocard schemes and advance directives are ones which many service users would like to see more widely discussed and publicised.

In conclusion

As this review of research and other literature has shown, although there are now opportunities for service users to participate in many different ways in social work services, these innovative initiatives often remain isolated examples of good practice. The reasons for this include patchy implementation of initiatives, a lack of commitment to the principles involved, inadequate funding, funding never made available or withdrawn early, and a lack of understanding of the development processes involved. Timescales are also important, with too little time allowed for new initiatives to find their feet.

There is a need for a more planned approach by social work departments and SSDs to facilitating user participation, with service users being involved in developing appropriate mechanisms to enable user consultation to take place on a regular basis within a wide range of social work activities. Attention needs to be given to the payment of expenses and consultation fees to service users.

Evidence of the impact of changes introduced so far suggests that services become more effective when users are involved in giving feedback on them, but that user views are often not listened to or acted upon in terms of determining priorities for service development.

With the shift of care from hospital to community settings, user participation in social work services within community mental health resources needs to be addressed more fully, particularly with reference to relationships between users and workers and ways of working which empower service users.

References

Association of Metropolitan Authorities (1990) *Contracts for Social Care – the Local Authority View.* London: AMA.

Audit Commission (1994) *Finding a Place. A Review of Mental Health Services for Adults.* London: HMSO.

Barker (1995) *Promoting Partnerships through Consultation.* London: Russell House.

Barnes, M. and Wistow, G. (1994) Listening to hear voices: listening to users of mental health services. *Journal of Mental Health 3,* 525–540.

Beeforth, M. *et al.* (1994) *Have We Got Views for You: User Evaluation of Case Management.* London: Sainsbury Centre for Mental Health.

Bewley, C. and Glendinning, C. (1994) *Involving Disabled People in Community Care Planning.* York: Joseph Rowntree Foundation.

Bleach, A. and Ryan, P. (1995) *Community Support for Mental Health. A Training and Resource Pack for the Care Programme Approach and Care Management.* Brighton: Pavilion Publishing.

Buglass, D. and Dick, S. (1992) *Not Just Somewhere to Go: A Study of Users' Views of Mental Health Day Activities.* Edinburgh: SAMH.

Central Council for Education and Training in Social Work (1994) *Changing the Culture: Involving Service Users in Social Work Education.* Paper 32.2. London: CCETSW.

Chamberlin, J. (1988) *On Our Own: Patient Controlled Alternatives to the Mental Health System.* London: MIND.

Connor, A. and Black, S. (eds) (1994) *Performance Review and Quality in Social Care. Research Highlights in Social Work 20.* London: Jessica Kingsley Publishers.

Cresswell, J. (1995) Straight into the pocket. *Community Care,* 6–11 January, 27.

Croft, S. and Beresford, P. (1990) *From Paternalism to Participation – Involving People in Social Services.* London: Open Services Project.

Dean, C. (ed.) (1994) *A Slow Train Coming: Bringing the Mental Health Revolution to Scotland.* Glasgow: Greater Glasgow Community and Mental Health Services NHS Trust.

Department of Health (1991) *The Patients' Charter.* London: HMSO.

Edinburgh Association for Mental Health (1992) *Who Cares, Who Decides?* Edinburgh: EAMH.

Ellis, K. (1994) *Squaring the Circle: User and Carer Participation in Needs Assessment.* York: Joseph Rowntree Foundation.

Evans, C. and Hughes, M. (eds) (1993) *Tall Oaks from Little Acorns: The Wiltshire Experience of Involving Users in the Training of Professionals in Care Management.* Wiltshire Community Care User Involvement Network and Wiltshire Social Services Department.

Flynn, N. and Hurley, D. (1993) Purchasing dilemmas no. 4. *Community Care,* 18 November.

Hannaway, J. and Kelly, D. (1994) If you can't beat 'em... *Care Weekly,* 17 February.

Harrison and Beresford, P. (1994) Using users. *Community Care,* 24 March, 26–27.

Health Education Board for Scotland/Community Development Foundation/Scottish Forum for Public Health Medicine (1994) *Community Participation in Health Needs Assessment.* HEBS/CDF/SFPHM.

HMSO (1983) *Mental Health Act.* London: HMSO.

HMSO (1984) *Mental Health (Scotland) Act.* Edinburgh: HMSO.

HMSO (1988) *Community Care: Agenda for Action. A Report by Sir Roy Griffiths.* London: HMSO.

HMSO (1990) *National Health Service and Community Care Act.* London: HMSO.

HMSO (1991) *Getting the Message Across.* London: HMSO.

Hudson, H. (1993) Needs-led assessment: nice idea, shame about the reality? *Health and Social Care 1,* 115–123.

Knibbs, S. (1994) User-run services. *Community Care,* 26 May, 18.

Leiper, R. and Field, V. (eds) (1993) *Counting for Something in Mental Health Services.* Aldershot: Avebury.

Lindow, V. (1991) Experts, lies and stereotypes. *Health Service Journal,* 29 August, 18–19.

Lucas, J. (1992) Piece of mind. *Social Work Today,* 19 November, 14.

Lupton, C. and Hall, B. (1993) Beyond the rhetoric. From policy to practice in user involvement. *Research, Policy and Planning 10,* 2, 6–11.

Lupton, C. and Taylor, P. (1995) Coming in from the cold. *Health Service Journal,* 16 March, 22.

Macdonald, C. and Myers, F. (1995) *Assessment and Care Management: The Practitioner Speaks.* Stirling: Social Work Research Centre, University of Stirling.

McCollam, A. (1992) *Community Care Plans.* Edinburgh: Scottish Association for Mental Health.

MIND (1986) *Finding Our Own Solutions. Women's Experience of Mental Health Care.* London: MIND.

National Institute for Social Work (1983) *Building Bridges between People who Use and People who Provide Services.* London: NISW.

NHS Executive Mental Health Task Force (1994) *Local Systems of Support: A Framework for Purchasing for People with Severe Mental Health Problems.* London: Department of Health.

NHS Executive Mental Health Task Force User Group (1994) *Guidelines for a Local Charter for Users of Mental Health Services.* London: Department of Health.

Prime Minister (1991) *The Citizens' Charter: Raising the Standard.* Cm 1599. London: HMSO.

Rogers, A., Pilgrim, D. and Lacey, R. (1993) *Experiencing Psychiatry: Users' Views of Services.* London: MIND.

Schneider, J. (1993) Care programming in mental health: Assimilation and adaptation. *British Journal of Social Work 23*, 383–403.

Scottish Association for Mental Health (unpublished) A Report on the Advocacy, Empowerment and Training Group by Sue Tait. Edinburgh: SAMH.

Scottish Association for Mental Health (1993) *Report of SAMH Advisory Council Meeting.* Edinburgh: SAMH.

Scottish Association of Health Councils (1993) *The Role of the Consumer in Health Needs Assessment.* Edinburgh: SAHC.

Scottish Council for Voluntary Organisations (1992) *Consultation and Community Care Plans.* Edinburgh: SCVO.

Scottish Office (1994) Community Care Planning. SW 14/1994.

Scottish Users' Conference (1993) *Care in the Community: 'Our Needs'.* Edinburgh: SUC.

Secretaries of State for Health, Social Security, Wales and Scotland (1989) *Caring for People: Community Care in the Next Decade and Beyond.* Cm 849. London: HMSO.

Sherlock, J. (ed) (1993) *Mental Health in the Countryside.* London: Good Practices in Mental Health.

Social Services Research and Information Unit (1992) *The Consumerism Project – the View from Service Users.* Portsmouth: University of Portsmouth.

Stalker, K. *et al.* (1994) *Implementing Community Care: Early Snapshots.* Stirling: Social Work Research Centre, University of Stirling.

Stone, K. (1992) The luck of the draw. *Community Care,* 30 January, 18–20.

Villeneau, L. (1992) *Housing with Care and Support.* London: MIND.

Wagner, G. (1988) *Residential Care: A Positive Choice.* London: HMSO.

White, J. (ed) (1995a) *On the Margins: Planning Mental Health Services in Rural Areas.* Edinburgh: SAMH.

White, J. (1995b) *Scottish Needs Assessment Programme: Report on the Involvement of Users in Assessing the Need for, Commissioning and Monitoring Mental Health Services.* Glasgow: Scottish Forum for Public Health Medicine.

Wilson, J. (1991) Giving in America. *Social Work Today,* July 14.

Wilson, J. (1994) Self help groups and professionals. In *Findings, Social Care Research 60.* York: Joseph Rowntree Foundation.

Winn, L. (ed.) (1990) *Power to the People: The Key to Responsive Services in Health and Social Care.* London: King's Fund Centre.

Wistow, G. et al. (1993) Where do we go from here? *Community Care,* 18–23 January.

York, A. and Itzhaky, H. (1991) How can we measure the effects of client participation on the effectiveness of social work intervention? *British Journal of Social Work 21,* 647–662.

CHAPTER 12

Afterword

Jim Kiddie

I am delighted to have a chance to offer comment on some of the chapters which have an impact on how users of mental health services view the various services which are provided. The recent launch by the Health Minister, Sam Galbraith, of the Advocacy Guidelines and Strategic Framework for Mental Health Services suggests that these are exciting times for the development of services which are in tune with the wishes of service users.

Increasing interest and participation in social work activities is the theme of Chapter 11 by White and McCollam. The chapter gives a good account of the history of the development of the user movement from its roots in Holland in the 1970s to the formation of the Scottish Users' Network in 1994. With the growth in local users' groups, users have developed confidence and now wish to become much more involved in planning the services they receive. The authors emphasise that progress is slow and patchy and funding often inadequate. There is no doubt in my mind that service users want to be more involved. This can only happen if adequate training and support are given. The authors give examples of how service user involvement can enrich the process and ensure more meaningful services result. This seems a sensible way of ensuring good value for money. As the authors highlight, many government reports emphasise the need for health and social work authorities to involve service users and, by so doing, empower them. It is now up to the social work authorities to respond to the challenge.

In their chapter dealing with the evaluation of social work services McCollam and White emphasise the need to ensure that users' views are obtained. As the authors themselves state, service users are becoming increasingly interested in evaluating services and in addressing the need to ensure that there are good and effective outcome measures. My own experience in evaluating day services, along with another service user, Maggie Keppie, and two social work inspectors, Tom Leckie and Mike Brown, showed that service users can enhance the evaluation process. The experience was productive and educational for all concerned.

Despite the potential danger of abusing evaluation as a rationing device, the authors see great potential in the evaluation process in empowering service users. By asking and involving service users in the services they experience, authorities stand a better chance of getting things right. When resources are limited, it makes good sense to make sure that services are properly evaluated. This can only benefit service users and for this reason is worthy of support.

Myers' thought-provoking article (Chapter 6) focuses on the dilemmas faced by social workers who are required to wear different hats and adopt different roles. Service users can on occasions experience great mental pain and anguish at a time of crisis. Their need for support from a trusted social worker who may be regarded in place of a nurturing parent is left unfulfilled as that same person is required to act as Mental Health Officer in restraining freedom and thus, in the eyes of the user, become the critical parent. The user can become extremely confused and angry by the whole process. New forms of crisis intervention have still to develop in Scotland. The dilemmas highlighted by Myers require to be addressed, and perhaps the specific mental health duties should be undertaken by social workers who are not directly involved in the care and aftercare of the users concerned.

Lines drawn between carers and users can often be blurred. Users can be carers and vice versa. In my own case, my 86-year-old mother is a constant reminder to me of how, as we age, we require individual help to retain dignity. She may be frail but she is still capable of giving much. O'Neill (Chapter 8) emphasises this aspect of individuality which so often can be ignored by professional staff. I found the chapter also gave a very good account of why older people can become depressed. I find it significant that while there have been advocacy developments in services for people with learning difficulties and mental health problems, older people have largely been ignored. In the Royal Edinburgh Hospital, for example, the Patients' Council does not presently cover the Care of the Elderly wards. Nor is there an individual advocacy service. O'Neill touches on preventive measures and includes the provision of social supports. Advocacy in its various forms should be part of this provision.

Fernando's chapter demonstrates how institutional racism exists in psychiatry. The research studies referred to show just how disadvantaged people from ethnic minority groups are in their treatment by western psychiatry. Fernando criticises the way in which the western medical model approach ignores the need for a holistic view of mental health problems, not just for those from the ethnic minorities but for the whole population. We all suffer at present, but those from ethnic minorities even more so.

There is a challenge to the user movement. Since my own work presently involves collective advocacy and campaigning, I do not personally subscribe to 'a western value system that emphasises individual empowerment' and excludes collective cooperative working. Nevertheless, I certainly understand how the Thatcher years reinforced this selfish approach, and their effect on our collective mental health and well-being has been significant. There is no doubt that ways must be found to involve people from the ethnic minorities in the mainstream user movement.

Conclusion

There is much in these chapters to generate thought and discussion. I personally hope that this material can be made available to service users. In this way the growing dialogue between users and professionals can hopefully produce a different kind of psychiatry which adequately reflects not just racial and cultural diversity but also addresses the wider 'religious, spiritual, philosophical, psychological' aspects of individual and collective behaviours highlighted by Fernando.

The Contributors

Anne Connor is an independent consultant and researcher. She was a health service manager with Lothian Health Board, where she commissioned mental health services and had a leading role in establishing the mental health joint planning arrangements. Before joining the health service she was a senior researcher in the Scottish Office, where she managed the social work research programme for mental health and other community care services. She has evaluated several major programmes of innovative community care services and ran a programme to help voluntary sector providers establish monitoring and evaluation systems.

Suman Fernando was a Consultant Psychiatrist in Enfield until July 1993 and is now a part-time Senior Lecturer at the Tizard Centre, University of Kent at Canterbury and Honorary Consultant Psychiatrist at Chase Farm Hospital, Enfield. He is the Chairperson of the Nafsiyat Intercultural Therapy Centre and a member of the Council of Management of MIND. He has written *Race and Culture in Psychiatry* (1988, London: Croom Helm) and *Mental Health, Race and Culture* (1991, London: Macmillan); he edited *Mental Health in Multi-ethnic Society. A Multidisciplinary Handbook* (1995, London: Routledge) and co-authored *Forensic Psychiatry, Race and Culture* (1988, London: Routledge).

Jim Kiddie started his working life in1966 as a graduate administrative trainee in what was then the Scottish Hospital Service. After holding a number of administrative and managerial posts he was appointed General Manager (Mental Health Services) in Grampian in 1987, a post which he held until experiencing a severe mental breakdown in 1990. Following a lengthy period of hospital care in Tayside, Grampian and Lothians, he was appointed in November 1993 as Support Worker with the Patients' Council at the Royal Edinburgh Hospital. He has just retired from this post and has recently been elected as the Vice-Convenor of the Scottish Users' Network. He serves as a member of the Scottish Mental Health Services Reference Group and various working parties on mental health issues. He was also a member of the management committee of the Scottish Association for Mental Health from 1993 to 1997.

Dr Allyson McCollam is currently Deputy Director of the Scottish Development Centre for Mental Health Services. She is a qualified social worker, who has worked for a number of years on mental health policy with the Scottish Association for Mental Health. During that time she had a part-time attachment to the Community Care Implementation Unit at the Scottish Office and was a member of the team responsible for drafting the *Framework for Mental Health Services in Scotland.*

Christine McGregor was the Social Work Commissioner to the Mental Welfare Commission for Scotland until June 1998. Previously she was employed as the first Social Work Officer to the Commission following on 12 years of social work in an Acute Psychiatric Unit of the Royal Edinburgh Hospital. Her MSc thesis was on the work of Mental Health Officers in compulsory detention procedures. She is a counsellor, a Trustee of the Sutherland Trust and Enable, and an Executive Member of Alzheimer Scotland – Action on Dementia.

Fiona Myers is a researcher who has contributed to studies in the fields of community care, mental health and learning disabilities in both Scotland and England. These include in addition to the Scottish Office-funded study of the role of Mental Health Officers, an evaluation of the effectiveness and efficiency of community care, and a study of the impact of moving from a long-stay hospital to homes in the community for people with learning disabilities. She has recently been involved in an evaluation of a Community Mental Health Team. She is currently working on a project exploring the practices of mediators and solicitors in the context of matrimonial disputes in the Department of Social Policy, University of Edinburgh.

Maureen O'Neill has been the Director of Age Concern Scotland since 1993. Previously she was Principal Officer Information and Policy at the Scottish Association for Mental Health. She has gained experience working in hospitals, and consumer, professional, medical and nursing associations. She has a keen interest in issues of ageing, provision of care services, and the mental, physical and spiritual needs of older people.

Michael Sheppard is Professor of Social Work at the University of Plymouth. He has published widely in social work theory, child and family care, and mental health social work. Among his books are: *Mental Health: The Role of the Approved Social Worker (1990, Sheffield: University of Sheffield Joint Unit for Social Services Research); Mental Health Work in the Community: Theory and Practice in Social Work* (1995, London: Whiting and Birch); and *Community Psychiatric Nursing and Care Management and the New Social Work* (1991, London: Falmer Press).

Marion Ulas is a lecturer in the Department of Social Work at the University of Edinburgh. Prior to this she worked as an Approved Social Worker in a psychiatric hospital in Hampshire. In her university post she supervised the study on the role of the Mental Health Officer funded by the Scottish Office. Her current research interests include professional practice under the Mental Health (Scotland) Act 1984, the Mental Health (Patients in the Community) Act 1995 and the inclusion of service users in planning mental health services.

Julia White is a freelance research consultant, specialising in evaluation and service user consultation and participation. She has previously worked with community development projects and as Policy Officer with the Scottish Association for Mental Health. She has recently been involved in a research and development project on good practice in mental health provision and is co-author of the Scottish Needs Assessment Programme (SNAP) Mental Health Portfolio.

Printed in the United Kingdom
by Lightning Source UK Ltd.
121115UK00001B/127-138